Sid Kimel
244-1761 Ext. 331

Risha
222-3110

The Intensive Group Experience

The Intensive Group Experience

Max Rosenbaum
Alvin Snadowsky

With Contributions by

Martin Lakin
Burton Giges and
Edward Rosenfeld
David Hays and Yael Danieli
Rosabeth Moss Kanter

THE FREE PRESS
A Division of Macmillan Publishing Co., Inc.
NEW YORK

Collier Macmillan Publishers
LONDON

The Free Press
A Division of Macmillan Publishing Co., Inc.
866 Third Avenue, New York, N.Y. 10022

Collier Macmillan Canada, Ltd.

Library of Congress Catalog Card Number: 76–8147

Printed in the United States of America

printing number
1 2 3 4 5 6 7 8 9 10

Library of Congress Cataloging in Publication Data
Main entry under title:

The Intensive group experience.

    Includes bibliographical references and index.
    1. Small groups--Addresses, essays, lectures.
2. Group relations training--Addresses, essays, lectures
3. Group psychotherapy--Addresses, essays, lectures.
I. Rosenbaum, Max.   II. Snadowsky, Alvin M.
III. Lakin, Martin.
HM133.I525   301.18'5   76–8147
ISBN 0-02-926950-4

Contents

Biographical Notes   vii

Preface   ix

Introduction   xi

Chapter 1. Group Psychotherapy   *Max Rosenbaum*   1

Chapter 2. The Human Relations Training Laboratory: A Special
            Case of the Experiential Group   *Martin Lakin*   50

Chapter 3. Personal Growth, Encounter, and Self-Awareness
            Groups   *Burton Giges* and *Edward Rosenfeld*   87

Chapter 4. Intentional Groups with a Specific Problem Orientation
            Focus   *David Hays* and *Yael Danieli*   111

Chapter 5. The Romance of Community: Intentional Communities
            as Intensive Group Experiences
                                    Rosabeth Moss Kanter   146

Notes   186

Index   206

Biographical Notes

Max Rosenbaum received his Ph. D. from New York University and was trained as a psychoanalyst. He is Clinical Professor, Post Doctoral Program, Adelphi University; Lecturer, Post Graduate Psychiatric Program, New York Medical College; and faculty, National Academy of Professional Psychology. He is author of numerous books and articles in the field of psychotherapy and group psychotherapy and Editor of the journal, *Group Process*. His current research interest is value systems in psychotherapy.

Alvin Snadowsky received his Ph. D. from the City University of New York and is currently Associate Professor at Brooklyn College. He is Editor of *Social Psychology Research: Laboratory–Field Relationships* and *Child and Adolescent Development: Laboratory–Field Relationships,* and co-author of *Social Psychology: An Introduction*. His research includes empirical analyses of communication structures, impact studies of social problems, and assessments of human potential groups.

Yael Danieli is completing her Ph. D. in Clinical Psychology at New York University and is a member of the faculty at Brooklyn College of the City University of New York. She contributed chapters on the conceptual and technical frameworks of the major schools of psychotherapy to an introductory psychology textbook and to *Three Psychotherapies: A Clinical Comparison*. Her current research interest is the phenomenological and psychological analysis of hope.

Burton Giges received his M. D. from New York University. He is Assistant Clinical Professor of Psychiatry at the Albert Einstein College of Medicine, Co-director of Training for The Institute for Human Relations Laboratory Training, and is engaged in the private practice of psychiatry. His interest is training psychiatrists and other mental health professionals in the newer approaches to group therapy.

David S. Hays received his M.D. from Tufts University Medical School. He is Clinical Instructor, Department of Psychiatry, New York Medical College; Medical Director, Cooperative Consultation Services of Westchester County, and engaged in the private practice of psychiatry. His interest is teaching the psychological aspects of medical practice in the general hospital setting.

Rosabeth Moss Kanter received her Ph.D. from the University of Michigan and is currently Associate Professor of Sociology at Brandeis University. She is author of *Commitment and Community*, and editor of *Communes: Creating and Managing the Collective Life* and *Another Voice: Feminist Perspectives on Social Life and Social Science*. Her research interests are the sociology of organizations and the sociology of law.

Martin Lakin received his Ph.D. from the University of Chicago and is currently Professor of Psychology and Psychiatry at Duke University. He is author of *Interpersonal Encounter: Theory and Practice in Sensitivity Training* and *The Experiental Group: The Uses of Interpersonal Encounter, Therapeutic and Sensitivity Training Groups*. He is currently working on an approach to developmental aspects of group processes and the life cycle.

Edward Rosenfeld is completing his Ph.D. in psychology at the Humanistic Psychology Institute in San Francisco and is a member of the faculty at the New School for Social Research. He is author of *The Book of Highs: 250 Ways of Altering Consciousness Without Drugs* and editor of *Real Time 1* and *Real Time 2, Catalogs of Ideas and Information*. His current research interests are the psychology of creativity and Gestalt Therapy theory.

Preface

As the United States of America moves past its bicentennial year, the value systems which served as a stimulus for the most powerful industrial society in the history of civilization are being severely challenged. The ideal of the affluent American is *not* acceptable to a good part of the world. Higher education is *no longer* seen as the goal of every child of the blue-collar worker.

The systematic erosion of religious authority has resulted in mass confusion. From this confusion stems the need for quick answers. More and more, people are searching for a meaning in existence. To a large extent this is the decade of the "group." It has become almost a magical word, and people flock to different kinds of groups to understand the significance of their lives. As in every age, there are those who claim to have the answers. "Join my group," they cry out, "and you will find the solutions to life's struggles." People join a group, but too often they do not find the answers, and the search goes on.

Disturbed by this chaotic search for the "magic group," we decided to offer some of our professional experience to help people clarify what they are searching for. While the hunger for meaning is understandable, the gimmickry used to satisfy that hunger is a "rip-off." Perhaps this book can be called a "consumer's guide" to the group experience. If it stimulates thought, caution, and further inquiry, we shall deem our efforts worthwhile. We have expressed our beliefs and opinions and have attempted to be fair and objective. Our colleagues in this endeavor have done the same.

We believe that intensive group participation can be an important and meaningful contribution to human welfare but *not* a religious experience. We hope that our opinions and guidelines and those of our colleagues will help the prospective group member.

We want, first of all, to express our deep appreciation to each

contributor. Their dedication and enthusiasm were important in-
gredients in bringing this project to fruition. We are particularly
grateful to Robert Wallace of the Free Press for his support and
editorial guidance. Special thanks to Barbara Braden, Vikki Del
Pellegrino, Leslie Felsher, Judith Rosenbaum, Rebecca Rosenbaum and Bonnie Weinstein for their dedication to the task of preparing this book for publication.

Max Rosenbaum
Alvin Snadowsky

Introduction

Profound change, freedom, unshackling the bonds of slavery are some of the terms used to describe the social phenomena occurring during the past ten years. Movements came and went—but their effects left their mark on the fabric of traditional society. The counterculture of the early sixties in the mold of nonconformity engulfed many of our institutions with tornado-like momentum, leaving many of them reeling.

Implicit in the counterculture was the concept of making one's own decision in a world that appeared to lack purpose. Behavior was aimed at maximizing one's life potential with the freedom to determine how this potential should be achieved—humanism often masked hedonism.

There are those commentators, however, who like to attribute the purported social changes of the sixties to small groups of *radicals:* angry students and militant Blacks, as well as women from the large urban areas of the United States. But only a cursory examination of the past decade will reveal the piercing and universal effects that events in the sixties had on our society. It should be remembered that one of the prevailing needs of man is *consistency,* and change must be looked at in this context rather than in the context of the radical fringe usually depicted in the mass media.

What were some of these changes and what were some of the institutional responses? The youth of the sixties fostered the idea of personal freedom: sex, drugs, dress. They questioned the term *normal.* Although obstacles were placed in their path, these soon crumbled. The university, center of reflective study, yielded to the demands of the students, in many cases beyond the students' wildest dreams. Many states passed liberal abortion laws although there was—and is—considerable antagonism to this legislation. The parent who condemned his son for wearing long hair and bizarrely colored clothing himself became a customer of "hair sculptors" and "male boutiques." Political leaders who a decade ago condemned the use of marijuana were calling for its legalization. And why not? American adults were "popping" more pills per capita than in any other nation although it was justified as medication. Of course, some legislators continued to press for strict drug control laws while at the same time minimizing the increasing concern with the rising rate of alcohol consumption. The contradiction was ignored. Young people joined in what some might consider the most massive world exploration ever known to mankind. Their parents soon joined them. Verities were questioned. Travel broadened horizons and awareness. Our natural resources in the United States were not taken for granted. A concern for the environment became apparent. Technological "advances" were seriously questioned. Is "bigger" really better?

The latter part of the sixties and the early seventies saw new manifestations of this quest for freedom: demands for removing the oppression from minority groups such as Blacks and Chicanos and the "oppressed" women majority. It does not seem speculative to predict that the aged, *our senior citizens,* a large minority, will soon demand that their esteemed title be replaced with more tangible rewards from a society to whose growth they contributed.

Why did the seemingly stable fifties erupt into the explosions of the sixties? Two explanatory factors often are given: the knowledge that the world as we know it can be destroyed within a few hours by manmade weapons, and technological advances that have provided heretofore unknown opportunities for leisure. These and perhaps other forces built the volcano-like pressure which served to pour forth the lava of the sixties.

What will the seventies, eighties, and nineties bring? How will historians classify a society where a significant portion of its members readily "light up" objects drawn from containers that are labeled "Warning: The Surgeon General Has Determined That Cigarette Smoking Is Dangerous to Your Health"? Predicting the future may be foolhardy, but the needs and desires of the present generation and of the immediate future generations seem self-evident.

People in the 1960s have tasted new pleasures and they have

craved more. But this is not the hedonism that led to the destruction of the ancient civilizations. This new self-orientation type of humanism that many have adopted has the potential, if adequately harnessed, for bringing people to new heights of growth, but it can easily become hedonistic.

One major attempt at restructuring the environment to meet the needs of this self-orientation took the form of a heightened interest in and creation of new uses for the intensive group experience. The intensive group experience has been a time-tested force for inducing individual and group change. Therapy groups, special interest groups, training groups, and communes have their roots in early history. Every significant cultural change involved groups. However, the 1960s brought an intensification of interest in therapy, training and special interest groups, creation of new types of groups such as the encounter group, and rekindling of the idea that the commune is the panacea for life's disappointments. The loneliness of people trapped in an impersonal industrialized society seemed relieved by these new kinds of groups.

Daniel Bell, an American sociologist, has applied the concept of the *double bind* to the American culture.[1] He has described the effect of the double bind where the individual receives two simultaneous and contradictory messages. Which one is he to respond to without being perceived as erratic? Is he to respond to the need for increased rational thought that technology requires or to the vision of personal fulfillment that capitalism promises?

The loneliness of our culture leads people to disown the past and to reject work for the sake of pleasure. As pleasure became the norm, people had to look for new ethical systems. Since the search for ethics is difficult, membership in a group seemed to supply the sought-for ethical system. Many group experiences are intended as a substitute for the ethical systems the individual has discarded in the search for the immediate experience and in the rejection of the concept of delayed gratification.

The Intensive Group Experience is structured in many ways. We have presented the leading approaches to group experiences so that the reader will have some idea of the kinds of groups people belong to in the search for answers.

There is such a plethora of techniques that professionals who approach the field of group process need a detailed sampling of which techniques are helpful. More important, there has to be some evaluation of the importance and limitations of a particular approach. For example, when is an approach based solely on charisma? We have evaluated the charismatic styles.

The informed layman who is in contact with group approaches will find an in-depth statement of various techniques. This is especially important at this time in our cultural growth because experimentation with different forms of human relating has led to an era of *the group*. Thus, included in this book is a statement of the communal approaches and extended family relationships that are part of these methods, as well as an evaluation of these communal modes. There is also a survey and delineation of the *new humanistic* approaches to relationships among people. In a time of social upheaval and personal loneliness, the humanistic techniques have attracted many adherents and many critics. The pros and cons have been evaluated.

Also covered are the current methods of coping with individuals who are in custodial settings. Current approaches to criminology and delinquency are opposed to *warehousing* of people. A variety of alternate modes, including self-help settings such as addiction centers and alcoholism treatment centers, are discussed.

In this book the various intensive group experiences will be explored through an historical review, an examination of techniques, and an analysis of current trends. When available, pertinent research findings will be cited to assess the efficacy of a particular intensive group experience for the needs that it was designed to meet. Thus the reader will be able to gain a perspective of both the old and the new, an understanding of those techniques that survived and those that failed, and an insight into how the methods of the past influenced the creation of the new.

Chapter 1.   Group Psychotherapy

Max Rosenbaum

SINCE WORLD WAR II there has been a rush toward the use of group treatment as a method of psychotherapy. At first glance, the visitor from another country would assume that we have become a nation of "groupies." Some people have promoted group psychotherapy as the ideal remedy for all kinds of problems. The experience of group membership is supposed to cure everything—from drug addiction to losing weight. The varied group methods overwhelm the onlooker and each day a new convert is added to the fold. It becomes more and more confusing for the public.

Much of the rush toward joining some kind of group experience appears related to the loneliness of many Americans. We are a very mobile nation. As small towns disappear and giant shopping centers dot the landscape, the impersonality of an urban society begins to make itself felt more and more. People seem to be looking for some place to go or somewhere to belong. Alienated people are searching for answers to living and joining a group seems to provide a solution to the loneliness many people experience.

There are basic questions. What is group therapy? How did it start? Who is it good for? What about the people with little or no training who lead groups? What about the groups that meet regularly for years? And the ones that meet for twenty-four or forty-eight hours at a stretch and let it "all hang out" to the point of sitting around in the nude—or touching—or Indian wrestling? This chapter should answer these questions and many more that will come to mind.

There are many techniques and maneuvers labeled group psychotherapy: encounter, sensitivity training, gestalt therapy, bioenergetics, family therapy, consciousness raising, transactional analysis, interactional analysis, psychosynthesis, theatre of encounter, group games, movement in depth, fantasy-imagery, Alexander techniques, rolfing, and

1

probably other terms that are being devised as you read this list. Because of the many techniques there are considerable misconceptions about group psychotherapy. Many people assume that when three or more individuals meet and talk about problems some type of group psychotherapy is occurring. This is false. While in the broadest sense a certain kind of therapy is taking place, it is generally unplanned and may more accurately be described as nontherapeutic group interaction. It's what may happen when friends or acquaintances unload their problems to one another in a neighborhood bar or at a dinner party.

The early history of group psychotherapy could be traced back to the ancient Greeks.[1] The all-day Greek drama with concern about family problems, the medieval morality plays, the groups of people who were treated by Anton Mesmer in the 1700s and who were instructed to hold hands as he hypnotized them (see the word *mesmerized*), all of these groups can be considered forerunners of group psychotherapy. Religious movements have sometimes been called a form of group psychotherapy as adherents gained emotional relief by professing religious faith. But modern group psychotherapy began in the United States in the year 1905.[2]

Pratt and the Inspirational Approach

Joseph Pratt, a physician who lived and practiced in Boston, Massachusetts, was treating tubercular patients.[3] He observed that most of his patients were disheartened. The community at large considered tuberculars some kind of pariahs. The tubercular patients were led to believe by the community that there must be something wrong with them socially as well as physically. Why else would they have tuberculosis? Most of the tubercular patients were so discouraged that they had begun to neglect themselves and ignored basic principles of physical hygiene. Pratt had read about a North Carolina physician, Charles L. Minor, who urged his patients to keep a daily record book of their everyday life in order to introduce some order and regularity in their existence. This gave Pratt other ideas and he decided to meet every week with groups of tubercular patients, usually twenty-five in number. He appealed to various organizations for financial support with his project but was unsuccessful. Finally Dr. Elwood Worcester, the rector of Emmanuel Church in Boston, granted him $500 to begin the project.[4] Pratt would lecture to his patients and tell them that he believed they would get better. He stressed the use of the daily record book to keep track of one's physical condition. He was at times inspirational and at other times supportive. The patients began to find that they were not alone in their suffering. Other members of the group were also discouraged and disheartened. A spirit of camaraderie developed that overcame ethnic, racial, and religious differences among the group of tuberculars. Pratt really didn't know what he was doing but he was prepared to try anything that might work. What he was actually doing was inspiring his patients. He was a forceful man and he believed that his patients could become healthy. In one of his first articles, where he described his work, he tells of the patient who came to him and later told a family member: "I don't think he is a doctor: he didn't say anything about medicine. He is more like a Christian Scientist, or a professor of physical culture, or something like that." And Pratt notes: "I did not make any impression upon him. My personality did not work that time."[5] Pratt's faith and belief were communicated to his tubercular patients. This, plus the fact that they found they were not alone in their misery, that other people were also suffering from similar problems, led to the awareness that they were all in the same boat.

By 1913 Pratt seemed to have become more sophisticated. He knew that he was doing something right since his patients were getting better. Now he wanted to find out why. He read in the field of psychiatry and spoke to a few psychiatrists but they didn't seem very helpful. Perhaps he sent off negative vibrations with them since he did believe that people with emotional problems are best treated by either an internist or the family physician. Besides, Pratt would on occasion meet with patients in a church, if he could not find quarters in a hospital. This seemed to strike some physicians as a rather strange alliance with clergy. At that time the Boston medical fraternity frowned upon the idea of clergymen becoming involved in treatment of anything related to health—either physical or emotional. One Boston medical journal criticized the alliance of physicians and clergy.

Pratt described his meeting with a Boston psychiatrist one afternoon in 1913 in some detail.[6] The man was Isadore Coriat, one of the first American psychoanalysts and he had just finished reading a book by a French psychiatrist, Joseph Jules Dejerine.[7] The book detailed the treatment of psychoneuroses by psychotherapy, and Coriat was very enthusiastic about the book, so enthusiastic that Pratt at once obtained a copy. He states: "It was a revelation to me." For the first time Pratt began to understand what he was doing, because Dejerine stated in his book that persuasion and reeducation was the way to treat patients with emotional problems. This is the line that Pratt had followed and continued to follow. He would persuade his patients that they could improve and would reeducate them to see things differently. Pratt called his method emotional reeducation and persuasion. It is interesting that the first physician who served as Pratt's assistant, John B. Hawes, lost faith in the method. He considered Pratt's success a matter of personality (Pratt's) rather than of method. Besides Pratt, few physicians in the United States before World War I used group methods in psychotherapy. The results of this work were published after the war. In 1921 Edward Lazell, a Washington, D.C., based psychiatrist who worked in a veterans administration hospital, described his group treatment of schizophrenics.[8] His group treatment consisted largely of lectures to his patients. Like Pratt, he found that his patients overcame their fear of loneliness when placed in a group; that they overcame their fear of the psychiatrist leading the group; and that, while they seemed to be sitting alone and mumbling to themselves, they seemed to hear and remember the material that the psychiatrist presented in the lectures.[9] Lazell was far better trained and aware than Pratt and appeared to know what he was doing.

Freud and Group Psychotherapy

Sigmund Freud had been invited to lecture in 1909 at Clark University in Worcester, Massachusetts, but there is no evidence that either Pratt or Freud had any contact with one another. When Freud came to the United States, he traveled by ship and there is a description of Freud sitting with several psychoanalysts who accompanied him, as they analyzed each other's dreams. Freud's biographer and co-worker, Ernest Jones, described this as the "first example of group analysis."[10] But this seems to be stretching it a lot. For, while Freud was interested in group psychology, he was not a group psychotherapist.[11] There are some writers who believe that Freud was inadvertently a group psychotherapist as he tried to control his followers, especially in the years 1900 to 1910, when they would meet with him every Wednesday night and present theoretical papers and discuss clinical problems.

These men later organized the Vienna Psychoanalytic Society and the original Wednesday night group was a creative, competitive, and sometimes very angry bunch of people.

Some writers have described Freud as a basic figure in group psychotherapy. This is inaccurate. He outlined a concept of group psychology in a book he wrote in 1921, but he focused on individual psychodynamics.[12] He spoke of a group of two but does not appear to have incorporated into his observations any concepts of group dynamics or cultural anthropology other than what he found in the writings of Le Bon, the French sociologist who used to write about the "mob."[13] It is possible that Freud's interest in the group was soured by his own problems leading *his* group of prima donnas.

In that setting there would be weekly struggles for power and approval. Alfred Adler, one of the group that met with Freud, later broke with him after some rather marked theoretical and personal disagreement.[14] But, while Freud may have had a tough time working with his followers and keeping them from destroying one another with their competitiveness, he was *not* practicing group psychotherapy. It is interesting to note that Adler was a political socialist, always concerned about bringing psychotherapy to the working class. He was attracted to the idea of treating people in groups and later encouraged his students to follow his approach. Freud's psychoanalysis was largely confined to more affluent patients in individual psychotherapy.

Psychodrama

Jacob L. Moreno, a Rumanian-born psychiatrist, grew up in Vienna. During his adolescence he enjoyed walking in the parks of Vienna and meeting with groups of children; he would talk to them, put on puppet shows, and listen to their problems.[15] He continued this interest when he entered medical school in Vienna and, after receiving his medical degree in 1917, continued to be interested in the spontaneity of children and adolescents. He claims that his meetings with groups of children and adolescents was the beginning of group psychotherapy. In 1912 he attended a lecture given by Freud at the University of Vienna and after the lecture spoke with Freud and told him what he was doing. He describes Freud as looking "puzzled." The group meetings must have seemed "far out" to Freud who was a careful and rather conservative practitioner even if he was considered a pioneer in the exploration of emotional problems.

Moreno was very interested in the theatre and founded a Theatre of Spontaneity near the Vienna Opera House.[16] In his theatre he would discard prepared scripts and the actors and the members of the audience would play events from the daily newspaper. There was no preparation at all. It was entirely unrehearsed and Moreno called this "The Living Newspaper." From all of this work, Moreno hit upon the idea of Psychodrama, a therapeutic theatre.

Moreno came to the United States in 1925. He actually came at the invitation of an industrialist to promote an invention that he had devised. He never got the support for his invention that he had been promised and continued to espouse his technique of psychodrama. He established a sanatorium in Beacon, New York, for psychiatric disorders in about 1934 and there he build the first stage theatre for psychodrama. He received financial support from a Mrs. Tone, the wife of a wealthy New York State industrialist and the mother of Franchot Tone, who later became a popular movie and stage performer.

Moreno died in 1974 and throughout his professional life he was a very charismatic and controversial figure. His technique has become established within the framework of group psychotherapy.[17] He was a dramatic, histrionic psychiatrist and his abrasiveness to some psychiatrists has obscured his genius. He was also a very dynamic man and his presence could not be ignored when he worked with patients.

What is the purpose of psychodrama? Moreno states that Freud and Joseph Breuer, who originally worked with Freud, were ignorant of the therapeutic implications of the Greek drama and that he was the first to discover this dramatic technique to effect mental catharsis or relief from tension. Since every form of human activity is believed to be the source of some form of catharsis, Moreno has attempted to find the different sources of catharsis and what catharsis represents. His aim is to define catharsis so that "all forms of influence which have a demonstrable cathartic effect can be shown as positive steps within a single total process of operation." The common principle which produces catharsis is spontaneity, according to Moreno, who also says:

> The treatment of audiences has become an important alternative to individual treatment. The relationship of the audience to itself in a psychodramatic session, being treated by its own spokesman on the stage, gives us a clue as to the reasons of the cathartic effect of psychodrama.[18]

He maintains that he has "put the psyche itself on the stage." Five instruments are used in psychodrama.

THE STAGE—THE FIRST INSTRUMENT

Moreno calls the stage an extension of life and beyond the reality of life. Through the stage the patient is provided a *space for living*. The first psychodrama theatre that was built in America had three stage levels, almost like three layers of a cake. The top stage—the balcony—was the superego or conscience that controls our impulses. A circular stage, when it is built in the psychodrama theatre, symbolizes the aspiration levels of the patient as he moves on stage from one circle to another circle.

THE PATIENT—THE SECOND INSTRUMENT

The patient is told: "Just be yourself when you are on the stage. Share your thoughts and feelings with us." This is where the skill of the director of psychodrama comes to the fore. The patient does *not* perform. The patient responds just as things come to his mind. This response which operates in the present relates to Moreno's theory of spontaneity. Spontaneity is related to readiness for the act and creativity relates to the act itself. Does this sound like playing with language? Remember that Moreno was striving to get freedom of expression. Now that the patient has expressed himself, he is urged to talk about a current anxiety or his concern about a future problem. He is encouraged to play the role of the people he fears or is anxious about. The patient is told not to perform but to feel the current emotion. He may be asked to take part in role and reversal. A mother and daughter cannot get along. They hate one another. Now the mother and daughter are on the stage. The mother is asked to become the daughter and the daughter is asked to become the mother. Think, feel, experience what a mother is going through, the daughter is told. Feel what a daughter is experiencing, the mother is told. Don't act—feel it.

THE DIRECTOR OF THE PSYCHODRAMA—THE THIRD INSTRUMENT

The director is the psychotherapist and jokes or laughs with the patient. He may, as he judges what is going on with the patient on stage, decide to be active or more passive. The director keeps the movement going in the psychodrama and maintains rapport with the audience which is considered part of the psychodrama. This is the director as the producer. The director also serves as an analyst. He works into the psychodrama all of the information that he has learned about the patient from family, neighbors, or friends. He also watches the audience and interprets the reactions of members of the audience who watch the psychodrama.

THE AUXILIARY EGOS—THE FOURTH INSTRUMENT

This group of people, on stage, serve as figures in the patient's world—they may represent people who are not present, the delusions of the patient, or the patient's hopes, aspirations, and ideals. They are an extension of both patient and director.

THE AUDIENCE—THE PEOPLE WHO ARE WATCHING THE PSYCHODRAMA—THE FIFTH INSTRUMENT

The audience is a sounding board for the patient. The members of the audience react to the patient and they may see in the patient(s) all of their own problems. The acutely disturbed, psychotic patient responds to the sympathetic audience which understands and accepts him.

Moreno has tried to expand the use of psychodrama, not only in psychiatry, sociology, and psychology, but in education and industry where people are encouraged to come together and explore their problems through psychodrama.[19] His technique has had its highs and lows. It is pretty well accepted as a method of helping unhappy people but not as the panacea to all of the world's problems—which is what Moreno claims.[20] Many current psychotherapy approaches owe a lot to Moreno's ideas.

Moreno's approach is action oriented.[21] He himself was motoric. The United States is a very action-oriented society.[22] The older European culture is far more reflective and is less receptive to what is perceived to be a less thoughtful approach to life. Of course, this was Moreno's complaint. He attacked psychoanalysis as being too passive a method of psychotherapy. It is possible that Moreno's technique was able to become established in the United States because of the action direction of America. However, Moreno did claim that his technique has been introduced all over the world—including mainland China. He also influenced prominent psychologists such as Gardner Murphy, who felt that his ideas could be integrated into personality theory.

Burrow's Method of Group Analysis

Shortly before Moreno arrived in the United States, during the mid-1920s, a physician and psychologist, Trigant Burrow, who became one of the first psychoanalysts in the United States, began using the term *group analysis*.[23] He was deeply dissatisfied with the emphasis psychoanalysis placed on the individual, an emphasis that he felt excluded social forces. He believed that behavior problems and all problems of living should be traced to social relationships and that effective inquiry into these problems was best carried out in a group setting. In 1914 he wrote:

> After all we are of one tissue. We have but to look about us at the so-called normal persons composing the community to see that life masquerades no less under the disguise of social make-believes than under the symbolic subterfuges of the neurotic individual.[24]

Burrow happened to be friendly with a family who had hired Clarence Shields, a quiet reserved Pennsylvania German who had agreed to be a companion to a psychiatric patient—one of their children. Shields seemed so thoughtful and intuitive that friends of both Burrow and Shields felt that each could profit from a meeting. Shields decided to enter psychoanalysis with Burrow and during the course of the psychotherapy Shields asked Burrow why he (Shields) should lie on the couch, as was the psychoanalytic procedure. Why, he asked, shouldn't Burrow lie on the couch while Shields sat up in the chair? These questions stimulated Burrow to question the whole fabric of human relationships. Why was he the doctor and what kind of authority did that imply and what kind of power had been granted to him? How did that apply in other human relationships?

He left private practice in 1921 and between 1923 and 1932 Burrow, in collaboration with Shields, embarked on group behavior exploration as a full-time activity. The research was carried out in the Adirondacks over consecutive summers with the entire families of patients at the sessions. We can observe, as we study Burrow's writings, the early phases of family therapy, face-to-face therapy, marathon therapy, and family network therapy. Toward the end of his life, Burrow became deeply interested in the biological principles underlying group behavior. Ironically, when the American Psychoanalytic Association was reorganized in 1933, Burrow was dropped from membership since he was considered *too biological* in his approach.

It is apparent now that Burrow was the first systematic student of group psychotherapy.[25] His emphasis was upon research and in his early work in the 1920s he was trying to define the word *group*. Unlike Freud, who stressed instincts, he believed that human violence and hostility was to be found in the social environment. In one experiment at the Adirondack camp, which he named Lifwynn Camp, after the Welsh words *joy of living,* twenty-four people would meet every morning and none of them would say "good morning" with the smile that usually accompanies the greeting. In this experiment, Burrow was trying to find out the signals that people used in their relationships. He minimized his role as a leader and encouraged patients to look upon their neurotic problems as part of the larger social illness. He encouraged participants in the group to listen to body signals. What is your breathing or eye movement telling you? What is the message? Today we call this *sensory awareness*. He was interested in the whole human race and when Freud read one of Burrow's papers he commented: "Does Burrow think he is going to cure the world?" When Burrow was told of the comment he answered, "Yes." He believed that, as a physician, this was his larger goal.

Participants in the groups that Burrow formed were actively discouraged from theorizing. A group member was encouraged to observe and study his own feeling but, unlike current encounter groups, Burrow did not encourage expression of emotion for the sake of expression. His writings are very complex and many psychotherapists are unaware of his pioneer work.

Group Psychotherapy in Hospitals

In 1935 L. Cody Marsh, a minister who later became a psychiatrist, described his group method.[26] He was essentially an inspirational psychotherapist and a preacher. Aware of the work of Pratt, he used every technique that he felt would contribute to the psychological well-being of his patients. He organized his patients into classes and enrolled them as *students*—the term he used. He gave a lecture course consisting of four meetings. He would discuss the structure of the family, how children develop, job problems, understanding one's emotional pattern, your social life, your religious life, your sex life, including a short history of the philosophy of sex, types of nervousness, and abnormality and the normal healthy personality. In some classes the students would be asked to repeat the course three or four times. After the lecture, questions and answers were part of the program. Marsh found that the people in the class were frank in asking questions and discussing their own problems. He always maintained the class in an "atmosphere of academic dignity" (his words). He emphasized teaching rather than treating and would assign tasks such as arrangement of chairs or cleaning the blackboard. Students were given notebooks to take notes and were graded on attendance, attentiveness, and cooperation. They were assigned outside readings and when Marsh noticed that a student was losing interest he would enlist the aid of another student in teaching the lackadaisical student. He stressed that his approach was educational rather than medical and should always be conducted in a group. In addition to his classes, he also formed art and dance classes. Patients were encouraged to help and support one another emotionally—a very early version of Alcoholics Anonymous.[27]

In the mid 1930s another psychiatrist, Louis Wender, reported on his work with borderline psychotics in a private mental hospital where he practiced group psychotherapy using psychoanalytic concepts.[28] Begun in 1929, the work was specifically described as psychoanalytic. He differentiated it from other group techniques which he considered educational and supportive. At that time he indicated that group psychotherapy was applicable only to disorders in which some degree of emotion was present and in which intellectual impairment was absent. Therefore, brain-damaged patients would not be treated. Nor would schizophrenics who were so withdrawn that they were flat emotionally. His article, "The Dynamics of Group Psychotherapy and Its Applications," was later reprinted as a manual for the use of psychiatrists and psychologists who practiced group psychotherapy with soldiers in World War II, and as a result a whole generation of professionals learned about group psychotherapy. Wender's group of patients ranged from six to eight in number and they were all of the same sex. Attendance was voluntary. The group met two or three times a week for one hour and they met for about four or five months. Once the group was formed, no new patients were admitted. The group members were told to hold in confidence what occurred in a group and not to discuss the proceedings with anyone outside the group. Wender began the sessions with lecture material: why we behave as we do, the meaning of dreams, the conscious and unconscious, and so on. From this the patients began to discuss their own problems in relation to the lecture or theory material. The patients were encouraged to understand the nature of their unconscious drives and needs.

He reported on seventy-five patients treated over a six-year period, concluding that the treatment helped the patients adjust socially and that they maintained a drive to remain well.

In 1934 Paul Schilder, a psychiatrist, decided to organize a project in group psychotherapy with fifty patients in the outpatient division of Bellevue Hospital in New York City. He established a definite plan of therapy.[29] Each patient was seen individually before he joined the group and the individual treatment continued after he joined the group. The groups met once or twice a week, with two to seven patients in attendance. The therapy emphasized the leadership of the physician, Schilder, who directed the group. He said that the therapist should not be an authority but a leader and that patients should not have blind faith in the physician who leads the group. He used psychoanalytic methods in his group treatment. With each patient the life history and early infancy was elicited and discussed in detail. After the patient gained some insight, he was asked to submit a written report where he described his entire life history as well as the relationship with his parents, brothers, sisters, and nurses. He also reported on his sexual life and development and discussed dreams and fantasies. His basic goals and life plan were studied. Schilder hoped eventually to treat both men and women in the same group but his premature death precluded this hope. He found that group psychotherapy was very effective with *social neuroses* where patients are uncomfortable with other people and develop as a result either anxiety reactions or physical symptoms such as sweating, stomach distress, or heart palpitations.

Schilder was a very well trained psychiatrist with an enormous grasp of philosophy as well as of psychology and physiology. His personality was a quiet one. His early tragic death was a great loss to behavioral science. He noted, in his work with poor people at Bellevue Hospital, the importance of motivation, travel, and the "symbolic significance of the carfare"—in this case, the subway ride fare—as the patient's therapy fee. Simply stated, he was claiming that a five-cent subway ride to a poor person, ostensibly being treated for nothing, was the fee since five cents was a lot of money in depression days. The fact that the patient expended that money was his way of paying the fee. More affluent patients may assume that the carfare has nothing to do with the fee or motivation for treatment. Indeed, the doctor may assume the same thing.

Schilder was steeped in Freud's contributions and Freud's theoretical paper on group psychology. But, beyond this, he was very concerned with the social milieu of the patients he was treating. Many contemporary group psychotherapists expose their own problems quite willingly in work with groups and Schilder would have supported this openness. He was forthright in expressing his value systems to his groups, and outspoken in defense of his values.

Activity Group Therapy

During the early 1930s John Slawson, a psychologist and executive director of the Jewish Board of Guardians (a child and adolescent treatment center that was strongly influenced by psychoanalytic concepts), encouraged by his wife, began to organize club groups in the agency. His wife led these groups and she would take them on picnics or organize social activities. These club groups were later taken over by Samuel Slavson, a brother of Slawson, who was originally an engineer with a great deal of interest in the youth activities of the Young People's Socialist League. He moved into group work and group education and developed a type of therapy at the Jewish Board of Guardians which he called *activity group therapy*. This was a blend of progressive education, psychoanalysis, and group work. It is primarily a therapy for children and adolescents from age 8 up to the age of 15.[30]

Slavson, who is still alive, describes his approach to activity group therapy as therapy *by* the group rather than therapy *in* the group. His treatment is *interpersonal therapy* and *situational therapy* and the emphasis is on *activity* as opposed to *interview*. The children are placed in a structured situation and the group leader works according to a theory. This is *not* a recreational approach to children. In the *activity group* the therapist sets a permissive environment. The children are encouraged to act out conflicts and emotions and the group therapist does *not* offer interpretations. He sets certain limits and ground rules—for example, no furniture is to be broken but you can work with modeling clay or finger paints. There is a lot of emphasis on arts and crafts in the activity group and this gives the children the opportunity to work out tensions. As the children play, the therapist observes the fantasy life that is at work. The activity group meets for about an hour and a half. This span of time does not exhaust the leader or the children in the group. After this period of time, the group leader provides a meal for all to eat. Everyone works at this task—the meal is prepared together, everyone eats together, and then they all clean up the dishes and utensils. The group leader is put into the position of providing food and therefore gratifies the oral needs of the child. He or she becomes the good parent. Sometimes there may be a planned picnic or swim party and all of this is done to educate and control the emotions of the child. The group leader has set up a warm emotional climate and the child begins to trust the therapist. As the child is accepted, it is believed that he or she develops insight. Through all of this, the group leader is studying the interaction of the children in the group and a comprehensive picture of the child's conflicts and emotional problems emerges.

Generally, the activity group contains children of the same age and sex. It rarely has more than eight children and there is careful structure in the group so that a good balance is set up. To achieve this balance, the group leader may place a very active and aggressive child in the same group with a passive withdrawn child.

Modifications of activity group therapy are used with children of preschool age and in this type of group the emphasis is upon play and the use of play materials: for example, in the use of play materials a very demanding child may indicate an unwillingness to share with other children. But, unlike individual play therapy where the child has the therapist to himself, the child has to share while a member of the group and cannot have the group leader to himself.

When the child grows older and may still require activity group therapy, the thrust is finally toward discussion. This is what happens in the adolescent group, where there is still some attention paid to meal planning, and so on. Feeding patients and planning meals and picnics are discouraged in the adult therapy group unless the patient is acutely disturbed and this oral feeding approach enables the therapist to make some type of contact.

Currently, there are arguments among those who work with activity groups as to whether adolescents of the same sex should be together in the same group. The arguments seem related to the therapist's personality and the goal of therapy. The results of activity group therapy seem to be good. The child or adolescent accepted in the activity group feels that he has found friends and his own latent growth possibilities are unlocked. Slavson stated: "Groups . . . especially activity therapy groups . . . have a releasing effect . . . a group is indicated for the shy and withdrawn."[31] Activity group therapy is devoted to "corrective relationships in the living situation," and encourages psychological awareness in group members. This type of therapy has a theoretical design and while the behavior of group members is not interpreted the principles and practices of activity group therapy are based on psychoanalytic concepts.

Slavson's ideas were adopted in hospitals, clinics, and social agencies. He has been very active in promoting group psychotherapy in psychiatry, psychology, and social work. He has constantly stressed the importance of a theory in any type of group therapy.

In his original paper, which he presented in 1943 at the annual conference of the American Orthopsychiatric Association, Slavson stated:

The opportunity we offer to each child to use environment in accordance with his particular needs is of immense importance. We believe that psychotherapy consists of removing the patient's resistance to the world, his self-encapsulation, as it were. Once this is done, living in a social environment is itself a therapeutic situation. As long as the patient isolates himself either through resistance, active aggression or withdrawal, the world cannot get at him. He remains in a state of isolation and develops or continues with anti-social attitudes. When we make it possible for our clients to go out into their environment to a degree to which they are ready and in a manner suitable to them, we not only give them release and comfort, but their perception of the world as a hostile destructive force to be feared or attacked changes. It is in this changed attitude that our therapy largely lies.[32]

Slavson was—and remains—concerned with proper selection of patients for all types of group psychotherapy. His experience is largely confined to children and adolescents, although he organized and led parent discussion groups and later worked with adult patients in a New York City mental hospital—Brooklyn State. He believes that psychoanalysis—dream analysis, interpretation, transference—cannot be practiced in the group setting. Currently, group treatment of children and adolescents has achieved wide application.[33] Most of this work is patterned on Slavson's activity group therapy.

Psychoanalysis in Groups

In 1938 Alexander Wolf, a psychiatrist and psychoanalyst, stimulated by the work of Schilder and Wender, began to work with groups. His original interest stemmed from his reluctance to turn away patients who needed but couldn't afford sustained psychotherapy. His sympathy for the poor led him to bone up on group psychotherapy literature and finally to devise a method. By the end of his first year with groups, he was so enthusiastic about the results that he revised his private practice; by 1940 he was working with five groups, each numbering eight to ten patients.[34] His groups met twice a week for one-and-one-half-hour sessions. In a meeting called the *alternate session,* group members assembled on their own—without the group therapist. This meeting was designed to stimulate group members to engage in peer experiences and discuss their reactions to one another, as well as to the absent group leader. The *alternate meeting* also encourages patients to evaluate how they get along without the trained group therapist and to rely upon one another. No fee is paid for the alternate meeting. Wolf called his method *psychoanalysis in groups* and trained an entire generation of psychiatrists, psychologists, and social workers.[35]

He stresses that he practices psychoanalysis *in* groups as opposed to psychoanalysis *of* groups and that he does not treat a group, but each individual in interaction with other individuals. Moreover, he does not believe that the *group qua group* (people being together) can be the instrument for resolving intrapsychic difficulties.[36] Wolf applied directly the principles of individual psychoanalysis to the group setting, using the major tools of the psychoanalytic method such as transference, free association, dreams, and historic development. He describes his therapy group as the re-creation of the original family where the patient works through his unresolved problems. He does this by reacting to other members of the group who remind him of important figures from his original family. His reaction to these people in the group is taken from the *here and now* and traced back to the historic roots. A man may overreact to a woman in the group and become very belligerent. Rather than just be encouraged to ventilate feelings, he will be asked: "Who does she remind you of? What are you feeling right now?"

Wolf states that his technique precludes the analyst's having a face-to-face confrontation. The group forces interaction. He uses the technique of *going around,* whereby each member takes turns at free associating about another member. Many have expanded on Wolf's idea, pointing out that asking group members to *go around* is asking them to participate fully and spontaneously in what they perceive to be a single member's problem, dream, fantasy, or interaction—either in or out of the group. The technique has been called an "ice breaker." The group's power falls upon a particular problem while at the same time group members are forced to become co-therapists. It is ego strengthening since patients come to realize that they can contribute to one another's welfare. Using the procedure of going around, the therapist, somewhat like the permissive parent, assures the child in the patient that his perceptions are important and even valuable. Going around provides a more accurate discernment of problems than does the perception of the individual therapist—a major advantage of group over individual psychotherapy.

Technically, going around is based on the transference relationship which occurs in the one-to-one interplay of individual psychoanalysis. In individual treatment when a therapist asks a patient "How do you see me, or what do I represent for you, or whom do I remind you of?" he is going around. The group widens this process.

One problem in individual psychotherapy is that a patient might become *fixed* in transference to the psychotherapist. The therapist may remind the patient of an unkind parent or teacher or sibling. In turn, the patient usually becomes very upset or angry with the psychotherapist. Nothing the therapist can do or say relieves the distress of the patient who ascribes to the therapist his own feelings (projects) and refuses to believe that the therapist doesn't share them. For example, an extremely distraught woman came to an individual therapy session and said, "Doctor,

you seem to be very uptight today.'' This was after she was twenty minutes late for the appointment and kept complaining that the therapist, who
was going to meet with her husband, might side with him. While some of
her anxieties might have been justified, most of her fears were based upon
her childhood experiences with a parent who consistently sided with an
older brother during arguments. When eight or nine other people are present in therapy and do not see the therapist as "uptight," the patient may
question his perception. Of course, some patients conclude that the entire
group has been influenced by the therapist and, occasionally, such a person quits treatment feeling that everyone in the world is against him.

While the patient may discuss the here and now in psychoanalytic
group psychotherapy, he is also encouraged to regress and reveal his early
life experiences, quite unlike *encounter-type groups*. His patterns of relating to other members of the group and the symbolic meaning of these
reactions, if they are distorted, are clarified. A man in a therapy group
always raised his voice when a woman in the group spoke to him. His
wife had complained of his browbeating her and he denied her complaint.
What came out in the group was his fear of his mother who would override
him completely. He was convinced that all women would do the same. He
felt that he had to speak in a loud voice in order to be heard. His behavior
was an overreaction based on his past history and this was pointed out to
him by other group members. Ventilation of feeling without exploration is
discouraged. It's not enough to say "I hate you." Maximum distortion
can be observed during periods of regression, but eventually there is a
move toward reconstruction, with patients seeing one another as they
really are.

Wolf does not believe in or encourage a group dynamic approach. He
says in his articles on group therapy, which later became part of his
textbook on group therapy:

> There is as yet no clinical evidence demonstrating that attention to these
> phenomena (group dynamics) is useful to the understanding and treatment of
> the patient in a group setting. How do group dynamics achieve a healing
> objective?[37]

Other Types of Groups

Before World War II there was the formation in the United States of
patient groups in and out of mental hospitals. The intent was to foster a
sense of group identification and the thrust was the *repressive-
inspirational* approach—repress the unconscious and inspire the patient.
Will training, organized by Abraham A. Low, a midwestern psychiatrist,
is an example of this.[38] The groups are generally large and self-directed,

part of a movement called Recovery, Inc. The emphasis is self-help and the membership is recruited from patients who have been discharged from mental hospitals. There is much use made of group camaraderie, with an emphasis on teaching and lecturing.

Since World War II there have been many new approaches to group psychotherapy and only a few have survived. One writer, Raymond Corsini, attempted to identify more than twenty-five different methods of group psychotherapy by name.[39] Today, many of the methods he listed have disappeared from the literature. This is because group psychotherapy is a field that is expanding in the nature of a geometric progression. The *practice* of group psychotherapy has been considerably in advance of its *theoretical* understanding and conceptual clarity. Since every major school of individual psychotherapy has begun to apply its methods of theory to the treatment of people in groups, a good deal of confusion has ensued.[40]

The Directive-Didactic Approach

In state mental hospitals the earliest use of group procedures involved organizing patients into a didactic group where the group leader presented material for guided discussion.[41] Such a group emphasizes a verbal and intellectual approach and is particularly useful with regressed, hospitalized psychotic patients.[42] It can also be effective with groups where there is a marked social distortion among patients. An effort is made to define the here and now very clearly. Such groups might include prisoners, paroled convicts, and juvenile offenders.

Didactic groups rely heavily on lecturing and conditioning (not unlike behavior therapy) as opposed to manipulation of instinctual drives and affects. Advocates of the didactic method equate motivated learning with the transference process as it occurs in psychotherapy that is psychoanalytically based.

The teaching method is used in a variety of ways. The therapist may depend upon the patient's bringing to class a problem for general discussion. A group of prisoners will meet and one prisoner will, let's say, tell why he beat up his wife, the crime that resulted in his being sent to jail. The discussion will focus on the lack of control involved in wife beating and, in all likelihood, on how to go about curbing anger. No effort will be made to interpret the prisoner's basic hostility toward women (or toward his mother, whom his wife probably symbolized).

The therapist serves as leader and moderator and, at times, interpreter. Such a technique is practical when patients are very inarticulate and may be repressing strong aggressive feelings. The therapist sometimes delivers a series of lectures. These lectures are organized so that there is maximum structure for the patients. The best method is to have these lectures printed in textbook form. The printed matter provides a systematic, logical, and planned sequence of material that the group leader wishes to cover. This structure both stimulates and controls the patient's ideas. Through this method the patients are encouraged to participate actively in the lectures—to read aloud, recite, and comment upon the materials presented. The approach is particularly important with regressed schizophrenic patients since there is structure and participation. The reader may note the similarity of the lecture and reading approach to a Bible-reading class in a religious setting.

Since organized material is readily available there is a continuity of program if a therapist leaves the group or is replaced. Another teacher-therapist takes over and continues the presentation.

This method is particularly useful in a state hospital setting, where there is a high turnover of professional staff, as psychologists and psychiatrists complete their training and leave the hospital. The organized material acts as a guide for changing personnel and provides a way to compare different patient groups. Also, the printed word carries additional authority.[43] Since material is always available, there are no periods of silence. (Silence with a group of neurotics may not indicate resistance to exploration of conflicts; rather, it may be a sign of reflection and assessment. Generally, this is not true with a psychotic population.)

During the *didactic* presentation no pressure is exercised, nor is any effort made to "cover material." The class may interrupt the leader at any time and he will encourage discussion, comment, and associations. Occasionally, the material previously presented will be reviewed. Besides the formal class "text" or materials, patients may be assigned books to read, a *bibliotherapy* for guidance in resolving personal problems. Debates, discussions, and analyses of autobiographical material by the entire patient group, as well as symposia arranged by the group, are all part of the didactic method. A group member may even be encouraged to present a case history based upon his life, which serves as a point of departure for a reading assignment and group discussion.

The structured presentation I have described lends itself to easy use in a mental hospital. Many mental hospitals are little more than big boarding houses with thousands of patients and strikingly few psychiatric and ward personnel. Often, the communication between ward personnel and the psychiatric staff is so poor that some patients never end up in the assigned therapy group. The situation seems to present complete chaos, particularly to the young professional. With the didactic approach there is an organized program that pulls the patients out of the back wards, where they have been deteriorating for many years. And the psychiatric staff gains the satisfaction of doing something besides administrating and dispensing tranquilizers.[44]

The directive-didactic approach seems to offer an educational experience to many patients who have never had any kind of system or order to their lives. A "looser" method of psychic inquiry simply ignores the limited background of many patients. The social and cultural background of patients cannot be ignored.

I have referred earlier to Dejerine's approach rooted in this principle: "Psychotherapy depends wholly and exclusively upon the beneficial influence of one person on another." It can be found today in diet groups such as Weight Watchers, Smokers Anonymous, Fear of Flying, and so on.

Behavior Therapy and Group Therapy

The recent work of conditioned-reflex therapists, such as Joseph Wolpe (behavior therapy), emphasizes the wisdom of treating certain specific symptoms with an intellectual approach.[45] Behavior therapists are opposed to *insight* therapies—know thyself. The behavior therapy approach seems to fall into the category of the didactic approach. In a recent application of Wolpe's system of *reciprocal inhibition,* a group of patients suffering from phobic disorders (e.g., fear of train travel or fear of elevators were presenting problems) were exposed to group desensitization.[46] The therapist constructed a group hierarchy of anxiety stimuli. The patients were then trained in intensive muscular relaxation, which they were instructed to practice morning and night. The desensitization was instituted with progressively stronger anxiety stimuli presented while at the same time the therapist named the muscle groups to be relaxed. The theory behind all this follows Wolpe:

> If a response incompatible with anxiety can be made to occur in the presence of anxiety-evoking stimuli so that it is accompanied by a complete or partial suppression of the anxiety-responses, the bond between these stimuli and the anxiety-responses will be weakened.[47]

This method incorporates the finding that muscular relaxation inhibits anxiety and that the expression of both at the same time is physiologically impossible.[48] The technique described does not attempt to effect basic changes in personality. It is devoted to relief of symptoms. The advocates of this approach believe that when disabling symptoms are eradicated the personality changes.[49]

Repressive-Inspirational Approach

A sense of group identification and the feeling of belonging is easily accomplished with the repressive-inspirational approach to patient groups.

This technique may be used with any population, whether it is made up of neurotics, psychotics, hospitalized psychotics, alcoholics, obese persons, narcotic addicts, criminals, or people with other problems. "Will Training" (Recovery, Inc.) and Alcoholics Anonymous, as well as the Christian Science religious movement, are repressive-inspirational. A supportive subculture is set up. The group is strongly leader led. The leader is vitally important because his enthusiasm establishes the original climate of the group. Some of the many mechanisms at work in the repressive-inspirational approach may be isolated: group identification, group status, esprit de corps, friendly environment, communal feeling, unification of the group, group socialization, loss of isolation, emotional acceptance of the group, ego support, social approval, realization that others are in the same boat, testimony and example of others, sharing of mutual experiences, and reassurance.

As my comments on previous pages indicate, there are three major approaches to group psychotherapy: the intellectual, the emotional, and the actional. The repressive-inspirational strongly emphasizes the emotional and the actional. *Parts* of the repressive-inspirational approach may be found in all of the techniques we describe in this chapter.

Client-Centered or Nondirective Group Psychotherapy

Carl Rogers encouraged his students to apply techniques of *client-centered* (the word *client* will be explained later) psychotherapy to persons seen in groups. Apparently, he originally viewed group therapy in terms of activity group therapy.[50] Those of his students who have engaged in group psychotherapy with adults have stressed a *phenomenological* point of view: the resolution of situational conflicts on conscious levels.[51] A problem that is thought to cause an individual or a group concern is the focus of attention. The therapist is accepting and permissive since any individual is believed to have the capacity to heal himself if given a secure environment where he can discuss his troubles. The terms *psychotherapy* and *counseling* are not differentiated since any relationship which permits the client to perceive his needs clearly is therapeutic. There is definitely no attempt to regress the patient emotionally: perceptions of the present are stressed and clarified. The rationale: the central problem of the patient revolves around his *self-concept*, thus threats to his self-concept must be clarified. The approach is strongly intellectual although advocates of this approach believe it to be *feeling* and humanistic.

The entire client-centered or nondirective approach is in marked contrast to a psychoanalytic approach, which applies depth therapy to effect personality change. Psychotherapy, as a psychoanalytically trained therapist uses the term, refers to personality change. Counseling, as seen by him, is supportive treatment for individuals whose problems seem based on reality or situational conflicts. Everything may be considered helpful and therapeutic—the friendly accepting counselor, whether he is a recreation worker, a nondirective therapist, or an intensively trained psychoanalyst who works in depth, either individually or in a group. But there are major theoretical differences behind the practices of these people. When the reader attempts to equate the work of a nondirective therapist with that of a psychoanalyst, whose goals are vastly different, confusion arises.

For example, a very agitated college student arranged to see a counselor at a university counseling center. The counselor was trained in a nondirective approach. The student said that he had been offered a high-paying job in a foreign country but couldn't decide if he should withdraw from college. The counselor listened sympathetically while the student talked about his problems. After several visits, the student decided to accept the position offered and attempt to continue a limited program of evening studies in the country to which he was moving. As far as the student and the counselor were concerned, this solution was reality based. From a psychoanalytic point of view, the more significant problem was that the student's divorced mother was about to marry a wealthy suitor. She stressed the suitor's capacity to earn large sums of money. The student was competitive and angry at his mother for marrying the wealthy suitor. He intended to earn large sums as well. None of this was brought up by the student, and the college counselor didn't inquire about deeper motivations.

A great deal of Rogers' approach has stemmed from his objection to what he calls the reductionism and determinism of psychoanalysis. He objects as well to the scientific objectivity of the psychoanalytic method or other psychotherapy approaches which are based on psychoanalysis.[52]

> From our observations we made only low-level inferences and formulated testable hypotheses. We might have chosen to draw high-level inferences and to have developed abstract, untestable, high-level theory, but I think my own earthly agricultural background deterred me from that. (Freudian thinkers chose this second course, and this marks, in my estimation, one of the most fundamental differences between their approach and the client-centered approach.)[53]

Rogers' comments about research in psychoanalysis reveal a certain naïveté, as he overlooks the most recent comprehensive report on research in psychoanalysis.[54] He describes the encounter movement in psychotherapy as the greatest breakthrough in contemporary psychotherapy.[55]

I recognize that while my whole approach to persons and their relationships changes but slowly (and very little in its fundamentals), my interest in its applications has shifted markedly. No longer am I primarily interested in individual therapeutic learning, but in broader and broader social implications.[56]

One writer describes a group encounter meeting as a "happening, a human adventure, a voyage, the destination of which defies determination."[57] However, another writer states that the encounter group

attracts the opportunist, the promoter, the self-styled healer, the charismatic would-be saint, the sick, and even the sadistic. It appeals to those who . . . go to encounter groups like some go to Arthur Murray Clubs.[58]

Group psychotherapy is quite flexible and therefore lends itself well to the theoretical direction of the group therapist. The Rogerian school of nondirective psychotherapy has served as a base for one type of group therapy. Here, again, there are many variations, since therapists perceive Rogers' work differently. The techniques espoused by Rogers appear to be easily acquired and have proved very popular with many American psychologists, who follow the philosophy of pragmatism.

The philosophical root of Rogers' approach lies in the idea that man is fundamentally good and constantly striving toward a more effective kind of life. Rogers views man as *self-actualizing*. Every effort is made in Rogerian therapy to offer an individual opportunities to recognize his needs and to test ways of satisfying them. Man is perceived as having a positive growth potential. Rogerian therapists claim that, as the client tests his needs in a group, he will find that he can get from others the things that he needs only when he has developed a relationship with them which will stimulate them to give him what he needs.

Many contemporary psychotherapists would accept the concept of man as essentially good and capable of growth, whether they are traditionally trained Freudian psychoanalysts or existential psychotherapists. Where nondirective therapists begin to differ from other schools of therapy is that the phenomenological or client-centered (nondirective) point of view seems to rely too heavily on some force in man to provide the solution of personal difficulties. The stress is upon *personal growth*. The *problem* or *therapy* is not the focus. The reasoning runs as follows: In order to help the individual, one must start with his perception of the problem. The problem that is causing the group (or individual) the most concern should be the focus of immediate attention. Groups (or individuals) have an innate capacity to heal themselves. As the group (or individual) feels more secure or accepted, more and more information is accepted. The egocentric individual resolves his paradox in living as he finds that his needs can be met only through other people. Throughout this nondirective therapy the emphasis is on the client (not the patient, since the term *client* suggests the positive potential, a good but somewhat over-worked point, for it often evades the patient's sometimes legitimate feel-ing that he is "sick"), who is believed to have the inherent ability to recognize and solve his emotional problems as he discusses them with a nondirective, accepting counselor.

The nondirective school argues that every individual has a drive to-ward health, growth, and personality maturation.[59] Change is believed to occur in counseling, which is *not* seen as a preparation for change. Since the counselor is permissive, the client matures psychologically under *self-scrutiny*. The counselor in the nondirective group is not a leader but a catalyst: he helps the client develop self-understanding. The counselor will generally say little in the group except to confront, clarify, and guide what the clients are saying, and presumably thinking. In one experiment client-centered group therapy was used with adult offenders placed on probation by a criminal court. The writers describe the theoretical ap-proach, upon which the group therapy was conducted, as based on the work of Rogers.

> Within this methodological orientation the therapist tries to convey to the client through gesture, posture, facial expression as well as by verbal means, the therapist's *congruence,* his sense of acceptance and of confidence in the ability of the client, with the help of the group, to resolve his problems. The therapist avoids interpretation and does not engage in statements of a probing nature, evaluative comments or reassuring remarks.

Further, these writers state that the

> most important function of the client-centered group therapist is to provide an atmosphere in which the group members feel free to explore their feelings and to communicate these reactions to the other group members. The therapist does not interpret, probe, evaluate or reassess, no matter how attractive the situation may seem for these kinds of explanation.[60]

In a group led by the counselor I have described, a group member may say to another member: "I feel like I want to hug and kiss you. But I'm afraid to." Often the group leader will say: "Why don't you?" The group member will be encouraged. The variety of trust exercises, body hugging, swaying, and so on are all intended to move beyond the verbal and the intellectual. Another group member might say to the group leader: "You make me feel so good, I just want to kiss you." Again, the individual will be encouraged to do so.

A therapist trained in the psychoanalytic method might fear the risk of intensifying homosexual problems or unresolved oedipal problems— incestuous anxieties that a son may have about having intercourse with a mother figure (a woman therapist) or a daughter with a father figure (a male therapist) when such techniques are used. The counselor who uses trust and nonverbal procedures will play down such fears, insisting that, more often than not, they only obstruct the natural growth of the group member. Of course, there are dangers in an approach which may permit a group leader to enjoy the praise of group members—like "Doctor, you're wonderful." When people in distress are grateful because they have found relief they may overreact and the therapist, without being aware of it, may foster such "grateful" behavior. Some lawyers exploit sexually unhappy women who come to them for matrimonial advice. Some physicians exploit women who come to them for aid with sexual problems. Teachers may exploit attractive young students—male or female. The risks are real.

Client-centered or nondirective group therapy appears to be primarily a *relationship* therapy, as opposed to a group therapy of an analytic insight-developing nature. The current interest among students of Rogers is in encounter group techniques. Rogers himself is an enthusiastic exponent of encounter group techniques; this enthusiasm seems to square with both his philosophy of humanism and his belief in *unconditional regard*. He claims that he accepts the client *unconditionally*.

The encounter group will be discussed at greater length in this book but it is important to underscore the fundamentally different philosophical views of human behavior that exist between group therapists who work from a psychoanalytic base and those who work from a nondirective base. This difference is generally overlooked by practitioners. Briefly, it is the difference in philosophy between Hobbes and Rousseau. Many who practice psychoanalytic group psychotherapy feel that they are realistic (Hobbesian) because they emphasize man's capacity to be quite bad as well as quite good. Rogers, stressing man's goodness, is the Rousseau optimist, while *I* have stressed the polarity of man, his capacity to move from goodness to badness quite quickly and easily. Of course, many followers of Rogers' approach feel that the usual *medical model* of psychotherapy tends to minimize the patient's resources and maximize his *illness*. Whether this is accurate, or a denial on the part of the Rogerian therapist of the individual's deep-seated confusion, I shall leave for the reader to judge.

Among the other types of group therapy emphasizing the intellectual approach is the group therapy based on the studies of learning theory developed by O. Hobart Mowrer.[61] Several other investigators have recently described activity in the field of group psychotherapy based on a learning theory approach. Their assumption is that patients' symptoms are learned maladjustments, subject to reinforcement, extinction, and new learning.[62]

Group Psychotherapy in England

The professional literature has paid so much attention to therapy in the United States that, until recently, one tended to think of such therapy as uniquely American. But group psychotherapy was practiced in Europe for many years, and after World War II reports of the exciting work carried out in England during the war reached the United States.[63] In World War II a few British psychoanalysts became interested in the therapeutic potentialities of group processes when they discovered that many soldiers became psychiatric casualties because they had been placed in the wrong jobs. New selection procedures were devised for choosing suitable candidates for officer training. The procedures made use of situational group tests, specifically the "leaderless group" test devised by W. R. Bion, a British psychiatrist. The test was one in which a particular task was given to a group of candidates. Observations were made of the way they went about solving the task. The group was unstructured and leaderless at first. But, as the candidates proceeded to carry out the task, a hierarchy of status developed. Some men chose leader roles, while others chose to collaborate with the leader or to obstruct him. This finding became important when Bion and John Rickman, an experienced and older psychoanalyst, were sent in 1943 to the Northfield Military Hospital to deal with unruly patients.

While Rickman followed a more traditional procedure of group discussions with the troubled men, Bion tried a more daring procedure. Since the men were obviously unhappy with army discipline and wanted to return to civilian life, Bion aimed at changing the traditional authoritarian setting of the military hospital. His goal: transforming the disorganized group into a responsible and cooperative community so that a healthy group structure and feeling of belonging would ensue. Bion therefore relinquished the authoritarian role of the doctor and military officer and gave the patients these options: suffering the discomforts of a chaotically unstructured community life or shouldering the responsibility of organizing communal activities themselves. Faced with these options, the men could no longer use the army as a scapegoat; they had to cope with their own disruptive and antisocial tendencies.

Bion stayed at the hospital for six weeks and succeeded in organizing the men. Later, in the second "Northfield experiment," he worked out a similar technique for a major London hospital; these techniques were linked with methods of small-group psychotherapy. The development of his approach to therapy group activities in Great Britain can be traced to these Northfield experiments. Before this, in 1938, Joshua Bierer had started group treatment in mental hospitals by means of therapeutic social clubs and small discussion groups. His influence was minor, however, and his *social clubs* will be discussed a little further on.[64]

Bion's second experiment led to a reexamination of the administrative structure of mental hospitals, which had grown in size and taken on the look of prisons. The hospitals were only segregating patients from society, not treating them. The work of Bion led therapists to encourage patients to accept more self-determination and responsibility for their activities in the hospital, so that today we have the open-door and open-ward policy, with very few locked wards.

At the Northfield Military Hospital, small-group psychotherapy was widely used. The group membership generally ranged from six to ten in number, similar to the size of the groups that Wolf organized. They met once a week for one and one-half hours. The majority of group therapists in Britain have modeled their work on psychoanalytic practice and generally follow the structure devised at Northfield.

BION'S SYSTEM

After World War II, in 1948, Bion was placed in charge of group psychotherapy at the Tavistock Clinic in London. This clinic stimulated many therapists to work with groups. During this period Bion trained in psychoanalysis, as did most of the other psychiatrists at the clinic. He was strongly influenced by Melanie Klein, who was his psychoanalyst, and her influence is reflected in the type of group psychotherapy practiced by many who work at Tavistock. Most of the American psychologists and psychiatrists who visited Tavistock, particularly the social psychologists, were ignorant of the subtle nuances involved as they observed the various techniques used with groups here. In a sense, more and more confusion found its way into the literature and history of group psychotherapy. Here are the facts: Bion's work has attracted the interest of many American researchers in the field of group dynamics but has been largely ignored by group psychotherapists.

Unlike most group psychotherapists who have concerned themselves with individual functioning in the group, Bion has concerned himself with the group context and has studied the group variables at work within group psychotherapy. In a series of seven articles that he wrote for the journal, *Human Relations,* and in a later article written for the *International Journal of Psychoanalysis,* all of which he later incorporated in a book, he attempted to set forth a theory of group culture and social structure which would apply to group psychotherapy.[65] By chance, researchers in group dynamics at Teachers College, Columbia University, as well as researchers working at the University of Chicago under the direction and stimulus of Herbert Thelen, an educator and social psychologist, stumbled across Bion's work. Thelen, who will be discussed a little later, has summarized Bion's speculations concerning group processes, and has attempted to coalesce Bion's theories with some of his own research on emotional dynamics and group culture.[66]

Bion worked with small groups of neurotic patients at the Tavistock Clinic. He decided to provide the group with no direction or structure. He probably did this for two reasons. First, he wasn't sure of what he was doing so he decided to remain silent. Second, he is a rather withdrawn individual. The patients, as a result of Bion's silence, were puzzled, upset, angry, and showed as well a variety of other reactions. Bion focused on the group's mood as well as the individual member's reactions to the group situation. As Bion became aware of the group's emotional state he interpreted for the group what he believed to be occurring. His emphasis was on the interpretation of group reactions rather than on the individual member's reactions. Also, he interpreted almost immediately the group situation to the group. The more Bion worked with his groups, the more he noticed certain intense emotional responses. At different times the members of the group seemed to desire much more direction from the group therapist, and at other times the members seemed to be expressing a desire to run away from the group. Bion speculated that the group was in a series of emotional states, or what he called *basic assumption cultures*. There seemed to be some emotional need tied in with what the group was trying to accomplish. Bion concluded that group members were reacting to these cultures. They seemed to form relationships with each other based on their reactions to the cultures. Bion called the individual member's relationship to the different cultures *valences*. (S. H. Foulkes, the British analyst, also an important figure in the history of group therapy, who will be discussed later, has stated his belief that what Slavson calls *social hunger* and Bion's concept of valency are closely related or even identical concepts. I would not agree.)

Bion observed that at times the group, while ostensibly involved in solving a problem, seemed to be moving further and further away from the ostensible problem and its possible solution. For example, the group might appear to be just sitting in silence unless one observed that the group members were preoccupied with their relationship to the leader. Why didn't the members speak up? Bion concluded that the group's behavior could be described in one of three cultures—work-*dependency* culture; work-*pairing* culture; work-*fight-flight* culture—or some aspect of these cultures. The members of the group have come together because of strong basic needs. The desire of the members is to find a leader and hold onto the leader who will meet their needs—direct them to fight-flight when danger threatens or help them find a sexual partner. Bion believed that the group members were engaged in a search for a leader. Now they were together and they could not exist without the leader. The silence was all related to culture present at that moment. If a leader were not present, an idea might be created to serve as the leader theme.

Rather than interpret the group's behavior based on the individual model of psychodynamics, Bion has constructed a group psychology of the unconscious. He has moved beyond Freud's limited ideas concerning group psychology. His fundamental concept is the description of valences in the group: pairing-counterpairing (movement toward intimacy or a desire to remain isolated); dependency-counterdependency (reliance on or rejection of external authority); and fight-flight (fighting or fleeing from stress).

What probably puzzles most people who study Bion's approach is their unawareness of how much of his work has been influenced by Melanie Klein, his psychoanalyst. Klein was an English psychoanalyst whose theories carry great weight among British and South American psychoanalysts. (The British trained the Argentinians, who trained the Brazilians, and so it went.) Her thinking is inbedded in Bion's view of human behavior. Essentially, she has modified the orthodox Freudian concept of personality. She believed that the ego exists *from birth*. The mother represents the external world to the infant who is in contact with her. Good and bad emotions come from the infant's contact with the mother. The infant's capacity to love as well as feelings of persecution stem from these early contacts with the mother, and these contacts are in turn influenced by environmental and constitutional factors. As the infant ego develops, two major processes appear—introjection and projection.

The situations, and more important, the people whom the infant encounters are taken up into the inner life of the infant. This is *introjection*. The infant attributes to other people different feelings. This is *projection*. The interplay of introjection and projection is basic to the infant's perception of the world and his personality development. The ego, which exists from birth, splits in the early months of life. Objects are divided into good and bad. The ego growth is accompanied by anxiety and destructive impulses. Klein labeled this the *paranoid-schizoid* position. Hopefully, there is healthy development and the infant is increasingly able to understand reality. However, from the sixth to the twelfth month of his life, the infant enters a depressed period which is related to his guilt and anxiety about his destructive impulses. The infant *never* fully recovers from this depressed period and this plays a fundamental part in the child's concept of social relationships. Human relationships, according to Klein, can be interpreted in terms of introjection and projection and splitting. Bion's approach is related to Klein's perception of social relationships.

Although Bion himself was rather quiet in his work with groups, the group therapist who follows Bion's approach (based on Kleinian concepts) will be much more active in his work with therapy groups. He will interpret much more quickly than other group therapists. Indeed, his interpretations will start from the very first meeting of the group. This is quite disconcerting to more traditionally trained therapists but is perfectly consonant with an approach that emphasizes group culture. A psychoanalyst described to me an incident where a Bion-oriented and Kleinian-influenced group therapist came to visit a group therapy session conducted by the analyst, who was trained in the Karen Horney tradition. From the moment the visiting analyst came, he was interpreting the group culture—in this case, that the group was in a murderous mood. The analyst, who had extended the invitation to the visitor, sat there petrified, worried about the impact of such interpretations upon the more depressed and anxiety-ridden patients. The visiting analyst felt that the rage of certain group members had to be brought to the surface immediately, else the group could not function. This would be an example of a fight-flight culture.

An analyst who followed Wolf's approach might answer that this early confrontation of patients' unwillingness to cope with rage merely helped strengthen their resistance to further exploration. Indeed, the group leader's unwillingness to explore his own anger might be the critical issue. This would be an individual-centered approach to the group.

FOULKES' SYSTEM

The outstanding exponent of group therapy in England is currently S. H. Foulkes, who founded the Group Analytic Society of London.[67] Foulkes was trained in neurology, psychiatry, and psychoanalysis in Vienna and Frankfurt, Germany. He was assistant for two years to Kurt Goldstein, the neurologist who followed the *organismic theory* of behavior, based largely upon his work with brain-damaged patients. Goldstein had also worked closely with W. Gelb, a gestalt psychologist, and Foulkes attended Gelb's lectures where he learned about the gestalt view of psychology—the whole is greater than the sum of its parts. Foulkes became the first director of the Frankfurt Psychoanalytic Institute and was there from 1931 to 1933.

The Frankfurt Psychoanalytic Institute was lodged in the same building as the sociological institutes of the university and these institutes were headed by two great sociologists, Max Horkheimer and Karl Mannheim. The psychoanalytic institute worked in close cooperation with the sociological institutes, especially the one headed by Horkheimer. Senior psychoanalysts at the institute, such as Karl Landauer and Wilhelm Meng, were well aware of the sociological and cultural factors in psychoanalysis. Erich Fromm and his wife at that time, Frieda Fromm-Reichmann, taught at the Frankfurt institute. But there was no discussion of or contact with group therapy or its concepts.

In 1933 Foulkes was invited to England by Ernest Jones, the pioneer psychoanalyst, and became a training analyst for British psychiatrists. By the time he became involved in work with groups in 1939, he was an established psychiatrist and psychoanalyst in England. He had read Burrow's papers in Germany during the 1920s. He states that he knew of other work through "hearsay." He knew Schilder since they had both worked in Vienna, and assumed that Schilder and he would work along the same lines since their views had much in common. But Foulkes states:

> Later post-war (World War II) experience showed that Schilder had not done anything near what I was doing. My own first post-war visit to the USA in 1949 made me aware that what was understood there at that time amongst analysts was very different from my concept. This led to a kind of defensive and erroneous equation on my American friends' part between my work and that of the Tavistock (and of K. Lewin) which I need not tell you is a very different approach—although I had influenced many of the original workers at the Tavistock during the war.[68]

Foulkes came to Northfield Military Neurosis Centre in 1943 and remained there until 1946. Apparently, he had had no knowledge of Bion's and Rickman's work in the very same setting. Perhaps it was so large that professionals did not keep in contact with one another. Foulkes was far more sophisticated than Bion when he began working with groups at Northfield, and introduced on a large scale the idea of group treatment and transformed part of the setting he was responsible for into a therapeutic community.

Foulkes describes himself as a psychoanalyst and bases his work on psychoanalytic concepts but states that he is also close to gestalt theory and the topological theory of Kurt Lewin. He does not appear to have been successful in fitting together psychoanalysis and Lewin's concepts. More recently, he has denied the relationship between Lewin's concepts and his clinical work. He uses the concept of *figure-ground configuration,* a term used in gestalt psychology. The use of the term has confused many people. He states:

> However, my concept of the group-as-a-whole and of a network were influenced by my teacher Kurt Goldstein who taught his students to consider the total organism as a whole, the total nervous system as a whole network, and the individual ganglion cells as centers, nodal points, inside this network. These notions, related in their holist point of view to Gestalt psychology are deliberately reflected in my use of the terms "network" and "nodal points" to refer to an interrelated group of individuals. This is probably the common ground which makes Americans feel that my approach is close to Kurt Lewin's. I know little of his approach, and as far as I can tell, Bion and (Henry) Ezriel (another leading group psychotherapist in England) know even less. Apart from this, I believe that Kurt Lewin turned his attention to groups about six or seven years after my own first manifest work with groups and after I already expressed these very same thoughts. As a lifelong psychoanalyst, I am concerned quite particularly with unconscious processes, which is the opposite of Kurt Lewin's approach.[69]

This is a very pleasant way to say that Lewin, the stimulus for sensitivity groups, was antipsychoanalysis.

What is the Foulkes approach?[70] He does not like to apply the word *psychoanalysis* to a multipersonal situation since he reserves the term for psychoanalysis in the classic sense—individual treatment where the patient is on the couch. He has speculated that over the course of the years psychoanalysis may be used less and less and only in special circumstances. This is the way he works.

The *group analyst* (a term he employs) meets with seven or eight patients for an hour and a half. The patients are seated in a circle and no directions are given. The idea is that this will lead to spontaneous reactions. The leader of the group is a participant observer who interprets and clarifies transference reactions as they occur in the group. He also points out the relationships between group members as well as the communications. The presence of other people in the group is supposed to discourage the regressive infantile relationship that a patient experiences in individual analysis. (The analyst who practices individual psychotherapy would answer that the regression is precisely what promotes deep-seated change.)

Members of the group react to all communications, just as if they were analysts reacting to individual free association. The group analyst, called a *conductor,* is a very important figure whose influence is decisive, for therapy is perceived as dependent upon the conductor being present at the group meetings. The conductor reveals very little about his own life but encourages and accepts fantasies and reactions to him. The group analytic meeting is called a T-situation, one in which therapeutic processes are at work. This kind of T-group has *nothing* in common with the T-groups of the National Training Laboratories in the United States which are based on Kurt Lewin's approach to groups and their formation.

The viewpoint of Foulkes is that emotional disturbances are due in large part to processes that involve a group of people who are in interaction. This network of interaction is of central importance, for a change in one member of the network results in a change in another member of the network. The patient wants to change himself or relieve his own symptoms without changes in the rest of the network. This cannot be. He has entered a therapy group from his own sick network and this must be examined in the new group of which he is a member. The group analytic situation is called by Foulkes the group *matrix* (a communicational network) and the network refers to the group where the patient became emotionally disturbed as well as the therapy group.

In many ways, Foulkes reflects Burrow's concern with the sick society. Although Foulkes describes himself as a Freudian psychoanalyst, he rejects two major hypotheses of Freud as far as groups are concerned. He rejects the Freudian concept of two basic drives in the individual—Eros (the life instinct) and Thanatos (the death instinct), which would be expressed in the group as the struggle between constructive and destructive forces. Eros represents the forces that bring people together to work with one another in a group. Thanatos represents the forces that lead to fear and consequently the fragmentation of group structure.

Foulkes also rejects a second hypothesis of Freud, that an independent social drive or herd instinct leads to the behavior observed in the group. He states that the group is a more fundamental unit than the individual: "Collectively they constitute the very norm, from which individually, they deviate. . . . The group tends to speak and react to a common theme as if it were—a living entity, expressing itself in different ways through various mouths."[71] Currently, Foulkes accepts completely Freud's statement that the death instinct hypothesis is necessary for a full understanding of the unconscious and is in fact a universal biological phenomenon. Konrad Lorenz, the ethnologist, disputes this theory and calls it biologically untenable. Foulkes also agrees with Freud that the superego (conscience) is charged with destructive tendencies.

Other British Approaches

Henry Ezriel, a British psychoanalyst who works with groups, is interested in the difference between the surface and unconscious processes that occur in the group.[72] He states that a problem common to all members of the group leads to tension. This tension is at the base of the unconscious fantasies of all group members. He is referring to a collective fantasy. He also states that members project unconscious fantasies upon one another, leading them to try and manipulate one another. Ezriel would stress exploration of the group tension and patterns of manipulation in his therapy approach. What he calls manipulation is actually not so different from the transference that Wolf has described which leads people to relate to one another on an unconscious level.

Joshua Bierer introduced the term *social psychiatry* in his work with groups in England in a mental hospital setting.[73] His orientation originally followed the concepts of Alfred Adler. His approach is social-educational and he favors a leader-centered and more active approach to work with groups. He has stressed the use of day hospitals—where patients only spend part of the day at the mental hospital—and strongly supports the use of therapeutic social clubs where patients develop the social skills needed to exist in an urban society.

Maxwell Jones began working with groups in England after World War II. He was originally more didactic in his approach and used class and discussion methods. He then became more psychoanalytic in his approach and moved on to work in mental hospitals where he organized *therapeutic communities,* somewhat related to Bion's Northfield Military Hospital experiment. He became very interested in the democratic staff functioning of psychiatric facilities. He stresses that the entire mental hospital staff should be involved in patient treatment with no hierarchies.[74] The person who is best equipped emotionally to treat a group of patients should do so—whether it be nurse, psychiatrist, or ward attendant. Recently, Jones feels that psychiatry should concern itself with primary school education as a way of preventing mental disorder and has become active in education.[75]

The culture of the country reflects the practice of group psychotherapy. The Americans seem to be more active and experimental. The British are more careful and reflective. Patients respond to a group leader in terms of their cultural background. In Greece a leader is expected to be very much in control in the therapy group. An American patient may more easily accept a group leader who does not exercise his authority. There is now more exchange of opinion between the United States, England, and Europe, as well as Australia.

Group Process and Group Psychotherapy

Shortly after World War II, Herbert Thelen, an educator at the University of Chicago, began a series of investigations in his Human Dynamics Laboratory. He was especially interested in group dynamics and studied the composition and developmental phases of a group, the formation of subgroups, and group culture, as well as how an individual learns and changes in a group. He developed a method of studying how group members perceive one another's personality and the sequence of group interaction. During his research, he came across the writing of Bion whose thinking seemed to fit into his own ideas about group interaction, the relationship between the individual personality and the culture of the group, and the importance of thought and emotion in the life of the group. He developed a theoretical position partially based on Bion's work and decided to subject Bion's speculations to systematic research.[76] Since Thelen is a modest and self-effacing man, his work is not too well known, which is unfortunate because it is a good illustration of group dynamics research applied to clinical practice of group psychotherapy.

The practitioner of group psychotherapy cannot decide to conduct research with patients he is responsible for just for the sake of research. In addition, many psychologists and sociologists who enjoy laboratory situations are uneasy about working with clinicians who do not present simple problems. While it is not important to describe Thelen's theories, his impact was particularly felt by two of his students, Morton Lieberman and Dorothy Stock-Whitaker, who published a book in 1964, *Psychotherapy Through the Group Process,* in which the group is emphasized as a social system.[77] They also included the ideas of Thomas French, a Chicago-based psychoanalyst, who wrote about *group focal conflict theory*.[78] The *focal conflict* in any meeting of a group is the most superficial conflict which explains all or almost all of the behavior and verbalizations during the group meeting. Rather than interpret the disturbing motive in any conflict, the group therapist interprets the reactions. Focal conflict was originally devised by French as a way of understanding dreams and the dynamics of individual psychoanalysis. He assumed that in an analytic session there appear to be many diverse and apparently unrelated elements which would also appear in a patient's dream. But he felt that there was an underlying relatedness and coherence. All of what transpires in the dream(s) and the patient's associations to the dream(s) can be related to a particular preconscious conflict which he called *focal* for that particular analytic session. During the group therapy session there is a slowly emerging and developing conflict situation, and the group members are making attempts by their behavior to solve the focal conflict. The here-and-now behavior of the patient is a method of solving conflicts that occurred early in his life and were buried.

An example of a focal group conflict is the group members' reactions to the inclusion of a new member. Their reactions are varied. The original members will try to keep out the new member by ignoring him or flooding him with anger. In Wolf's approach, the group leader would explore the historical reaction to the birth of a new sibling (brother or sister) as represented by the new member. The original anxiety or anger has now surfaced. In the focal conflict approach, the group therapist would elicit and define the reactions of the group members toward the new patient. In another group the patients seemed to be in turmoil. It became evident that the patients were upset because the group therapist was leaving for an extended vacation. The patients felt abandoned. For some, it was a sense of distrust and they felt betrayed: "You are leaving when I need you." For others, it was "What's the use. I knew it would happen. That's why I'm depressed." The focal conflict would be the sense of abandonment. Another approach would be to trace back the earlier experience of abandonment, possibly by the parents, and relate this to present-day behavior.

The approach of Lieberman and Stock-Whitaker stresses the stereotyped response of the group member, and the group behaves in such a way as to reduce the fear that the patient experiences. Essentially, it is an oversimplified approach to deeper conflicts and avoids the larger question of what keeps the therapy group together.

Gestalt Therapy and Group Psychotherapy

Frederick S. Perls, who liked to be called "Fritz" Perls, was born in Germany. He claimed that he was trained in the psychoanalytic method by "outstanding teachers." He moved to South Africa and developed a theory of *gestalt therapy*. It is rather obscure as to why he chose the word *gestalt,* which is a term used first by psychologists in Germany who wanted to describe the holistic quality of the human organism—the whole is greater than the sum of its parts. Perls later claimed that he selected the name gestalt therapy because he admired the gestalt psychologists who, according to him, believed in the wholeness of man.[79] Gestalt therapy encompasses a highly flexible approach to intensive psychotherapy and Perls believed it to be a theory of personality. Some of his students use the term to describe an entire approach to life.

Perls and his wife moved to New York City where both of them trained psychotherapists. He moved on to Miami, Florida; to Cleveland, Ohio; to Carmel, California (Esalen), the home of the encounter movement; and, just before he died, to Vancouver, British Columbia. Everywhere he lived and practiced he trained psychotherapists who became very devoted to him and gestalt therapy. He was a charismatic individual and was very intuitive. He could become bored with a patient quite easily and would simply state that he was bored and dismiss the patient. Ultimately, he believed that individual psychotherapy had outlived its usefulness and became attracted to group therapy. What he called group therapy is actually one-to-one therapy conducted in a group setting.

In 1951 Perls, Ralph Hefferline, and Paul Goodman published a book called *Gestalt Therapy: The Excitement and Growth in the Human Personality*.[80] The theory set forth in the book was that the normal individual reacts as a whole organism and not as a fragmented and disorganized person. The organism forms figures and grounds, according to Perls. A figure is defined as any process that emerges, which becomes a foreground and stands out against a background. The person is concerned about the figure. In the normal person a constant flow of figures emerges from the background, fades away, or is destroyed. If a need is gratified, the old gestalt is no longer needed and is destroyed. A new gestalt emerges. Perls referred to aggressive destruction and reconstruction and this is the destruction of the old gestalt and the emergence of the new gestalt. The organism needs healthy aggression in order to survive and the individual must be encouraged to express aggressive feelings in an appropriate fashion. The goal of gestalt therapy is for the person to form figures and grounds, to destroy gestalts, and finally to be able to use his aggressive feelings appropriately. All of this is believed to help the person find his potential.[81]

In gestalt therapy the *here and now* is stressed and the individual is always asked to examine how and what he is doing. He is encouraged to be *responsible* for his own behavior. Questions that the patient asks are discouraged. Many of Perls' students like to call the people in gestalt therapy *clients*. Perls believed that the individual would regulate himself if left alone. Clients have been encouraged to think too much. Perls called this "mind fucking." They must be encouraged to experience emotions and senses.

In actual practice, Perls would sit next to an empty chair with a group of patients (clients) watching. The chair was called the *hot seat* and Perls would work with the person who volunteered to sit in it. Those who observe are getting therapy. Dreams are stressed as very important and there is great emphasis on the voice patterns or posture of the individual in the hot seat. The patient is responsible for his own participation and no one is encouraged to participate. An important goal in gestalt group therapy is the awareness of the moment. The participant is asked to explore fantasies and dreams in front of the group. A group leader will actively encourage the patient to express his pent-up anger in front of the onlooking group. Or the patient may be asked to take on different roles in order to evoke intense emotions. A man might be asked to imagine how it felt to be dominated as a child and now he will be encouraged to express his rage at this domination. The catharsis was believed to lead to a basic change in personality. In a dream exploration, the patient is asked to express each of the dream symbols since Perls believed that each part of the dream represented a part of the patient.

While Perls never stated that he was influenced by psychodrama, many of his techniques are very similar. He did not settle for abreaction as a cure and at the end of his life expressed himself bluntly by attacking practitioners of psychotherapy who espouse instant cure or instant joy. He described them as "phoney therapists."

In his practice of group therapy, Perls was in control and discouraged free group interaction. If a group member volunteered a comment, Perls would consider this as interference. He spoke simply and used vernacular expressions. Many of the people who took part in his group therapy believed that they were helped by empathic identification. He was impatient with a more introspective approach and patients who desire a good deal of interaction with the therapist appear to be responsive to gestalt therapy. The detached patient would simply get lost. Currently, Perls' students appear to have modified his approach. They spend more time with clients and are less critical.[88] His technique attracts both therapists and patients who seem more active and motoric.

Perls described the neurosis as consisting of five layers. The first is the layer of social behavior which consists of meaningless mannerisms. Perls would attack this behavior immediately. Second is role playing. Perls would point out the role engaged in by the patient. Third is the impasse when the gestalt therapist refuses to accept behavior which is stereotyped; as a result the patient becomes upset, fearful, and experiences intense loneliness. The fourth stage results in implosion and the patient is locked in battle with intense opposing forces within his behavior. He believes that he will die. The fifth stage is the explosion, which may manifest itself in anger or grief. This is what the therapist aims for.

The technique of gestalt group therapy is abrasive and the theory seems very oversimplified. Many patients probably enjoy the intense attention that they receive when the hot-seat approach is used.

Transactional Analysis and Group Psychotherapy

Transactional analysis began to be used in 1954. It was developed by Eric Berne, a psychiatrist who was from Montreal, Canada, and who moved to New York City where he began training as a psychoanalyst. He continued his studies in San Francisco, California, and claimed that he *was* trained as a psychoanalyst. The institutes that he attended have stated that he was not accredited by either as having completed his training. His work stemmed from articles published in 1949 where he was concerned with intuition, the capacities of the ego, and the importance of the child ego state, which he considered the most important part of the personality.[83]

Berne organized study groups of professionals who lived in the San Francisco Bay area and met with them from 1958 until his sudden death in 1970. After this, his students organized into more formal training groups which offer accreditation to those who study with them. The strongest influence of the transactional analysis approach is to be felt in the western United States, especially California, although more recently it has gained favor in the Southwest.

There are three forms of ego function according to transactional analysis: the parent, the adult, and the child. Berne was impatient with what he felt to be the overintellectual approach of Freud. He described the concept of superego, ego, and id as too abstract. Berne felt that the states of parent, adult, and child are observable states. The *parent* ego state is fashioned after parent figures or those people who served as parent surrogates. This state is basic to the survival of civilization. The *adult* ego state gathers data and is arbitrary. It is rational but cut off from feelings. The *child* ego state is the way an individual behaves when he is a child. Adults are not supposed to engage in child ego state behavior except at parties, athletic events, or festivities. If a person is in a child ego state, he will walk or sit like a child or use child expressions such as "gee whiz." According to transactional analysis, people can obscure ego states by sometimes behaving like an adult while actually being in the child ego state. An example of this would be a person who has learned to speak in a reasonable adult-like fashion which obscures the changeable behavior of a child.[84]

In many ways, Berne has reformulated the role theory stated by social psychologists. A woman can be a mother, wife, and mistress all at the same time. People are engaged in different role relationships in everyday life. Berne's approach appears to be oversimplistic.

When a patient enters group therapy with a practitioner of transactional analysis, his behavior is examined as a transaction that occurs in the ego states of adult, parent, child. The transaction occurs *within* one person rather than transactions *among* people. People, according to Berne, live by engaging in a series of games which are repeated again and again. Freud would have called this the *repetition-compulsion,* the unconscious need to repeat certain behavior. But Berne stated that his approach is more comprehensive. He claimed that the repetition-compulsion covers the reenactment of past experiences in life which the patient never worked out while his description of games that people play looks to the future as well as to the past. According to him, a person follows a script based on a blueprint for living. The script, like a stage script, is based on decisions made in early childhood. In the group, the transactional analyst observes the transaction, explores the games that are played, and works out the script that the patient has established. The group therapist is very much in control of the group, not unlike gestalt therapy, and the group is leader oriented rather than peer oriented. The leader works with each group member in turn and therapy is conducted *in* the group rather than *with* the group. The therapist exercises control of the group and does not give up his strong leadership role. If he does, the therapy group becomes a "party," according to Berne.

The group in transactional analysis is heterogeneous in composition. Selection procedures are not considered important. In actual practice, Eric Berne did not work with patients who were manic, obsessional, hysteric, or phobic. He recommended that those patients be treated by psychoanalysts, many of whom in turn recommend that phobic patients are best treated by behavior therapists. The goal of transactional therapy is *cure,* a term which means many different things to different patients. In order to follow the goal of cure, when patients meet in a group setting they have agreed to a contract with the transactional therapist and the patients may decide which material is not relevant. All of what has been described is a very pragmatic approach to psychotherapy. It seems to work best with patients who are motivated and verbal, who need a structured approach, and who desire a strong therapist. The more withdrawn, introspective person would have a difficult time in transactional group therapy. Although Berne stated that *no selection* of patients was the clinical rule, his approach has attracted verbal patients.

Gestalt therapy and transactional analysis owe much to the work of Wilhelm Reich, a psychoanalyst who introduced many innovative ideas into dynamic psychotherapy.[85] Among his ideas is the analysis of *body language*—how you sit, gesture, and so on—and *body armor*—the tightness or looseness of your posture, whether you are "tight-assed," walk with mincing steps, or stride along, and so on. Reich, who practiced psychoanalysis from the mid-1920s to the early 1930s, formulated an *or-*

gone theory related to the sexual orgasm. His views began to veer off markedly from traditional psychoanalysis and he was expelled from the analytic societies. Since he was a Marxist, he stated that his expulsion was motivated by politics. Toward the end of his life, he stated that he was able to cure cancer. This led to prosecution by the U.S. government, imprisonment, and a heart attack which he suffered while in jail. It is not clear as to whether Perls, the basic figure in the gestalt therapy approach, or Berne, the founder of transactional analysis, knew of Reich's approach because neither expressed indebtedness for many of the ideas they incorporated.

The Marathon Group

The marathon group is an accelerated interaction group. It has gained popularity over the past five years. The origin of the marathon group can be traced back to 1963 when Frederick Stoller and Gene Waller participated in a sensitivity training laboratory conducted by George Lehner at the University of California in Los Angeles. The sensitivity group extended over a weekend and this stimulated Stoller to apply a time-extended experience to the group psychotherapy he was practicing. During this same period of time, George Bach, a group psychotherapist, had also been experimenting with the idea.[86] Bach and Stoller began to use the technique with Bach's patients. Stoller has stated that his approach avoids the mental illness model. It is based on an ahistorical focus. It emphasizes for each group member the responsibility for his own fate. It concentrates upon the potential of the group member and the future rather than emphasizing past and current difficulties. The philosophical approach is humanistic and the orientation is here and now.

The marathon group is not bound by traditional procedures used in psychotherapy. Over a period of time, intense reactions are generated. The group meetings can last anywhere from 12 to 72 hours with some breaks for eating and sleeping. The setting is informal and food and drink are served. The group leader interacts and exposes himself to the scrutiny of the group members. Defense mechanisms are explored immediately by the therapist and the group members. Therapy is limited to the specific time period and occasionally there is a followup about six months later.[87]

The theory behind the marathon group approach is that the long time period which group members spend with one another leads to a speedier dissolution of neurotic defense mechanisms as well as a more intense and effective therapy experience. The theory may be accurate but I am skeptical. Lifelong defenses are not dissolved by accelerated interaction. Like gourmet cooking, where the food has to simmer and be brought to a slow boil, the individual cannot be "cooked" quickly. Often the patient is incapable of absorbing the insights that are presented in a short time span. Up to this time of writing, marathon group therapy practitioners do not report adverse reactions. It is interesting to note that current techniques are not at such great variance with the more traditional techniques. The marathon group members are encouraged to penetrate façades quickly. Yet as far back as 1949 Wolf, who is considered one of the *traditional* advocates of group psychotherapy, described his technique of *going around* and stated: "A by-product of the going around technique and free association is the penetration of facades to reveal each member's inner conflict trends . . . (and further) . . . (stressing that rehearsal of the patient's past is useless and time consuming) . . . transferences that occur at the moment should be analyzed and if these are connected with the history of the patient's past, then the history becomes meaningful."[88]

Videotape Approaches

In 1970 the first text devoted to the use of videotape techniques in psychiatric training and treatment, particularly in group psychotherapy, appeared in the literature.[89] The use of videotape techniques has spread quickly in the fields of education and psychotherapy as well as in research in human behavior.[90] When one considers that the first use of closed-circuit television to describe five surgical operations at Johns Hopkins Hospital occurred in 1947, the growth of videotape has been enormous.

The videotape approach tends to emphasize confrontation as a technique. In a group session, portions of the videotape will be played back for the group to study. The patient is able to observe immediately what he has done in relation to other members of the group. When used with a family or group composed of couples, the patterns of behavior are captured and played back for analysis. But there are large problems involved. The issue of privacy and the invasion of privacy is of great concern. The "cooperative" patient who participates may be too frightened, grateful, or upset to object. Does the videotape technique stimulate change or does the patient get caught up in a "Hollywood production" where he is gratified by the filmed image of himself? There are no easy answers. Videotape techniques are being used by therapists who subscribe to a psychoanalytic point of view as well as by those who emphasize operant conditioning where the group therapist actively manipulates the patient's behavior.

Family Therapy—Different Approaches

Psychoanalytic psychotherapists, until very recently, did not treat members of the same family. Indeed, they avoided the idea, even going so far as to refuse to meet with members of a patient's family. The situation has changed. Today families are treated as a unit.[91] Nathan Ackerman was one of the first psychoanalysts who insisted that the patient could not be understood apart from the family and he moved toward treatment of the patient and the patient's family.[92] Another psychoanalyst, Martin Grotjahn,[93] noted that there was a precedent for family therapy since Freud treated "Little Hans" in 1909 by asking the boy's father to serve as a psychotherapist. There are many radical changes predicted and at work in the family structure of Americans. It appears that family therapists will have to help families adjust to the radical changes. The family therapist of the future will have to be a figure who embodies the warmth, wisdom, and experience of the old-time family physician and the psychodynamic skills of the psychoanalyst.

Some family therapists study the families in terms of transference phenomena. Members of the family are perceived by the individual *not* as they really are but as representative of important figures of the person's own childhood. The individual then transfers images of his inner childhood family, as he recalls them, to the outer realistic family of adult life. For each individual, then, there would exist: his real childhood family, the unconscious image of that family within himself, and the projection of these images onto the family of the next generation. If an individual has not worked out a conflict between himself and some other member of his childhood family, the conflict is reenacted with family members of the next generation. The individual projects onto these people unconscious images. Conflicts that exist in all families are worked through in a healthy family without conscious insight. The individual comes to a realistic view of his family. But in the unhappy neurotic family the conflict is endless.

More recently, there are some group psychotherapists who attempt to utilize general system theory[94] in order to gain a broader perspective of the family in therapy or of a group of patients.[95] The culture is perceived as a system with checks and balances and certain feedback. Indeed, Speck involves the larger family in his network therapy—grandparents, aunts, uncles, cousins, close friends.[96] The surface has hardly been scratched in many of the innovative approaches.

Recently, there has been a good deal of attention paid to nonverbal communication in families. This is generally what goes on in human relationships and especially in families. People don't spell it all out but there is a nonverbal language at work—a wink, a sigh, a facial grimace, and so on. This permits ease of functioning in the family. If nonverbal communication is disturbed, serious conflicts may result. Sometimes one member of the family is picked as the sick one. The entire family works out conflicts by focusing on one person. This person is believed to be the cause of all the family's problems. A hidden compact is made. The neurotic wife of an alchoholic may maintain her stability by catering to a drunken husband.

As soon as he becomes healthier in his patterns and stops drinking, she begins to fall apart.

In one family in therapy Bryan, age 17, was defined as the psychotic teenager. His father Michael, a businessman, was completely unethical in his business dealings. He would deny oral contracts or contracts sealed with a handshake and spent his life "wheeling and dealing." Bryan's mother Gilda was completely narcissistic. She would spend her days playing tennis, or if the weather was poor she would go to fashion shows. Any other free time was spent sunning herself. When Bryan began to act erratically, failing in school, distorting and threatening to stab his mother or cut off his penis, his father, away from home at the time on a business trip, was contacted. He would not interrupt his business trip but suggested that it was time to "fix Bryan up with a whore." Bryan's older sister Jean was married to a lawyer and lived 2,000 miles away from her parents in order to *preserve* her sanity. When mother and father and Bryan were in family therapy the focus was on Bryan's "craziness," and yet the father kept asking if there "was any way for the doctor to fix it so that Bryan could get his driving license." This at a time when Bryan was acutely disturbed and a risk to both pedestrians and other motorists. The father needed someone to help him drive an auto so that he could make business deliveries. It was difficult to decide who was the most disturbed in the family, yet Bryan was tagged with the label since his unhappiness was most obvious.

John Bell has recently formulated a theory of family therapy where the small-group theory of social psychology is applied to the natural family group. The social systems of the family are explored in his approach.[97] Currently, married couples are being treated in groups. This works well with many couples as they observe other people in patterns of relatedness. If a divorce occurs in the group of married couples, other couples often view it as a disaster and become discouraged about treatment, and the group may dissolve.

Over the last ten years, many articles have been published describing new breakthroughs in group psychotherapy. Most of them are long on testimonial and short on theory. There is much more use made of two therapists at the same time in both individual and group psychotherapy. The names given to the techniques of using multiple therapists are dual leadership, co-therapy, multiple therapy, role divided therapy, three-cornered interview, joint interview, and cooperative psychotherapy.[98] The techniques appear to be exciting but it is still not clear as to whether treatment is more intensive, shorter, or in any way significantly improved. Often the use of co-therapists helps clinics and hospitals train new personnel—one works and the other trains by observing. While this benefits professionals, what about the patient? Does it mean anything as far as the patient is concerned? The reports indicate that it can be helpful, especially in working with families, couples, or a group of patients where there is an impasse.

Researching the Encounter Group

In 1973 Morton Lieberman, Irwin Yalom, and Matthew Miles published the results of their research on encounter groups.[99] This research, which has evoked protests from many encounter group practitioners, has been largely critical. It points out that much of the success of the encounter groups is based on charismatic leaders and a short-lived state of euphoria which participants experience. It is doubtful as to whether the human potential movement will offer anything of substance to group psychotherapy.

The Current Scene

It is difficult to state what is truly new in group psychotherapy today. The strong impression is that a "hard-sell" campaign exists for many group therapy practitioners.[100] Modesty does not appear to be the strongest point. The old arguments continue. Michael Farrell wrote in 1962:

> The manifestations of transference interaction among group members constitute the therapeutic climate in group therapy, and the resolution and understanding of these multiple transference constellations which exist in simultaneous interaction among group members is the unique therapeutic task of the group therapist.[101]

Helen Durkin wrote in 1962 and 1964: "The question, therefore, becomes not *whether* transference develops in the group, but what form it takes."[102]

Remember that many British group therapists have stressed the phenomenon of the dynamic totality of the group. They view the combined group process rather than in terms of transference to the whole group. S. H. Foulkes and E. J. Anthony have summed up their positions as follows: "Transference phenomena do occur in the group but they are not of paramount importance for the therapeutic trend of the group."[103] Pavlovian concepts dominate group psychotherapy which is practiced in the Soviet Union and Czechoslovakia.[104] After many years of group therapy practice, there is still a dearth of reputable training facilities for those who want to study group psychotherapy. The American Group Psychotherapy Association has recently set up a guide for such training centers. The inexperienced group therapist is often left to work out his own training and discovers through trial and error what special problems he will encounter, how to handle these problems, and what the probable effects are of different styles of therapeutic leadership.[105]

The literature indicates that the move is toward sound conceptualization, research, and the advantages of thorough training.[106] Yet lavish testimonials are to be found in articles and books.[107] There is a sense of excitement and vitality in the field of group psychotherapy.[108] Marriage counselors, drug addiction counselors, and family life educators are all being trained in techniques derived from group therapy.[109] Many school guidance counselors are using group techniques in colleges and high schools with students who are underachievers and want to drop out of school.[110] All of the major religious faiths have used variations of group therapy techniques in the training of clergymen in order to help them with their problems.[111] Many clergy are exposed to and trained in group therapy methods for use in pastoral counseling and in other work with parishioners. Prison guards and wardens, as well as prison inmates,[112] are increasingly exposed to group experiences which are therapeutic.[113] These approaches are very helpful in defusing tensions which build up in prison facilities.[114] The custodial staff, when placed in group settings with a modified therapy approach, become aware of the feelings and sensitivities of inmates. Many police departments are using modified group therapy techniques with police officers.

The proliferation of different group approaches to the problems of people leads to confusion when someone needs help. People want a group experience for treatment, personal growth, or education. Whether the experience is labeled encounter, sensitivity training, or group therapy the people who participate in such a group take part in an emotional experience. It is often confusing as to what needs are being met. Some people avoid the need for more intensive therapy in a group by entering a sensitivity training experience.

The current arguments concern the whole concept of normal and abnormal. Do people join therapy groups because they are lonely? Are they searching for friendships? The problem is the followup. What exactly was the benefit gained from the group experience? Since psychotherapy is such a personal and subjective experience, the problems involved in researching the results are formidable. If a person reports that he feels "better" as a result of treatment in a group, how is this to be evaluated?

Intellectual brilliance does not appear to be the important factor for a good group therapist. More important are qualities such as warmth, humaneness, and an intuitive approach to people. Research indicates that not every good individual therapist has the qualities that make for a good group therapist. Often the therapist is more at ease with a one-to-one relationship and is threatened by having to cope with a group of patients. His personality may not be able to withstand the anger or attacks of a group of patients. Sometimes a therapist is drawn to work with groups because of a need to dominate a group of people. There are many positive as well as neurotic reasons that may draw people to want to lead therapy groups.

Overview

The observer will find today the following major types of group psychotherapy. (The popularity of certain "schools" of group therapy hits highs and lows. I have covered the major trends and approaches. Others have also dealt with the more peripheral approaches.)[115]

GROUP PSYCHOTHERAPY FROM A PSYCHOANALYTIC BASE

This is group therapy based on psychoanalysis. The general thrust is to engage in long-term treatment with the goal of achieving major personality change. The patients are usually highly motivated. The effort is made to achieve insight. Transference is explored as are resistance mechanisms, dreams, and a group version of free association. Many group therapists were originally trained as individual therapists in the Karen Horney approach, the Sullivan (interpersonal) approach, and the Adler approach, as well as spinoffs from each of these approaches. The approach to the group will depend upon how the group leader integrates his original psychoanalytic approach. The Horney-trained group therapist will emphasize self-realization and the here and now. The Adler-trained group therapist will emphasize self-confidence and self-respect. The Sullivan-trained group leader emphasizes the interpersonal mechanisms at work. Some combine group dynamics and individual psychodynamics.

EXISTENTIAL-EXPERIENTIAL APPROACHES AND GROUP THERAPY

The group leader focuses on the immediate experience. Many of the practitioners who use this approach have become disenchanted with what they feel is the static approach of the Freudian view of behavior. Their practice is more a reaction *against* rather than a statement *for*. This is understandable because existential philosophy embodies many points of view, from the positive existentialism of Martin Buber to the negative existentialism of Jean-Paul Sartre. The approach may encompass therapists originally trained in psychoanalysis as well as those trained along Rogerian concepts. There is much emphasis placed on the individual's despair at *being-in-the-world*. Feeling experiences are stressed and the goal of *authenticity* is stressed. Some experiential group therapists stress transference and resistance mechanisms while others reject this as meaningless. There is little effort made by some to select or screen group participants. For them, the regressive experience is deemphasized and the group therapist is a very active participant, making full use of his personality.

TRANSACTIONAL ANALYSIS AND GROUP PSYCHOTHERAPY

This technique has become very popular. The group leader emphasizes the *games* that people play and the *script* of life is analyzed. The unconscious or the root of the patient's problem is not stressed. The group is heterogeneous and there is little or no effort made at diagnostic classification. The techniques of transactional analysis are easily learned, which seems to account for its enthusiastic supporters. Berne, the founder of this approach, stated that his goal was cure: "to transform schizophrenics into non-schizophrenics." He justified every technique which would help him get to his goal as quickly as possible. The effort is made to work on patterns of maladaptation.

GESTALT THERAPY AND GROUP THERAPY

Group members are encouraged to work with feelings they want to get away from. There is an effort made to heighten awareness and strong emphasis is on the here and now. The game characteristics of human behavior are noted and quickly identified by the group leader. If a patient states that he wishes to withdraw from the group, his wish is respected. Rather than encourage actual physical withdrawal, he is asked to share his fantasy with the group and reveal the *feelings* that he is experiencing. The emphasis is on the *how you feel* and *what are you feeling* as contrasted with *why you feel*. This is believed to make you more at ease with your feelings and increasingly self-confident. There is no effort to work out old conflicts and these areas are avoided. The approach is very exciting, especially with people who have great difficulty in coming to grips with basic drives. It may open up feelings which will come to the surface too quickly, with painful and possibly destructive results.

PSYCHODRAMA

This technique has been gaining new adherents during the past decade after a period of relative inactivity. It is being used more frequently in France and some parts of the United States. Its current renaissance may be related to the encounter movement and the human potential growth movement since the psychodrama therapist aims for the individual to express himself with greater ease, and to be spontaneous and creative. The technique has attracted vocal exponents and it is even claimed to promote healing of a broken leg.[116] While this may appear to be a rather extreme statement, there is indeed a report in the medical literature which maintains that the use of psychodrama hastened the healing of a fractured femur.

GROUP PSYCHOTHERAPY BASED ON HUMANISM AND THE ENCOUNTER GROUP

The group leader constantly stresses acceptance and respect for the group member's feelings. Basic growth is believed to be lying dormant in the individual. For many people this is an important experience, particularly if they come from environments where they have been minimized, negated, or generally disregarded. There is no attention paid to diagnostic procedures. The same approach is believed applicable to normal, psychotic, or neurotic people. Classification is believed to imprison both patient (client) and therapist in preconceived notions as to the client's potential. Hostile and disruptive clients are excluded from the group—in theory. In practice, this doesn't seem to happen.[117] The group therapist constantly emphasizes that the client is a responsible individual who, when exposed to unconditional positive regard, will find his own growth potential.

GROUP THERAPY BASED ON BEHAVIOR THERAPY

The stress in the group is upon the treatment of disabling symptomatology. Short-term procedures are used. The therapist is interested in changing specific patterns of behavior. The main techniques used are group desensitization and group self-assertion training. It is similar to a classroom situation. The group leader lectures a great deal at early meetings of the group, which meets about twenty times. Later group meetings involve some interchange among members.

The use of the term *behavior therapy* is very confusing since what really happens is that the group meetings consist of *learning how to relax*. Since the patient is motivated to initiate self-assertive behavior through persuasion and reasoning there is no Pavlov-type conditioning involved.[118] Behaviorism is supposed to be the "doctrine that the behavior of man and animal can be fully understood without the use of explanatory concepts referring to states or actions of consciousness, namely by studying only observable behavior." Recently Arnold Lazarus, one of the more active exponents of this approach, has expressed the belief that there is a common field of overlap between the psychoanalytic and behavioral approach to group therapy. Since behavior therapists state that relief from disabling symptoms is personality change and question the importance of unearthing unconscious feelings or repressed impulses, his statement seems inappropriate.

SUPPORTIVE AND ADAPTATIONAL APPROACHES TO GROUP THERAPY

The strongest recent advocate of this approach was James Johnson.[119] He was very specific as to the practical nature of his approach, which is used in clinics as well as hospitals and other institutional settings. There is no effort made to achieve change of personality or resolution of deep-seated conflicts. Patients are encouraged to practice new methods of *adaptation*.

There is strong emphasis on homogeneity of patients. Neurotic and psychotic patients are carefully differentiated and placed in separate groups. The therapist who leads the group is a definite authority figure, very much the all-knowing doctor. He is in control of the group and has carefully formulated his goals and the way he plans to proceed for the group. He wants to promote socialization and reality testing, and to have group members note the relationship between anxiety and feelings. The patient is very dependent upon the group. The effort is made to strengthen defenses of the patient and there is emphasis on the repression of the unconscious. There is no effort made to unlearn long held patterns of self-destructive behavior.

Some Concluding Thoughts and a Look to the Future

Group psychotherapy is an exciting technique and often stimulates over-enthusiasm in its practitioners. But enthusiasm, while pleasant to observe, does not take the place of a mature, trained group therapist. The depth therapy which I practice is regressive and reconstructive and is based on psychoanalysis. The patient, after such an experience, should become responsible, not only for himself, but to the society he lives in. After he leaves treatment he continues to change and evolve.

Today we may find group therapists and patients who hope to find the answers to life in a group therapy experience. Effective treatment should equip the individual to cope with the pressures, paradoxes, absurdities, duplicity, and despair of living in a time and era overshadowed by the atomic bomb. From the logical positivism of Freud, who was so concerned with objectivity, we have moved to advocates of humanism who promise self-actualization. I am skeptical about these new preachers of humanism who stress group therapy as a panacea.

A meaningful group therapy experience based on regressive-reconstructive lines offers the individual an opportunity to explore his uniqueness. After this, he must decide how to use his uniqueness in the struggles of contemporary life. I believe that the trend will be to coalesce group therapy and social psychology, particularly group process and group dynamics. This should prove to be a meaningful cross-fertilization. The current interest in community mental health, treatment of drug addiction, interracial tensions, school dropouts, and crimes of violence should intensify the research needed for the most effective use of intensive group therapy as well as its more diluted applications. The new kinds of living relationships, such as communes, will call upon experts in small group relationships. Group psychotherapists should play an important and responsible part in ascertaining some answers to new styles of life.

Chapter 2. The Human Relations Training Laboratory: A Special Case of the Experiential Group

Martin Lakin

THE AIM OF THIS CHAPTER is to present the human relations training laboratory as a specific type of experimental group. Under the rubric *experiential,* I include group experiences known as *therapy groups, sensitivity training, encounter, personal growth, self-study,* or *T-groups.* Attenders of all of these are usually volunteers who participate in them for different reasons, some seeking psychological relief, others pursuing opportunities for emotional expressiveness or for close and meaningful association.

The human relations training laboratory is related in a number of ways to the various kinds of group experiences listed above. To understand the rationale of laboratory groups it's necessary to have an idea of the commonalities and differences among experiential groups. We may approach the problem by comparing the aims and philosophies of the groups, and by tracing their historic relationships. Let us begin by placing the human relations training laboratory in a historical context.

Experiential Groups for Therapy, Human Relations Training, and Personal Growth

The urgencies of treatment and rehabilitation needs during and after World War II, plus the shortage of trained manpower to meet these needs, were major factors in promoting the wider use of groups for therapy. In Great Britain, postwar experiments in psychological rehabilitation of veterans generated a broad interest in self-governing therapeutic communities, as well as a specific technical interest in the group as a psychological treatment method. In the United States, too, group methods began to be used in rehabilitation efforts. Among the British pioneers to adapt group work for therapeutic purposes were the psychiatrists Bion and Jones. Both have written accounts of their work.[1] The latter, in particular, was convinced that a *therapeutic community* made up of one's peers was a more effective curative agent than the individual therapist could possibly be.

But, in general, group therapy met considerable resistance as it tried to establish itself as a respectable form of psychological treatment. Many patients, as well as their therapists, regarded assignment to group therapy as consignment to second-class treatment. In addition to feeling deprived of the traditional doctor-patient relationship, many individuals were understandably reluctant to accept the premise of benefit to themselves through disclosing inner feelings to strangers. After all, as they perceived it, other group members, besides being demonstrably and self-confessedly poorly adjusted, possessed no obvious helping competencies and expressed no great eagerness to be of help to anyone! This resistance has only gradually been overcome through demonstrations of benefit from patient-patient interactions. No small part of this benefit has been the gratification obtained by patients through helping other patients.

At first group therapies developed around accepted theories of personality, as if the group forms of treatment were merely pluralized individual forms. Thus one could follow the developments of *Freudian* or *Adlerian* group therapies as extensions of traditional dyadic treatment principles. Very early on—in fact, prior to the great post–World War II expansion—some psychotherapists experimented with group treatment. Trigant Burrow[2] and Paul Schilder[3] tried out group methods on various psychiatric populations, but it was mostly through the systematic efforts of the psychodrama therapist Jacob Moreno[4] and the aforementioned W. Bion,[5] as well as two other British therapists, S. H. Foulkes and E. J. Anthony,[6] that attention was forcefully drawn to the usefulness of integrating group dynamics processes with contemporary personality concepts. Interactions in any group, according to Bion, occur simultaneously at an unconscious emotionally volatile level and at a level of conscious understanding. The latter are accessible to rational communication and analyses, whereas the former, consisting mainly of shared dependent, sexual, and aggressive impulses are, of course, largely unconscious. Periods when activities of the group are dominated by irrational impulses may be contrasted with more mature periods when analysis is possible. In the former, oscillations in mood predominate; surges of activity alternate with sieges of torpor and boredom. In the latter phases, when cognitive understanding can be coordinated with affect and enhanced through analyses, the group is said to be *working* (in contrast to operating impulsively on the basis of irrational assumptions).

The pioneer group psychotherapists, Foulkes and Anthony, systematically tried to integrate Freud's psychotherapy concepts with the social field theories of the psychologist Kurt Lewin and to relate the hybrid to their background of clinical experience in multiperson treatment. The group was conceived as a symbolic extension of the family whose members assume sibling-like roles and functions. The designated leader is attributed sometimes benign, sometimes malevolent traits of previously experienced parental authorities by the members. This *transference* of traits to the leaders is of course reminiscent of what occurs in individual psychoanalytic treatment with respect to the therapist. The group naturally evokes certain characteristic conflicts because the members as well as the leader come to symbolize a sibling or an authority figure toward whom one has ambivalent attitudes. Of course, at the same time and for identical reasons, the leader also evokes in members many of the more positive sorts of familial feelings. These ambivalent feelings develop to a very considerable intensity and can generate rather profound responses. Gradually, it became apparent that the dynamics of the group had the capacity to affect drastically group members' feelings, attitudes toward themselves as well as toward others, and, ultimately, their beliefs regarding desirable and undesirable modes of behaving.

Increasingly, mental health workers came to recognize the utility of this fusion of personal dynamics and group processes. Finally, many became convinced that the major *curative* factor for psychological distress in groups is not so much the *therapeutic* technique of interpretation of the leader-designate but the interactions among the group members themselves. In this view, the effective group therapist is one who can help his group become an effective agency of therapeutic change.

How does the human relations training group relate to therapeutic uses of group dynamics? The human relations training laboratory group was a product of serendipity. In 1946 a group of academic psychologists and federal government officials met at a conference in Connecticut. Their avowed purpose was to plan concerted action for reducing racial discrimination in government and public employment practices. Their conference took place in a setting away from habitual work places so that the consulting psychologists and the officials of the participating agencies could interact informally. Several participants happened upon a postmeeting staff-research session and proceeded to give unsolicited views of what had gone on during the meeting. What was especially noteworthy was that hitherto unreported thoughts and feelings were now acknowledged as influences on what ultimately transpired. For instance, the participants' retrospections included subtle undertones, hidden meanings, and emotional effects of interactions of which the researchers had not been aware. For the research staff this participant input was an eye-opening account of subsurface reactions to interactions in groups. This unanticipated discovery led to more systematic attempts at on-the-spot analysis of group processes by participants. Such efforts at systematic analyses in the *here and now* by the participants themselves were an educational innovation. An old-new form of learning from experience, participant action followed by reflection, was rediscovered. Especially impressive was the relative impactfulness of what was learned in this way and the individual's greater commitment to it.

For a group to provide the possibility for such learning, it has to meet certain criteria. For one thing, it must be composed of people who can tolerate a minimum of conventional organizational structure and, corollarily, who are committed to permitting relatively spontaneous behavior. Thus the members have to be ready to cope with feelings normally hidden and to at least agree to foster frankness rather than the innocuous chitchat that is typical in conventional social intercourse.

It is perhaps no accident that the human relations training laboratory began in the wake of World War II—a war against fascism—and that other forms of experiential groups received a great impetus at the same time. The idea of democratic participation in a pluralistic society with contending pushes and pulls was anchored, at one end, in the ideal of free individuals competing in a free society and, at the other, in acknowledged responsibilities to community, job, and family. As it developed, a large number of personal and organizational goals was subsumed under the rubric *human relations training*. But the purpose, most generally stated, was to foster effective relating, effective participation, and effective organization in democratically oriented associations. Therefore, its coordinate ideal was the safeguarding of individual integrity while achieving social and organizational objectives in a time of ever accelerating social change. It was believed that, in the absence of effective personal participation, members would become mere cogs. At the same time, for effective teamwork, members had to learn to cope with the various admixtures of competition and cooperation found in the various work units.

While the human relations training laboratory was rooted in concern for improved relationships, the viewpoint of its early practitioners was that the need for improved relations is almost universal and not a problem for the psychologically impaired alone. This attitude gave it an educational and social interest outlook rather than an explicitly therapeutic one. It also had several strong ideological commitments. These are: (1) use of scientific methods to facilitate human problem solving for any significant interpersonal problem; (2) an ideological adherence to democratic interchange, including a willingness to evaluate and influence leadership as well as to parcel it out among members or, if maladaptive, to jettison it altogether; and (3) the development of adaptive and helping capacities among ordinary people to facilitate social and technological change.

Abandonment of conventional models of organization, transfer of the responsibility for the content of agendas to group members, and the instruction to try to learn from personal experiences were leader stimuli that elicited characteristic responses from participants. These responses were basically looked at in one of two ways: (1) how the member affected others in the group, and (2) how he or she was responded to by fellow members.

Notwithstanding the general and inclusive nature of their goals, human relations training practitioners became polarized in the early phases of the group movement. For those chiefly concerned with each individual's inner experiences in the group, a person-focused approach that tended to improve feelings about one's self, to reduce anxiety, or to nourish greater authenticity in relationships (much as a psychotherapist would attempt) was quick to emerge. For those who thought it more important to develop understanding of intraorganizational patterns of behavior, personal style and personality were important primarily as they figured in the group's development or were reflected in the roles taken by the member. Advocates of the latter view saw role in the group as more significant than inner self or personality. This is not to say that these different emphases were ever really mutually exclusive. In point of fact, the human relations training laboratory group tried to comprehend both of them. As conceived, the lab could be used to achieve process insights and to ameliorate organizational conflict, but at the same time it could also be used to explore interpersonal problems or to try to remedy personal difficulties arising from characteristically ineffectual relating.

Although human relations training groups distinguish between overt and covert behavior and between conscious and unconscious processes, little attention is devoted to unconscious processes in human relations training groups. The reason is pragmatic rather than theoretical. To do so would detract substantially from the impact of here-and-now interactions. By contrast, there are careful efforts to distinguish between the content, or *what* happens, and the process, or *how* it happens. These distinctions are carefully drawn early in the group, and they are repeatedly made the basis of much of the reflections the members engage in about the nature of their interactions. Additionally, group processes, including characteristic group dynamics such as conforming, subgrouping, scapegoating, and so on are highlighted for learning purposes. This means they are pointed out when they occur, questions are asked about them, and they are frequently discussed at length. Analyses of significant interactions are immediate and the consequent emotional arousal is accepted as natural. *Feedback* (the relay of immediate feeling reactions) is typically given as information to be assimilated by the member. Not infrequently, such feedback is regarded as the emotional fulcrum of the group experience and the most impactful learning which occurs. Often it is also treated by members on the ''receiving end'' as if it were the critical confirmation or disconfirmation of *self-image*.

The Laboratory Concept

Many people are puzzled by the use of the term *laboratory* in connection with human relations training. The image of white-coated staff handling scientific hardware, monitoring carefully standardized procedures, and studying the laboratory animal's behavior is, of course, grossly inappropriate, but the aspiration to experimentation is not. Although the laboratory concept is primarily symbolic and suggestive, the participant *is* conceived as engaging in a self-initiated experiment in personal behavior manipulation. The notion of personal self-study and personal change in the light of self-assessment is entirely consonant with the approach. Since these processes are held to lead to objective assessment, the term *lab* fits the aspired-to image.

The founders of human relations labs held that their processes should be open to public scrutiny and validation like any other experimental approach to human welfare. Various assessment devices such as self-description forms, daily diaries, rating scales, and other measures are used to foster systematic self-reporting and objectivity toward the events of the group. Supplementing the experiential core, the occasional use of lectures and readings are also intended to provide additional tools for thinking about the issues of group interaction, self-in-interaction, and change.

Regardless of the specific objectives for which the group sessions are being held (improvement of race relations, community improvement, organizational development, self-development, learning about group processes, etc.), members of human relations groups get caught up in the more personal aspects of interaction in their groups. Interest in their own personal feelings and those of their co-members is often the most compelling feature of the human relations group, just as it is for participants in any of the other kinds of experiential groups.

Historically, the overlap between training lab purposes and an explicit therapeutic intention has been integral to experiential groups from the beginning. This overlap has also had advantages and disadvantages. For one thing, a participant could be rewarded by unanticipated therapeutic benefits in any experiential learning group. For another, self-disclosure could lead to a more involved participation, hence firmer commitment to the group's success. This also benefits the learning goals of fellow members. Finally, the overlap generates a multidimensional perspective on interaction problems. On the other hand, it is probably true that this overlap also confuses a number of participants. Persons seeking relief are sometimes frustrated by the emphasis on learning in human relations groups while those searching for the knowledge promised by the latter are put off by the intense emotionalism generated in the efforts to ease emotional distress. As a matter of fact, it has proven to be more difficult to establish a productive balance in learning and corrective purposes than anyone anticipated.

From the early 1960s on, there were qualitative changes in human relations labs. Two major offshoots developed: one, the personal growth or encounter branch, which emphasizes individual expressiveness; the other, organizational development, which specializes in diagnosis and improvement of the communication and interaction problems of work units of various types and sizes in industrial and educational settings.

In personal growth groups, there has been a diminution of interest in the group experience per se. Verbal interactions in general have been subordinated to emotional expressiveness, the latter sometimes fostered directly through touching, embracing, wrestling, and other means as well as through conventional speech. Clearly, such methods encourage a conception of the group as an instrument for disinhibiting the "uptight" individual. Some of the proponents of this point of view have abandoned participant observation and jettisoned learning goals. The group is not to be studied under such circumstances; rather, it becomes an arena in which the "authentic" encounters are to take place. The leader's functions become increasingly suggestive in nature, and he does what he thinks necessary to generate emotional intensity; some dramatically and self-consciously lead participants toward exploration of inner experiences or join in collective emoting. The most publicized examples of such approaches have been identified with Esalen and other "growth centers."[7] However, there are signs of recurrent schisms with some leaders now abandoning encounter in favor of group sessions geared to self and body awareness training rather than to social interaction at all.

Philosophic Backgrounds

In their therapeutic, learning, and expressiveness functions, all experiential groups confront the paradoxes and contradictions inherent in modern attempts to integrate cooperative and competitive aspects of living. These conflictful, if complementary, aspects of human experience were discussed in general terms by the psychologist David Bakan. Bakan[8] described the social dynamic as a ceaseless contention between *communitarian* and *agentic* impulses and the outcome as a necessary compromise. For instance, the urge toward merging with others battles needs for salience and personal recognition. Thus a member's wish to belong contends with his wish to be independent. The therapeutic group, the human relations training group, and its offshoots, encounter, personal growth, and organizational development groups, all involve these conflicting tendencies within and among persons.

Psychologist Kurt Lewin's social outlook on dynamic change, philosopher John Dewey's insistence on learning by experience, and their shared concern with preserving a vital democracy influenced the conceptual basis of human relations labs. Dewey's faith in the ability of ordinary people to guide themselves was also reflected in the way the leaders, known first as *trainers,* tried to conduct their groups. In fact, they tried to concretize and to actualize Dewey's ideas as they sought ways to increase self-governance and mutual responsibility among members. Since knowing and doing were seen as interdependent, solving problems among people was, in the final analysis, perceived as dependent upon accurate diagnosis and effective communication.[9]

Earlier, I mentioned that there were marked changes among lab leaders since the early 1960s. For one thing, the desire to use the group as treatment and as opportunity to further emotional self-expressiveness among attenders became even more pronounced within the group movement. Also, since about the mid-1960s, a number of human relations lab leaders began to show enthusiasm for quasi-therapeutic elements in certain Asian philosophic systems, notably yoga and Zen Buddhism. For instance, they *imported* meditation and consciousness-expanding exercises to their groups as relaxation and *growth* techniques. This practice of importation was not really new. Previous imports of psychoanalytic practices and theory had also taken place at earlier stages. Nevertheless, these particular imports and the decisive shift toward a therapy emphasis (even though termed growth) constituted a severe challenge to the balanced *group-person* focus of the original human relations idea.

Let us now leave the changing historical scene and turn to human relations groups as they are practiced. We shall return, as we must, to a view of the historical context later on in the chapter.

What Can the Observer Note in Human Relations Groups?

The student of human relations groups can analyze them from several vantage points. He can consider such total group questions as How are its norms or ground rules established? or What causes its emotional atmosphere to shift from warm to cold from one session to the next? Alternatively, he can focus on individual reactions among the personalities in the group. From the latter perspective, he might try to evaluate the controls the group members exercise over each individual. The interplay between personal disposition and group controls is exemplified where A's hostility toward B appears to be kept in bounds of civility only by the norms of his group which place clear limits on overt displays of anger. The observer would note repeated instances in groups where leadership aspirations of one individual are repeatedly frustrated because his "bossiness" is resented by fellow members, and he is denied what his talents, under other circumstances, might achieve.

Human relations group processes should be understood in group *and* in individual personality terms. To the group that provides acceptance and fulfillment for their personal needs, members give loyalty. As members, they in turn provide the group with its unique spirit. A group viewed as a developing social system progresses, stabilizes, stagnates, or disintegrates with changes in member involvement and interest. Where membership is valued, a cohesive group *aura* is created. The cohesiveness is valued for its own sake in terms of the good feelings generated, but it also makes possible effective group actions.

Paradoxically, group membership threatens one's autonomy at the same time that it seems to offer security of a kind. The wish to be nurtured and supported warmly is offset by the fantasy of being overwhelmed and stifled. In ordinary life one can discern a similar ambivalence in the individual's relationship to his family or some other social unit. Most persons experience real deprivation when excluded from groups they want to be part of. On the other hand, many people also *defend* against being enveloped by a group, especially when they fear they might be subject to its controls and denied the expression of their own individuality.

One way of avoiding absorption is through personal recognition for talents or skills. This involves evaluation whether overt or covert, as is most frequently the case in the "real world." During the group experience, member evaluation of one another becomes increasingly explicit. (This is so despite disclaimers of a "nonjudgmental" atmosphere. Evaluation is, as a matter of fact, most explicit in the process termed *feedback*.) The impelling factors are two: an almost irresistible tendency to engage in social comparison (comparing one's self with everyone else), and a tendency to assess the effects each member has on every other member. A member can be valued by his group for a variety of reasons: one may be outstanding for his communicating abilities; another may be respected for his insights; a third appreciated for stimulating others or for getting things started just when people seem to need active direction. In human relations labs, credit accrues especially to those who practice effective altruism, that is, who are able to extend help to others at the right time and without sign of immediate personal payoff. Generally, evaluations tend to be of behavior effects rather than of motivations, of how one's actions made another feel rather than *why* one did what he did (although motivational considerations are never completely absent).

The transaction between member and group involves group acceptance in exchange for member commitment, intimacy in exchange for personal disclosure and a role in the group for each member. As a matter of fact, some participants are so anxious to feel a sense of belonging that they complain at the very onset, ''I don't feel as though I'm really a part of this group.'' Such individuals are usually expressing a lack of understanding of how, in fact, one becomes an effective part of the social organization through helping to build it. Such a seemingly simple learning may be an important one for them with ramifications for their participation in other groups.

The conditions for membership in the group are more or less the same for all members. They are as follows: (1) to contribute to the shaping and coherence of the group, (2) to invest in it emotionally, (3) to help move it toward a goal, (4) to help establish its rules and to obey them, (5) to take on specific roles in the group, (6) to strive for deeper levels of intimacy, and (7) to give help to other participants. Groups may be distinguished by the conditions which are most salient for them, that is, those which are most emphasized. A group which is high on conditions 2 and 6 would demand relatively high emotionality. Collaboration and cooperation would be most important for the group which stresses conditions 1, 3, and 7.

The human relations training group requires the exercise of reflection as well as emotional commitment. With *only* intellectual comprehension the process becomes sterile. Emotions and intellect are both needed for a balanced and meaningful experience. Group effects interact with individual needs. How these effects are experienced in a specific group is partly the result of the mix of the personalities in that group and partly due to the influence of its leader. The core processes themselves, however, occur regardless of the quality of members or leader. Let us consider some of these core processes and see how they might interact with personal responses. The general point should be made that these core processes take place in all types of experiential groups that permit the development of group processes.

A. Achieving and Maintaining Cohesiveness

Group cohesiveness is the collective expression of personal belongingness. It leads to deeper association and concern about one's fellow members. Demonstrably, group cohesion (1) binds members emotionally to the common task as well as to one another; (2) assures greater stability of the group even in the face of frustrating circumstances; and (3) develops a shared frame of reference which allows for more tolerance for diverse aims of group members.

A negative attitude toward one's group reduces one's participation in the group task, but valued membership in that group leads to a greater commitment to its values and to the tasks the group undertakes. When membership is highly valued, the productivity of the group may be expected to rise. In human relations groups, the wish to be accepted is especially strong, and participants are anxious to assure themselves that all members have in fact been "accepted," that is, the group's "success" is measured in terms of cohesion. Concern over the degree of success is epitomized in the question, "How successful are we in having become a group?" The potency of this concern is evidenced in the fact that one can even censure one's fellow members by complaining: "I don't feel as though we have become a 'real' group."

B. Behaving in Conformity with Group Norms

All experiential groups encourage expressiveness, warmth, openness, and the like. In fact, such attributes become standards by which to evaluate the progress members are making. In these groups such *norms* are expected to evolve organically. As a result, the individual participant has a feeling of commitment to them because, after all, he has participated in their development. Partly for this reason, the norms are compelling in influencing individual behavior.

C. Consequential Validation of Personal Perceptions

Another group effect is a press toward agreement. Members continually compare interpretations of events in order to establish confidently meanings of events for themselves. Tracing the consensus processes that develop among the members of the group is in itself an absorbing learning process for attenders. "How did we come to agree on Fran?" is one form of the question. "Why do we all feel the same way about Tony?" is another. *Feedback* is often given as a type of consensual reaction summary. To discover how this consensus is achieved, and with what consequences for each participant, is the learning objective. Ideally, each participant should be able to see himself in the consensus and evaluate the part he plays in arriving at it. This self-conscious view of group consensus process offsets the tendency for consensus to become merely another mechanism for increasing or enforcing conformity.

D. The Expression of Emotional Immediacy

Any experiential group generates emotional expressiveness in participants. Hostile or affectionate feelings are evoked with fewer inhibitions than in most other interpersonal situations. There are, however, factors which discourage emotional "binges" such as the media often portray. Concern for one's standing in the group influences one to monitor personal outpourings. The rapid spread of emotionality among the members of the group *is* helpful in freeing a participant who is constricted in expressing feelings, and it is readily apparent that in such cases the unblocking of "frozen" feelings is a desirable development. This does not mean, however, that any display of emotionality is necessarily helpful, so that there are constraints upon emotionality just as there are facilitating elements for its expression.

E. Group Perception of Problem Relationships

In what sense is it appropriate to talk about the group as a *problem-solving* experience? Human relations training groups deal supportively with problems of human relationships and investigate the mutual perceptions which determine their problematic status. For instance, to Phil's query, "How am I perceived?," he is told, "You come on too strong," or "Your pompousness turns us off." Through discussion of how his behavior affects his relationships within the group, he is stimulated to try alternate ways of relating that could be more effective. The assumption is that problematic interpersonal behaviors are most effectively looked at from fresh vantage points provided by the views of other group members. While "many heads" do not necessarily come up with solutions to problems, they provide alternative perspectives on them.

F. Dominance Alignments

In human relations groups, leadership and influence positions rarely remain static. This is because any member can legitimately try exercising power and influence. His efforts are at best ambivalently received because the other participants are also impelled to try to assume *their* habitual positions of power. With the help of the leader, the group should develop flexibility in power allocation or *ownership*. Thus a number of persons, regardless of "real life" position, simultaneously experiment in the roles of decision makers or influencers or are treated as objects of influence. This contrasts with enduring self-perceptions as either "boss" or power victim. Even the *naturally* dominant member must, after all, garner support from others if he is to continue to exercise leadership. Thus the group provides a multiple perspective on power and influence transactions.

G. Role Differentiation

A group stagnates where there is no diversity of functions and, especially, where members feel stuck in undesirable and unproductive roles. In human relations groups, the functions of initiating, clarifying, harmonizing, and so on are easily recognizable. Other roles emerge, depending on group composition and purpose. This availability of roles does not mean, however, that role interchange is easily or effortlessly achieved. As in the uses of power, participants gravitate to accustomed roles. Groups especially tend to locate and keep individuals in extreme roles, such as "the blocker," the group "clown," or the group "foul-up," perhaps to provide some elements of constancy and predictability. This tendency is counterproductive, however, from the point of view of the participant who gets stuck in them for the aim must be to enable him to experiment with *different* ways of being in the group. In the absence of such experimentation, a stereotypic role stabilizes with little by way of constructive exchange, and consequently produces a profitless learning experience.

H. Movement toward Intimate Disclosure

Objective *change* indices following training routinely demonstrate increases in feelings of intimacy.[10] We cannot be sure whether these represent only a temporary emotional state precipitated by the experience. In expressiveness forms of experiential groups, especially, members are enjoined to push toward greater intimacy on the assumption that it will have considerable *carryover* beyond the life of the group.

The interaction between group effects and personal responses is singular for each participant. Thus the same group experience may have rewarding and punishing consequences for two different members. For example, a person with a great need for belongingness may experience the cohesiveness of his group (group effect A) with a positive response of relieved belongingness while another may have a negative feeling of being overwhelmed. With respect to effect B, conformity, one participant could respond by becoming more aware of the need to be accountable to his fellows; whereas another simply brings his behavior into line with everyone else's by uncritical acceptance of group standards. With respect to effect C, consensus, although its achievement feels satisfying, there is the risk that it may come about at the cost of denying real differences in order to achieve it. What is the range of possible responses to the group effect of emotional immediacy (effect D)? On the positive side, one is likely to feel freed emotionally. On the negative side, one could be coerced into expressing group-evoked emotions. Effect E (group perception of problems) may facilitate one's thinking about one's interactional problems, and it stimulates different perspectives. On the other hand, pressured sharing of problems arouses defensiveness.

With respect to dominance alignments (effect F), the important thing is to endeavor that no one remain permanently at either extreme, that is, feeling either constantly manipulated at one end or freely able to dominate the group at the other. Group effect G (role differentiation) stimulates the individual to try himself out in hitherto unaccustomed ways. The negative side is a tendency of the group to stereotype the individual or "pigeonhole" him into a pattern or category in order to reduce cognitive and emotional problems in defining the group. In regard to group effect H (movement toward intimate disclosure), a desirable result is intimacy, when based on meaningful feedback. On the other hand, there is risk to self-esteem unavoidably associated with self-disclosure.

The human relations group departs somewhat from other experiential groups in its emphasis on group dynamics theory, illustrative lectures, and the discussions which accompany the core group experience. The character of each group and its use of these supplementary techniques is determined by its specific goals. For instance, a group organized to foster organizational development for a large industrial corporation and a group organized to achieve better police-citizen relations will employ somewhat different admixtures of theory and experience even though both rely on similar experiential principles.

The reader may find it helpful to imagine being present at an orientation session for a human relations training program in which the purpose, the format, and the contractual relations are outlined. In most cases, lab attenders have an idea long in advance, however vague, of the kind of sessions that they have chosen to attend. They have read about them in the popular press, and usually they have also heard about them from friends or co-workers who have previously attended. While there are no surprises for them in the orientation, the fact of its actuality—of the incipience of the sessions—does generate some anxiety and a good deal of excitement. The orientation given usually takes care to emphasize each individual's responsibility for participation and learning and to point out the shared stake in developing a learning community. The leader is also alert to the tension of beginning and tries to reduce it with some humor but, hopefully, mainly with solid information.

The leader may begin as follows: "This is an opportunity for learning *in* the group and *about* the group, for seeing yourself as a learner, even as an experimenter, if you will." He continues, "There are three basic things that can be learned here: (1) how a group develops and functions, (2) how you yourself come across or are perceived by other people, and (3) how you might think about changing in order to be more effective interpersonally. My job is to help in that process, mostly by raising questions from time to time, perhaps by encouraging you to examine your own behavior, but I certainly don't expect to bear this responsibility all by myself. Each one of us has to get into the act. Keep in mind that the success of this experience for all depends on all." The leader then describes schedules and any other details. It is something approximating a tradition that schedules should be tentative. The reason is the central conception that learning should be partly determined by participant needs and aspirations rather than purely prescribed by staff. If a special concern develops that is not being addressed by the scheduled program, there are often efforts to alter the prearranged program within limits to accommodate this concern.

Continuing with our picturing this human relations approach, let the reader imagine that fifty managers and administrative directors from industrial and educational organizations have gathered for the lab. The leader-dean introduces staff members, announces the various group compositions (roughly ten persons per group with an assigned leader), and gives room assignments for the small groups. Participants are informed of session recordings to be made, if any, and about the presence of observers. In a residential laboratory there are also "housekeeping details" to be attended to. These include restrictions on free time, trips outside the lab, and so on. (We shall return to the special problems of distinguishing between residential and nonresidential groups in a later section.) The schedule for a one-week residential lab might well be one such as I have sketched out on the opposite page.

The alumnus of a human relations training laboratory knows that there are opportunities for relaxation and that the group or theory session totally bereft of entertainment value is the exception rather than the rule. Amusing interactions enliven many of the group sessions and theory lectures as well as the between-session interactions between participants. The learning design is to integrate the socializing experiences and the theory sessions with the unstructured groups as a total learning environment. The group sessions and the informal interactions between sessions are of

FIGURE 2.1. Typical Schedule for a Residential Human Relations Training Laboratory

TIME	SUNDAY	MONDAY	TUESDAY	WEDNESDAY	THURSDAY	FRIDAY	SATURDAY
8:30–9:45		Group	Group	Group	Group	Group	Group
9:45–10:30		Pairings	Pairings	Pairings	Trios	Trios	Trios
10:30–12:00		Group	General Session	General Session	General Session	General Session	General Session Closing
12:00–1:30	LUNCH	LUNCH	LUNCH	LUNCH	LUNCH	LUNCH	LUNCH
1:30–3:00	Group	Group	Group	Group	Project Consultation	Project Consultation	Departure Time
3:00–4:30	FREE	FREE	FREE	FREE	FREE	FREE	
4:30–6:00	Project Formulation	Project	Project	Project	Group	Group	
6:00–8:00	DINNER	DINNER	DINNER	DINNER	DINNER	DINNER	
8:00–10:00	Group	Group	Group	FREE	Group	Group	

course influenced by what is being absorbed by way of participation in the structured theory sessions. The knowledge imparted in them derives from psychology, psychiatry, sociology, and related fields. Typically, they are in the form of short talks and are followed by discussions about group dynamics or dealing with specific areas of difficulty such as problems in trust development, useful versus ineffective feedback to individuals, or even alternative interventional strategies for organizations. These presentations are generally intended to stimulate thought rather than to develop elaborate formulations or to resolve issues. They usually lead to spirited discussions among staff and participants. The hoped-for result is the integration of behavioral science theory with the experiences in the human relations groups.

One way of concretizing the relationship of the human relations experience to the individual's back-home situation is in the formulation of individual projects. These are developed around an interpersonal or intraorganizational problem of the member's choosing. These may be tentatively stated at the lab's inception. Then the participant can, if he wishes, use this initial formulation of a problem as a continuing point of reference throughout the laboratory experience. When this is done, coffee breaks and mealtimes, as well as other relatively free periods, are used for further reflection on the "homework" problem. Paired or "trio" interactions may be scheduled in order to facilitate the comparison of the current experiences and their implications for the back-home problems. Often this is best accomplished in pairs or in trios where the parties agree to consider first one, then another's problems in the light of demonstrated, that is, lab, behavior to date. Sometimes the same issues are talked about among larger numbers of individuals. Certain communication skills—for example, more effective listening, greater sensitivity to emotional issues, more skillful interventions, and the awareness of better helping strategies—are being practiced even as more adequate formulations are being developed and tentative solutions proffered.

The *cultural island* laboratory, a residential setting away from home and work, seems to make possible a more *total* learning experience because one is away from daily commitments and distractions. On the other hand, these advantages of the relief from everyday concerns and relationships are to some degree offset by the expense, the emotional distance from the real world, and the summer camp atmosphere which encourages a kind of adolescent regression. Still, the value of the residential laboratory is that it permits an intensity of experiencing which is unlikely to develop elsewhere, and this intensity is useful in generating the kinds of interactions from which one learns most.

Despite the advantages, nonresidential human relations groups have increased over the past few years. Some meet as infrequently as once weekly over an extended period, sometimes as long as a year, and some intersperse intensive weekend sessions. There are all sorts of in-between arrangements. All of them, however, try to compromise the desirable and the expedient in terms of atmosphere, duration, and expense. At present, there are no solidly based conclusions as to the efficacy of one or another frequency of meeting. In the absence of definitive research, one must reserve for future consideration the questions of efficacy of duration and setting.

Human relations lab group participants are enjoined *not* to use agendas, administrative hierarchies, or rules of order, and so on, in structuring their interactions. The suggestions they receive from their leaders on *how to learn* discourage them from doing so. For this reason, getting things moving is invariably an awkward experience. In the vernacular of the participants, the very early interactions are described as "sparring" or "sizing up" one another. The attempt to assess one another's intentions is unmistakable: "Who are you?" "What will you do to me?" are the two questions which are psychological constants in the situation. Eventually, egocentric self-concern broadens to comprehend the welfare of others rather than simply fending off possible aggressive probes.

As the group process develops, each member comes to be recognized in terms of characteristic effects upon others. Sporadically, at early states, but later in more systematic ways, others' reactions to these effects are relayed back in what we have already referred to as *feedback*. This feedback usually consists of emotionally toned reactions which have been generated in others by one's ways of relating to them. It is a truism that members' behaviors determine the quality of the group atmosphere and its productivity. For instance, if all the members of a group are combative individuals, mutual defensiveness becomes so extensive as virtually to preclude any probing interactions, even relatively innocuous ones. A group composed mainly of passive security seekers, on the other hand, is likely to develop an atmosphere of stifling "togetherness" because of its collective veto on conflict. Even mildly competitive interactions would be ruled out.

To describe fully a human relations training laboratory is to present the laboratory itself—from the moment of arrival to departure. In one sense nothing is irrelevant to the program. One's habits, conversations, recreations, appetites, political attitudes, values, and so on all relate to the central topic of conversation—personal style and group effect. The centerprice of activity is the small-group sessions. It is the arena for considering all the interactional problems which arise in the course of the lab. Thus Phil's (the names are, of course, fictional; the events are actual) "arbitrariness," which he himself identifies as a major interpersonal problem in his usual management function, is considered in the light of the moment-to-moment interactions which have occurred to that point in the group. Evidence of the generality of this behavior tendency is likely to have been observed elsewhere: for instance, in theory sessions, discussions at the dinner table, on the golf course, and so on. Chip gives the impression of being rather "timid." In fact, he confesses to characteristic insecurity on his job and in social gatherings. Not surprisingly, he perceives the group as a competitive environment in which he is at a disadvantage owing to his lack of assertiveness and self-confidence. From the beginning he is outspoken in his admiration of Phil's "toughness." These self-presentations and self-disclosures begin the process of problem identification and indicate the personal style characteristics which are almost certain to become subjects of discussion in ensuing discussions in the group.

Dag started off as a self-described "tough guy." He shocked his group by asserting that he and his superior had no respect for one another. In the second session Dag stated boldly that his boss even feared him because he was so much more competent than the latter. Yet his participation belied this self-presentation. For instance, when Dag's toughness was questioned, he withdrew into a morose silence. This led members to suspect that beneath the incongruity in his self-presentation there lay substantial intrapersonal problems. It was, in fact, Phil who reacted most strongly to Dag's initially "cocky" self-presentation. He challenged Dag repeatedly thereafter. Finally in the third session he erupted, "Well, if I had a subordinate like you, I'd kick his ass. Either he would fit into line or get out!" This explosion had an immediate effect upon Dag. He seemed curiously respectful toward Phil after this. Was Dag a "gutsy" risk taker or was he really seriously unstable? The group is understandably leary about directly testing such questions because they do not know what kind of problem they are confronting in Dag or how stable he is. This is an example of a problem in which the leader's help is essential in signaling the group either that in his opinion Dag can "take it," that is, can usefully deal with the issues in a constructive way; or that the members should be aware that the problem may be too severe to be aired in the expectation of any useful outcome, that is, they should "lay off."

Interpersonal problems owing to one's personal style regularly arise. As an illustration, let us consider Jack, a key executive of a national corporation. As appraised by fellow members, Jack analyzes people constantly and then, to their discomfiture, he states his formulations in an irritatingly condescending manner. At one point, in trying to explain how he interprets Phil's behavior, his comments manage to anger every other member. He perceives that this is happening. He asks for help because, as he puts it, "It's happening here just like it happens everywhere else. Whenever I talk I seem somehow to turn people off. Look how I made everybody mad just now."

The human relations training approach requires that participants identify personally significant interpersonal problems. The style-of-relating problems represented by Phil, Dag, and Jack are samples of such a pro-

cess. The leader's focus upon the group processes which are shared enable the members to more readily identify their personal contributions to
these processes, and they are thus able to also identify *problems* reflected
in the style of participation of each person. There is usually small need for
the leader to pinpoint a problem posed by a particular member; these are
typically self-evident. They are grounds for prolonged and involved discussions without leader intervention. On the other hand, members often
do need help in being able to give feedback constructively. It is also not
easy to receive feedback undefensively and to assimilate successfully all
that is being *fed*. The leader can help somewhat by making sure that the
feedback communication is as clear as possible. Needless to state, what
reduces mutual defensiveness usually also facilitates good feedback.

The leader also keeps issues in focus when they might be avoided or
prematurely dropped if he feels they are important. The commonly used
strategy of keeping attention focused on issues or specific interactions is to
make well timed queries. For example, a leader asks why a line of discussion was precipitously dropped when it had seemed so important to the
group only a few moments before. He may inquire into the feelings with-
held during moments of tense, anxiety-filled silences, or ask about the
feelings behind hostile interchanges. The point is to get these out into the
open where they can be aired. Sudden explosions of hilarity are also
important indicators of subsurface feelings. During all of his inquiries, the
leader tries to exemplify openness and willingness to engage in interchange as useful interpersonal tools, thus demonstrating his conviction
about what participants can learn from the experience.

The process is facilitated if members are genuinely willing to explore
their problems in interaction. Jack tries to do this. So does Phil. Dag,
however, presents us with an enigma regarding his state of mental health.
Is he able to use this group experience constructively or is his a personality problem for which the group setting is insufficient and inappropriate?
(In the ensuing days it became apparent that the latter assessment was
correct. Consequently, Dag must be numbered among the failures of
human relations training. More about this later in the chapter.)

Byron, a government official, achieved a great deal by age 40 by dint of
his intelligence and diligence. Yet Byron's career is at an end, according to
his own statement, unless he can improve his recurrent problems with
authority. How do his problems manifest themselves in the human relations group? Byron shows an overriding concern with whatever the leader
does. He constantly calls attention to what he interprets as "unfair" and
"sneaky" maneuvers by the leader and protests repeatedly that the group
is being gulled and dishonestly manipulated. These include any slight
variation in the timing of opening or closing of the meetings (a matter of
minutes), any query by the leader, and focus on any problem area. This
unusual preoccupation with authority catches the attention of the group

and becomes one of the continuing points of discussion during the lab. It is joked about, occasionally responded to with annoyance or anger. Byron remains defensive, asserting to everyone's incredulity that he behaves differently back home, where "the boss is no problem to me." His response to the group's growing criticism is to become even more defensive. For instance, when taxed with not being emotionally open in the group, he claims that he is a very emotional person back home and that the present group particularly inhibits him. When told he is consistently diffident about asserting what he himself wants the group to do, he insists that he is the very opposite, indeed very assertive back home. The "group humorist" once described Byron as the "guy who could really play a great game of golf . . . back home!" Since he plays golf not at all, the description made the point and quickly became a group joke.

Dag and Byron represent the nexus between learning potential and therapeutic needs encountered in human relations labs. The question which naturally arises is: Is the individual participating in ways that will benefit him? And is the person's problem sufficiently severe to require treatment rather than learning? Is the human relations group the appropriate therapeutic vehicle?

My view is that the human relations leader who is adequately backgrounded professionally recognizes the difference between deep problems of long standing and those which, while nontrivial, nevertheless don't impair the individual's learning capacities and particularly his ability to learn from experience by remaining open to it. He is in a better position to diagnose such problems than is a relative novice. It happens, of course, that useful insights may be garnered by even disturbed persons in human relations groups; however, it is exorbitantly expensive in terms of time and energy for the group which, of necessity, must preoccupy itself with the problems they pose. Faced with a deep-seated personality problem, even the most capable and best intentioned group becomes frustrated to the point of impatience and anger. The fragility or defensiveness of the psychologically impaired member renders him unable to detach himself from his own preoccupations to perceive what transpires with others or what they require of him, and this defeats the learning goals of the lab.

In the cases of Dag and Byron, the leader tried to maintain communication between them and their increasingly irritated co-members to see if they could ultimately assimilate the messages the group was trying to convey. In Byron's case this appeared to work. In Dag's it did not. It became quite evident with time that his disturbance was rather severe, and he had fewer resources to call upon in coping with the situation.

One experiential group theorist, Chris Argyris,[11] contended that human relations lab experiences should always be success experiences. The question naturally arises: What would constitute a "success" experience? From my point of view, it could only be one which leads the individual to review his previous subjective assumptions about his level of interpersonal competence. Surely it could not be merely a hedonically pleasurable experience. Indeed, it is difficult for me to imagine a worthwhile human relations experience that is all "good feelings." The only way to have a positive hedonic experience under human relations group conditions would be to counterfeit one's interpersonal approach since authentic interpersonal experiences are bound to be fraught with ambivalence. This issue is an important one for all types of experiential groups. If it is to be an authentic experience, any experiential group must reflect the vulnerabilities and ambivalences that are true of real life relationships.

Some aspects of the behavior of Chip may be used to illustrate the problem. Chip comes as an eager participant, already speaking the "injargon" of human relations before he has even been involved in the group. His familiarity with the terms is not difficult to trace. It turns out that he is a minister by profession so that practical concerns of psychology and interpersonal relations are part of his everyday professional experiences. He suggests in the initial sessions that he wants to "get in deeply quickly" so as to build on what he already knows about human relations. Despite these professions of readiness for "deep encounters," the fact is that he shrinks from confrontation and, most particularly, from conflict. Whenever he asserts himself, he just as quickly withdraws his assertion. In his own words, he "runs for cover" if challenged. This pattern is demonstrated repeatedly and with such regularity that almost everyone comes to feel he can predict its occurrence. Additionally, his emotions are expressed as copies of other people's. Thus he becomes angry, but in the wake of someone else's irritation as if he were tagging along and echoing the latter's resentment. For example, when Byron attacks the leader, so does Chip. When Dag shouts his resentment of the group, so does Chip. When Jeff complains that Phil has been unfair, so does Chip, and so on. However, the instant he is asked "Why are *you* mad?" Chip typically first appears confused, then stammers apologies, and finally lapses into an embarrassed silence until the next round of similar behavior. This kind of surging into the arena and repeated withdrawal earns him some condescension. In response to this he compares himself to the others, as though he were a lesser being and seems to invite their compassion—or is it their pity? Phil tells him, "You remind me of a six-year-old who whines all the time about not being invited to play even after he has been told dozens of times that he *is* included in the game." Doc adds that Chip seems to act solely in terms of his own insecurities, that is, asking for reassurance when no one could see that he needed any. Jeff imparts a more manipulative element to his behavior. He sees in Chip's pattern a veiled bid for power through repeatedly demanding support and pleading weakness. Chip does perceive a congruence between his pattern in the lab and its consequences for him and those groups in which he operates on his job. This perception is the beginning point in his project for change.

The tendency to express direct dependency toward the leader is characteristic of human relations groups, especially at the outset. At first, the tendency takes the form of sometimes reasonable, sometimes unreasonable demands. The frustrated feelings which underlie them are very general but occasionally are specified as complaints about *ineffective leadership* or even against the leader's *irresponsibility*. Members resent what they take to be a lack of appropriate responsiveness and/or direction on the part of the leader. At the same time, of course, members do have some idea and perhaps even a rudimentary, albeit grudging understanding of the necessity for self-reliance and self-direction, and at least of trying to move toward group independence of the leader. These expressions of dependency and their underlying resentments diminish somewhat as the group progresses until finally they remain prominent features only among those individuals with deep dependency or counterdependency interpersonal problems.

If individual help for persons who respond consistently in a dependent or counterdependent way is not limited to the immediate here-and-now situation, there is considerable risk of a shift in focus from group process to interest in purely personal problems. Indeed, if the latter interest is much reinforced by the leader, a certain general *magical* expectation develops, and it tends to defeat the self-help orientation in the group. I term this the "make me a miracle" reaction in which the member prefers to wait for leader initiatives rather than acting himself. In experiential groups there is, to be sure, an inevitable transference-type expectancy built up from the beginning. One may think of it as the fantasy that *if* only he *would,* the leader *could* "change" members directly by virtue of his personal charisma. This somewhat messianic fantasy tends swiftly to become powerful for the entire group as it represents a shared motivation. In any group this transference-based fantasy is prepotent, but there is little opportunity to work it through and, thus, to resolve it outside of long-term therapeutic groups. This is, in my view, an underdiscussed and nonresearched area of concern for human relations labs. The ubiquity of this tendency makes the discouragement of attendance by severely disturbed individuals all the more necessary because they are more readily enmeshed in it.

In the present illustration, Phil, Ralph, Doc, Jeff, Jack, and, to a lesser extent, Chip, effective individuals to begin with, are less caught up with transference problems than are Byron and Dag. Also, they are able to profit directly from the feedback they receive from fellow members. Finally, they learn vicariously from others through observing what happens to them as well as through personal experiencing.

The Uses of Exercises in Human Relations Labs: An Illustration

Let us return to imagined participation-observation in the lab. It is the third day of a six-day lab. The participants have spent several days in feeling each other out and in trying to establish norms of what is called *leveling*, that is, relating honestly and communicating in emotional terms to one another. Whereas some are able to *open up* emotionally, others have withdrawn to the comparative safety of silent observation. While some take initiative in trying to be self-disclosive about their own feelings, others remain determinedly opaque. It is usual under such circumstances to compare the respective contributions that various members make. For instance, some are seen by most of their peers as moving the group forward in some vaguely defined, desirable direction, however diffidently. At the same time, others are seen as retarding the group's progress toward the same goals. All are bound to be subjective evaluations, to be sure. However, it is worthwhile to check whether these judgments may be consensually validated. In such events the leader may introduce an exercise, when appropriate, intended to concretize and visualize this subsurface process of mutual assessment.

The task given the participants is to rank one another in terms of the combined criteria described above. In this instance, as may be seen from inspection of Figure 2.2, there is a relatively high degree of concordance among members. There is a general consensus about who are perceived as major contributors and who are perceived as contributing little to the progress of the group. The rankings are, in fact, faithful reflections of the feedback each had been getting to that point from other members.

The kinds of feedback offered were not restricted to evaluation of contributions to the group as such. They also included reactions to the salient problems reflected in the manner of approach to others or in the ways one reacted to others. A pattern usually developed between members which illustrated typical problems for each. By way of illustration, Chip revealed that he feared Phil was always evaluating him. One session he braced himself and asked Phil directly, "What do you think of me?" Phil was almost brutally critical, saying, in effect, "In this group, you hardly exist for me; you're always late in coming into the action. By the time you get around to saying what you have to say I figure I have heard it already many times. By then I find I'm not even interested in what you have to say." Chip had in fact already tipped his hand by confessing, "You intimidate me; you scare me with your readiness to evaluate me, to write me off," so that Phil's response merely reasserted what both knew was the situation. Their interchange confirmed that Phil's "evaluative set" did

FIGURE 2.2. Exercise in Group-Member Evaluation

QUESTION: Who moves our group in desirable ways?

Evaluation is always a difficult task, but it is true that in our human relations groups different members make contributions which are valued differentially. For example, some help move the group toward more open expression of feeling reactions. Others are supportive in a timely way. On the other hand, some members may withhold comments, don't seem as perceptive, or are less willing to risk showing reactions that may reveal their own feelings.

At this stage of the group let us try to do a bit of self-evaluation. You are asked to rank yourself and your fellow group members on the following combined criteria:

    A. Makes perceptive comments that help the group achieve more genuine understanding.
    B. Gives feeling reactions that keep group open and leveling.
    C. Supplies timely support when necessary.

I. Using the three criteria above, rank order (from most contributing to least contributing) yourself and *all* other members of your group.

GROUP RANKINGS

Rankings By:	Byron	Jeff	Phil	Chip	Jack	Ralph	Dag	Doc
Most 1.	P	B	R	C	C	P	R	P
2.	R	P	P	R	B	B	Do	B
3.	C	C	B	P	P	R	P	C
4.	Do	R	C	B	R	C	B	R
5.	Da	j	Ja	J	Do	J	C	Ja
6.	B	Do	J	Ja	Ja	Da	J	J
7.	J	Ja	Do	Do	J	Do	Ja	Da
Least 8.	Ja	Da	Da	Da	Da	Ja	Da	Do

unnerve Chip. The change comes because at this point *other* members tell Phil that *they* also experience him as overly judgmental and that he inhibits *them* just as he does Chip. As an example, Jeff puts in, "You are the kind of guy who will allow a subordinate just one mistake . . . then he gets it—you are just unfair." After similar comments are made to him by others, Phil acknowledges, "Yes, this is a problem for me; in fact, my staff has almost quit trying to work with me because of it." He claims he wants productive contention and challenge, not merely abject capitulation. In contradiction to his expressed aims, here in the group he obviously continues to elicit submissive or avoidance reactions similar to those he ostensibly dislikes in his own staff. Is it true that there is little joy or stimulation in such "victories"? Regardless of the possible pleasure in them, such victories are surely costly in terms of staff morale and efficiency.

Should the leader push the group to query Phil's pattern of proving his superiority again and again if it appears that the group wishes to abandon the problem or continues in yielding to his dominance? This is the kind of strategic choice a human relations leader must make many times if the group does not. In this case, the group has already made the choice, and it *holds* steady on the issue. The leader is merely called in to help structure the problem as a role play. The problem-solving context suggested is a simulation of Phil's staff situation. Members of the group take roles as if they are staff members working in Phil's organization under his direction. Each role player gives feedback to Phil from the perspective of the role he takes as one of Phil's "boys" in the course of a week's experience with Phil in the group. This is then translated into the terms of the home organization for Phil.

Jack discloses a tendency to be devious and manipulative, in his own words, "pretending to be dumber than I am." Phil portrays himself as a "tyrant." Chip pictures himself as "Mr. Milquetoast," timid, frightened, insecure. Doc labels himself "just an old-fashioned type." The human relations training experience purposely upends self-pictures—negative ones as well as positive ones. One way to deal with such self-stereotypes, whether positive or negative, is to shuffle and recombine groups to form N- or new groups. Such N-groups are even more temporary than regular human relations groups. In a lab the function of such N-groups is to provide fresh vantage points for considering how to be more effective in interactions and for a *second chance* to those who have gotten *locked-in* in their initial groups. For members who have had little impact, the problem is how to make themselves felt in the group. For those evaluated as already participating effectively, the challenge is to facilitate the interactions of those who have been too frightened to try. Low-ranked and high-ranked members are grouped together for this exercise. The questions listed in Figure 2.3 are put to the participants following the three *N-group* sessions.

These questions are intended to help members to use the N-group experience as an opportunity to test out the generality of the feedback received by them to that point in the lab. If one does not like the way he is being responded to by others, how should he react to alter that response? For the "effectives," the question will be interpreted quite differently, that is: Can I help others to feel free and more self-confident and to relate more effecively?

As a final exercise in applying the lessons of the lab to one's back-home activities, members are directed to design a personal back-home project.

FIGURE 2.3. Maximizing Learnings from the Evaluation Exercise: What Can Be Learned in the N-Group?

1. What can be learned from the N-group about interpersonal skills or the lack of them?
2. What did I learn about myself?
3. What did I learn about how I facilitate others in their interactions?
4. What did I learn about group interactions and my usual role in them?
5. What did I learn about organizational life in comparing human relations group and N-group processes?

This "tailor-made" project provides for direct translation of lab learnings to the organizational setting or to any other interpersonal context the participant chooses. This attempt to transfer learnings is a key feature of human relations training labs. Learnings from them are deemed important only insofar as they are tried out in real life give and take.

FIGURE 2.4.   Top Secret! ! !

My Very Own Special Planned Change Project Involving Me and My Organization*

This exercise can have very real consequences. You are asked to design for yourself a project which you really intend to carry out. It should be, to some extent at least, contingent upon its human relations aspects even if the processes involved are technical (i.e., its success should depend upon good teamwork or interpersonal cooperation). It should also reflect your personal experiences here at the lab.

Do *not* try it out immediately. Wait two to three weeks. *Then* put it into operation. It should be a project involving a trial period of at least several weeks or even months before you decide about its success or failure. If it fails, try to assess *why*.

Outline Details of Project

   Criteria for Success or Failure

   The Meaning of the Project to Me Personally

   How Does the Lab Experience Relate to My Anticipated Behavior in Relation to This Project?

   Results of Discussions with My Planning Consultant

   Circumstances of Project Initiation (describe)

   Progress Report (halfway)

   Final Report and Evaluation

* The questions are spaced over several sheets when assigned as a project.

This project, as well as the evaluation exercises, suggests how self-monitoring during a lab is adapted to an individual's needs. The general objective is the one in which all share, that is, to utilize laboratory learning in one's back-home situation. The continuing question which each must answer for himself or herself is How? The notion of personal experimentation receives considerable reinforcement from the personal research and self-assessment that is fairly frequently employed. Systematic efforts to follow up such projects lead us to more soundly based conclusions about the lasting values of human relations training.

An Image of Human Relationships in the Social Context

Human relations groups emphasize the interplay of communitarian with personal needs among people. This idea of interplay between these forces shapes the general goals of human relations experiences, and it also influences its theory of practice and prescribes what is possible to achieve as well as clues as to how a leader works toward such goals. From the perspectives of members, human relations labs seem to convey the demand that every participant should regard every other as accountable and self-responsible. On the basis of such an *image* of human responsibility and accountability, one expects rather different leader-member relationships to develop than in those experiential groups where the aim is to generate emotionally expressive responses in the interest of *personal growth*. In order to clarify this point, it will again be necessary to refer to some recent developments which have influenced practices in experiential groups.

I remind the reader that the experiential group from its early years embodied the aspiration that since man's combative nature was the product of frustrated inner needs, in the wake of satisfaction of these, competition had eventually to yield to collaboration. The human relations lab idea held further that the achievement of a good balance between rational and emotional aspects of self in turn would be reflected in a productive balancing of competitive and cooperative strivings. A genuine interdependency could be actualized in the human relations group where any single member ignored the welfare of others only at peril to his own. Group gain ultimately meant personal gain for one's self while personal gain came about at least partly as a result of group gain. One might temporarily have harsh feelings about another, but ultimately there was a coming together on the basis of a deeper and more genuine mutual understanding.

This *balanced image* ideal was overshadowed by a late sixties surge toward emotionality and expressiveness. In the wake of this development associated with general societal turbulence, the experiential group movement as a whole shifted to an explicitly more disclosive and a programmatically expressive emphasis. This general tendency affected human relations labs, influencing them to take on more disclosive aspects, to use more dramatic exercises, and even to employ body awareness training.

While this tendency has not everywhere had precisely the same effects, its effect in experiential groups generally has been to fuse therapy and effectiveness training purposes and to reduce the importance of understanding per se as part of the process to the status of an academic interest. As a consequence, critics have tarred human relations groups with the brush applied to all experiential groups in general, terming them "confessionals," "middle-class recreations," and denying them any significant social value.

One such critic's assessment is particularly vivid. He calls the groups "psychic strip-tease."[12] Broad-brush treatments like this miss the point. Excess in the conduct of experiential groups does not mean that they are necessarily exhibitionistic or without social merit. The balance model of relationship in human relations labs represents the viewpoint that man is at neither extreme—neither solely reasonable nor completely irrational—but that he needs to blend his human propensities for feeling and thinking into constructive and effective forms for relating to and working with his fellows. In this context, emotional and disclosive sharing can be constructive. On the other hand, self-disclosure can certainly be cheap theatrics or maudlin self-display—but it can also be employed in the interests of self-conscious and responsible interdependence and cooperative action.

Failures in Human Relations Laboratories

Earlier in this chapter I alluded to the problem of failures in the human relations training laboratory. Although the criteria for success in human relations laboratories are general, it seems unarguable that Dag's withdrawal from active participation should be considered as a failure. One could suggest other indices of failure, for instance, an increase in defensiveness over time rather than its diminution. Or one might consider an index of relevance, that is: If a participant does not relate the events of the laboratory to his own life in any meaningful way or treats it as an isolated experience without significance in his real world, I would regard his human relations experience as a failure. How many such failures have human relations training laboratories had by these criteria? This is an issue to which no ready answer is available. We shall deal with the reason why this is so in the section on research.

There are some failures and psychological casualties due to poor leader practices. Standards of leader training and practice should be increasingly more rigorous. Certainly they are too casually treated today. Among desirable criteria are backgrounds in personality theory, psychopathology, and group dynamics taught in behavioral science disciplines such as psychology, psychiatry, and education. A minimal formal educational requirement would be the equivalent of the master's degree. The leader should have a sequence of participative and supervisory experiences in the conduct of groups and in psychotherapy as well. The reason for the latter requirement is not so much the acquisition of skills as to prevent the exploitation of the group situation for personal psychological needs.

Qualifications of Leaders

We have seen that the primary mediator of interactions in any type of experiential group is the leader. The clarification of theoretical issues and the evaluation of group forms may take years, but we can begin at once to insist on better standards of practice and preparation. Since rigorous standards of practice have not yet been sufficiently well established and because there is a relatively laissez-faire attitude toward qualification, many essentially unqualified persons now conduct group experiences. Enthusiasm for the helping role is a natural consequence of learning to listen better to others, experiencing empathy oneself, and having the satisfaction of giving support effectively. Participants are naturally attracted to the function that seems to repeat such experiences. A talented participant should be encouraged to seek higher levels of preparation, but he must be dissuaded from assuming a function for which he is inadequately prepared, no matter how much native skill he may have. For the leader's training I suggest what I believe to be desirable.

A. Leader-Investigators

In the category of leader-investigators I include persons who approach experiential group practice from fields broadly designated as education, health, or social sciences. Ordinarily they are specialists in such disciplines as psychology, psychiatry, or intergroup relations and hold advanced degrees. They should be able to contribute conceptually or through research to our knowledge about processes and interactions, and they should participate in the preparation of group leaders.

B. Leaders

Leaders should have a background in personality theory, psychopathology, and group dynamics, including extensive supervised practice centered in any of a variety of disciplines and fields. Although there could be exceptions, they should in general hold the equivalent of a master's degree. If they lack adequate background in the areas specified, they should be required to take relevant courses.

Before a person in either category functions as a leader, he should have a three-year sequence of practical experiences in something like the following order:

1. Participate as a member in at least two groups conducted at the highest possible level.
2. Observe group meetings and meet after sessions with their leaders to discuss the interactions of members and other processes. This should be done with at least five groups.
3. Co-lead five groups with experienced leaders.
4. Lead five groups as leader but be *consulted* for the purpose of monitoring his functioning in the leader role.
5. Have psychotherapy or some equivalent *individual* experiential self-study. (A group experience, in this sense, is not equivalent.)
6. Be evaluated by experienced, well qualified leaders, who focus on his general fitness of character, background, and preparation and review evaluations and recommendations that others make about him.
7. Keep his functions as a leader refreshed by periodic seminars and containing education which includes reviews of the ethics of the leader function.

A recent publication of facts on psychological casualties in encounter groups indicates that they are more likely to occur as the result of the activities of charismatically enthusiastic leaders. Even without these disclosures on casualties, it seems obvious that the leader role is a sensitive and potent one which affects participants in a variety of ways. Therefore, ethical standards for leaders who conduct any kind of experiencing groups should be as rigorous as those for medical or psychotherapeutic practitioners. For further details on this point see Lakin.[13]

Organizational Development: A Human Relations Technology

Organizational development is lab training applied to organizational settings. Its processes parallel those of the human relations lab in attempting to generate productive changes in an organizational system through improved communication diagnoses of the system's problems. Solutions to them are worked out cooperatively. Diagnoses are mainly focused upon interpersonal problems as they are reflected in decision-making systems and organizational structures. Organizational development programs are mainly aimed at reinvigorating a sluggish system by making its decision processes increasingly responsive to organization participants, not merely to rapidly changing technology requirements.[14]

An organizational development *consultant* functions in various ways, mainly interviewing members of teams and departments and counseling with department heads as needed. Only when he feels that there is the need for a general airing of a problem does he try to organize what are called *confrontation* groups (essentially short-term human relations training groups). The interventions of the OD consultant are usually more directive than those of the human relations group leader. For example, the former does not hesitate to propose provisional solutions to problems, suggest specific learning experiences he thinks are corrective, or undertake counseling which becomes a form of time-limited therapy in one-to-one relationships with members of the organization.

OD theory is an admixture of human relations training formulations resulting from early human relations laboratory experiences and the teachings of the late Douglas McGregor, an industrial psychologist and an advocate of shared management responsibility. In his *The Human Side of Enterprise,*[15] he presented two contrasting motivational theories of why people work and of their satisfactions from working, terming them *theory X* and *theory Y*. Those who act as though the first one were more correct hold that man is motivated solely by economic need or by fear of deprivation, that is, for material gain or out of fear of punishment. Those who act on the assumption that theory Y is predominant assume that an individual needs intellectual challenge from his job, seeks a share of responsibility for the fulfillment of organizational objectives, and may be trusted to work toward them.

The second theory does not deny the potency of material rewards or deprivations. However, its major consideration is that, once the point is reached when material needs press less urgently, the satisfactions an individual seeks will be egotistical rather than solely material. The person's priority of motives then shifts to more abstract goals such as the intrinsic challenge and prestige social utility—in short, the *meaningfulness* of the job. Theory Y motivations are more likely to be recognized in organizations where innovation, initiative, responsibility, and self-direction are also prized.

To McGregor the main way to build an effective organization was to meet the members' needs for challenge and involvement in decision making. One had to create a problem-solving climate, especially at higher policy levels where the sharing of decision making could take on reality. In the light of such aims it is understandable that the organizational development approach stresses team building, identification of specific intra-

and interdepartmental problems, and, most of all, effective intraorganizational communication. The uses of confrontation group experience vary widely in form and duration. An occasional weekend confrontation group is arranged as a problem-solving vehicle. On the other hand, role plays and psychodrama techniques may be used occasionally to highlight a recurrent problem. Exercises, when employed, are used to practice such specific skills as listening, organizing, and leading others effectively and learning how to negotiate conflicts involving task priorities.

The Relationship between Human Relations Labs and Therapy Groups

The commonalities among the various kinds of experiential groups have naturally led to a shared image of treatment groups. In all of them, remedial and self-improvement goals are facilitated by the generation of intense affects among the group members—the like of which are routinely experienced only in treatment contexts. This admixture of purposes has always been a characteristic of experiential groups. I am convinced that this does no harm but, rather, good because the role of learner is more self-reliant than that of patient. However, in human relations labs the failure to specify the priority of goals clearly—that is indeed for learning, not for treatment—and to insist on the primacy of a learning rather than a reparative goal results in the vitiation of the learning values. While the therapy intention must be mainly corrective, the learning intention is more broadly gauged and centers on enhanced effectiveness. Granted that the tendency toward fusion is inevitable, nevertheless, the goal priority, therapy *or* learning, is important to reinforce if only for the relative security this provides for participants. Few experiences are less fruitful than a group which finds itself torn between conflicting intentions and protagonists who push for the fulfillment of quite different objectives on the basis of conflicting priorities. Leaders can help by establishing contractual clarity so that the participants have as clear a conception as possible of what they are entering into and what they may expect from it.

Evaluation of Human Relations Lab Training

There is no separate evaluation data pertaining to human relations labs as distinct from other forms of experiential groups. This fact reflects the lack of differentiation among different experiential groups in the minds of many researchers in this area. On the other hand, looking at the general class of experiential groups, there is no dearth of evaluation research. Indeed, in one form or another, such groups have been heavily researched beginning with the early 1950s. Campbell and Dunnette[16] have summarized much of the early evaluation research under the rubric *sensitivity training* and Jack R. Gibb has used the term *human relations training* but obviously includes a broad range of experiential group experiences in his chapter on evaluation.[17]

When Dorothy Stock[18] first categorized the early evaluation attempts of various kinds of experiential groups, it seemed almost certain that solid bases for evaluating process and outcomes in such groups were imminent. That early optimism has vanished several hundred studies later in the mid-1970s. One is still bedeviled by questions such as "What good is it?" This question, in turn, cannot be satisfactorily resolved until "What is it?" becomes considerably clearer.

Why is it so difficult to resolve these issues? The earliest handful of promising process studies sketched the complexities inherent in lab interrelationships among group composition, leader personality and style, and group purpose. Instead of continuing to flesh out these areas, evaluation leapfrogged the issues of process ("What is it?") to concern about outcomes or effects in all kinds of settings: schools, government, businesses, churches, and the military ("How good is it?"). Most effects studies had methodological shortcomings in terms of design, sampling, and inadequate or nonexistent controls. But, most important, they were hobbled from the outset by their fundamental lack of clarity about the process counted on to generate the anticipated effects. Without a clear understanding of what goes into training labs, how can there be great confidence in measures of what results from them?

Logically, of course, one could still conduct evaluations of a pre–post type. However, as could be predicted, they have no anchor in the lab experience itself. Consequently, they use many outcome variables which, while they express all manner of desiderata, may have little to relate back to in the lab. Thus we see a great number of studies seeking such changes as gains in salary, profit-making capacity of the work unit, improved interpersonal behaviors as rated by peers (who usually *know* the individual attended a human relations lab!), and various measures of emotionality, personal happiness, and/or adjustment. There have been a few sophisticated studies of outcomes of certain types of experiential groups (aside from therapy groups where the outcome research is, of course, focused on improved adjustment), and we shall refer to one of them in some detail. It is a fair criticism of the entire experiential group movement that its evaluation efforts have failed to specify adequately the processes which make possible meaningful assessments of outcomes.

The most thoroughgoing evaluation of experiential groups to date is by two psychologists and a psychiatrist, Lieberman, Yalom, and Miles.[19]

Although their book's title refers only to encounter groups, it is in fact a study covering at least three different types of experiential groups and within them an array of leader orientations and styles. No one of their groups was actually termed a human relations lab. However, their findings are relevant to human relations groups as well as to other experiential groups.

Lieberman and his colleagues took the position that the groups they studied are committed to changing people. On this basis, they devised a composite index of change according to which they compared participants and a matched group of controls—all college students. The index used four perspectives: (1) benefits as seen by participants immediately following the group and six months later; (2) benefits as seen by the group leader; (3) benefits as seen by friends or relatives of participants; and (4) those seen by co-participants.

The self-ratings are consistent with the typical post–human relations lab self-reports. They are overwhelmingly enthusiastic and the general tenor is that of "satisfied customers." A decrease in positive evaluations over a six-month period from a ratio of five to one to a ratio of two to one suggests either that the initial enthusiasm was not quite so well founded in a great number of cases or that there is significant slipping away of gains. Leaders see the vast majority of their members as gratifyingly successful. Participants are also seen by friends and relatives as having achieved significant positive change. However, the same is true of the friends and relatives of controls who have gone through no group experience at all! Finally, co-participants estimate one third of their colleagues to have benefited really significantly in terms of learning. However, the last finding used the more ambiguous term *learning* rather than *change,* so we are not quite clear about its implications.

In a careful analysis of their composite indices which now included the consideration of such factors as respondent success ratios and dropouts or attriters, the researchers conclude that short-run positive changes occur in about one-third of those beginning the group experience; that about one-third are relatively unchanged; and that, among the remainder, some simply drop out while others are negatively affected. This gives a more conservative picture than self-reports usually do and a considerably less rosy picture than conveyed in the popularized versions of encounter groups.

Another contribution from this evaluation report tends to confirm apprehensions that some styles of leader intervention are poorly suited to the psychological needs of certain participants. Of the groups producing psychological casualties—that is, breakdowns, depressions, suicidal feelings, and so on—those with the greater proportions (8–14%!) were led by *charismatic* leaders who were the most probing, intrusive, and directive. It is a curious fact that this high casualty rate was obtained among charismatically led groups in the part of the country most saturated by growth centers using dramatic encounter groups; however, one cannot know cause-and-effect relationships without further study.

This research has made some effort in the direction of retracing process aspects in its attempts to characterize leader style and in the uses of questionnaires and checklists designed to tap some aspects of ongoing process.

Future evaluations of human relations labs must surely take account of this pioneering study in designing methods which go beyond the usual testimonials or rely solely upon immediate self-report. They should also define in specific terms the *kinds* of change intended by the human relations experience as contrasted with other kinds of experiential groups and match them against back-home behavior criteria. Most of all, there is the need to do what the previously cited study has also failed to do: to relate the process to an anticipated outcome through more thorough mapping of the process.

There are encouraging signs that in various kinds of experiential groups these criteria for meaningful evaluative research are becoming recognized. Comprehensive understanding is needed to trace out the important variables involved. Variables of human relations training processes are interwoven in the complex interaction of personalities, group dynamic processes, and leader action which is intrinsically difficult to research. However, the large financial and emotional commitment on the part of so many persons and institutions to this type of educational experience demands continuing efforts to arrive at meaningful answers to the questions of process and utility.

The Outlook for Human Relations Training

In these times of rapid change it is difficult to forecast the career of any idea, let alone an idea which has taken on the cast and substance of a social movement. Who in 1946 and 1947 could have foreseen the vicissitudes of the human relations lab eventuating in the hybrid admixture of psychotherapy, body awareness training, and Eastern philosophies called *personal growth group,* on the one hand, and in organizational development serving Business America on the other? The dynamic interplays between therapy and learning, group process and personal inner experience, and individualism and communitarian impulses have all proven very difficult to balance off in a planned learning experience. Their explosive dynamics are genuine, not just figurative. Then, too, the changes in the society have had enormous influence upon experiential group forms. There is bound to be less patience for a human relations lab which takes a more academic approach to the antinomies of person and group, and studies the accommodations of person and social order in a time of rapid change. On the other hand, the human relations group, precisely because of its learning stance, is perhaps the best suited of experiential groups to contribute understanding regarding these vital relationships. The conception that human relationships can be improved through mutual understanding of what passes between people is the humanistic task of the human relations lab and is its credential of social relevance.

Learning through shared experience and sharing candid reflections on mutual experience remains the distinctive characteristic of human relations training labs. Because they foster candor and mutual acceptance not through maudlin sentimentality but through give and take, they continue to be important educational experiences, *particularly* in a time of fluctuating social values. If the ideas animating the human relations lab can be reestablished for the experiential group movement as a whole, understanding of individual and group relations among groups and the processes in organizations would have a brighter outlook.

The conception is as valid now as it was in the 1940s. It remains for the priorities of this conception to be reasserted and for its forms to be so clear that contractual agreements between leader and member may be firm. The past few turbulent years have witnessed immense growth and popularity of experiential groups, but not the validation of the conception of human relations groups for mass education toward comprehension of person and group relations and person-societal relations. One may hope that the present decade will witness more solid if less spectacular development with accompanying confidence that we shall know more about what the human relations group is and measure more meaningfully how it will achieve its purposes.

Chapter 3. Personal Growth, Encounter, and Self-Awareness Groups

Burton Giges and Edward Rosenfeld

PERSONAL GROWTH can be viewed as making new connections in any of several directions: upward, to achieve one's full potential; outward, to make contact and encounter others; inward, to increase our awareness of who we are, and what we want, need, sense, feel, think, and do; and downward, to touch earth, to be grounded, and to connect with the universe. Such growth involves increasing the range of perceptions, thoughts, and feelings we experience, developing new ways to express them, and making choices and decisions about the direction in which we wish to move. This leads to increased flexibility as we create and recognize our alternatives; greater spontaneity as we stretch our boundaries and free ourselves from fixed patterns of behavior; and enhanced self-esteem as we begin to sense our mastery, use our ability to effect change, and take responsibility for the outcome. Ultimately, these processes lead to increased acceptance of ourselves and others, as we come to know who we really are and where we want to be in this universe.

The purpose of this chapter will be to show how these processes are enhanced and facilitated by a variety of approaches, methods, and techniques generally referred to under the grouping of the *personal growth movement* or the *human potential movement*. Elements of these approaches embrace self-awareness, living in the here and now, body work, movement, play, meditation, and encounter.

The origins of group psychotherapy, in general, and the personal growth movement, in particular, can be traced back to the nineteenth century. However, the real emergence of these movements begins following World War II.[1] The aftermath of the devastating global warfare brought many serious thinkers into profound consideration of basic questions and facts of individual existence.

Existential Origins

The burgeoning of intellectual interest in phenomenology and existentialism created an intense and fertile environment for the development of new psychotherapeutic tools. The post-war existential vantage point was of a world never again to be safe from the threat of total and instantaneous holocaust. Thus the daily life of an individual is a microcosm of potential oblivion and, conversely, of potential joy.

Philosophers and psychotherapists alike began to reexamine the very stuff of existence, the moment-to-moment phenomena of daily life. Rather than attending only to the client's verbal report, therapists began to emphasize other perspectives of the client: style, manner, and, most especially, his* body. Soon after the war, Sheldon pointed to the possibility that the body may be what psychoanalysts had been calling the unconscious for so many years.[2]

By attending to the obvious, the a priori given of daily existence, therapists began breaking ground in a new, decidedly phenomenological field: the field of awareness. The attention of the developing therapies in the personal growth movement was centered on awareness of the present, the here and now. Such awareness does not ignore the past and the future. It integrates them with the knowledge that cognizance of the past (memory) occurs in the present as does expectation of the future. Thus the present is seen to include representations of the past and the future.

By focusing on the present, and introducing techniques for developing and enhancing awareness, the therapies of the personal growth movement developed a new style of helping the client that has come to be known as the *safe emergency*. The safe emergency lets a client experiment with awareness of his feelings, awareness of his life style, and new ways of being within the context of the therapeutic situation. By experiencing his new ways of being and integrating feedback from the therapist and the group, the client has a base from which to operate when taking this new behavior out into the world at large. By being himself, by being real in an experimental situation first, the client can safely approach new ways of being.

Authenticity

The concept of authenticity is fundamental to understanding what is meant by *being oneself* or *being real*.[3] To be authentic requires an awareness of

* For convenience, the authors will be using *he* and *his* in writing about a client's experience, with full awareness of the fact that there is no satisfactory simple pronoun that includes both sexes.

one's deeper feelings and needs, those which may have been buried early in life, behind a façade that was more palatable to others or less uncomfortable for ourselves. Everett Shostrom[4] focused attention on how this leads to manipulations; Eric Berne[5] introduced the concept of games; Ronald Laing[6] and Arthur Janov[7] described the unreal self, the façade we develop to hide the pain we originally felt.

To know what one really wants is not always immediately apparent. Being authentic is not necessarily presenting ourselves with our first feeling. Sometimes we may wish to cover our deeper feelings to avoid embarrassment or anxiety, or we may express anger to cover hurt feelings, irritation to cover sadness. It is erroneous to equate authentic behavior with immediate gratification. Authenticity often leads to a choice which may postpone being satisfied immediately. The first feelings we are aware of may not be any truer than those which emerge if given time. Hugh Prather[8] expresses it this way:

> At first I thought that to "be myself" meant simply to act the way I feel. I would ask myself a question such as, "what do I want to say to this person?", and very often the answer was surprisingly negative. It seemed that when I looked inside, the negative feelings were the ones I noticed first. . . . But I soon found that behind most negative feelings were deeper, more positive feelings—if I held still long enough to look. The more I attempted to "be me" the more "me's" I found there were. I now see that "being me" means acknowledging all that I feel at the moment, and then taking responsibility for my actions by consciously choosing which level of my feeling I am going to respond to.

An authentic relationship is one in which each person is seen as separate, and acknowledged as having his own needs and feelings, rather than merely being the object of the other's needs or feelings. Martin Buber[9] identified the former as an *I-Thou* relationship, a mutual attempt to know and be known, and the latter as *I-It*. The I-Thou is the core of a meaningful encounter between two persons. To allow another to be different and to accept that difference forms the basis for an authentic relationship, one in which intimacy becomes possible. George Land calls this ability to accept differentness the *mutual phase* of growth. In this phase, one can use similarities as a beginning basis for a relationship, and differences to deepen it and allow for mutual growth.[10]

Personal Growth

Being authentic is an aspect of personal growth emphasized by Carl Rogers.[11] He describes such growth as moving away from façades and *oughts*, being self-directed, opening to inner and outer experience, being capable of intimacy, with sensitivity to and acceptance of others. The aspects of personal growth which Jack Gibb[12] considers as central and of critical importance are trust, openness, realization (what I want to become), and interdependence. He believes that the basic dynamic process of growth is the change from fear to trust, and that progressive changes in the other aspects can be described as fulfilling, emerging, and becoming.[13] These processes are characterized by an increased capacity to express love and warmth, an enhanced sense of power and influence, a greater freedom from role, and increased ability to live fully in the present moment.[14]

The ability to initiate action is emphasized by William Schutz and Charles Seashore[15] as an essential element in personal growth. This requires a heightened awareness of alternatives which provides the opportunity to make decisions. In developing the concept of self-actualization, Abraham Maslow[16] states that we are capable of functioning with far more intensity, creativity, and vitality than we realize. He sees personal growth as the process by which we can approach our full human potential. While he describes growth as intrinsically rewarding and delightful, he recognizes that it requires effort and self-discipline, and may involve pain and sorrow.

According to Clark Moustakas,[17] personal growth has two major components: self-growth and growth in human relations. The former requires self-awareness and self-understanding, and often leads to periods of loneliness and solitude; the latter becomes possible when each person recognizes others as they are and accepts their otherness. Sidney Jourard[18] writes that "growth is the dis-integration of one way of experiencing the world, followed by a re-organization of this experience, a reorganization that includes the new disclosure of the world." He believes he has personally grown when he perceives changes that have occurred, decides how he wants to be in this world, how he wants the world to be for him, and then acts.[19]

In thinking about his own personal growth, Moustakas writes:[20]

> Many times in my life I have overcome obstacles to my own growth (after) I discovered resources when none appeared available. Many times, too, I have felt emptiness, boredom, triviality, repetitiveness, sterility and meaninglessness—momentarily; but when I transcended the mood or feeling or situation, when I became involved, spontaneous and free, suddenly I was seeing with different eyes and hearing with different ears . . . boredom dissipated into interest, sadness into joy, emptiness into excitement.

Alan Watts[21] has also commented on the ever changing process involved in feelings, and the importance of allowing a natural flow from one to another. To allow this flow requires awareness and acceptance of these feelings as a natural part of one's moment-to-moment existence.

Awareness

We believe that awareness is central to the concept of personal growth: awareness of feelings, thoughts, needs, senses, and bodily messages. In gestalt therapy, awareness = experience = reality = now.[22] If awareness is blocked, growth stops. Awareness is essential in enabling us to deal with whatever the most important unfinished situation is from moment to moment.[23,24] It is necessary to provide us with the opportunity to see alternatives and make choices,[25] and to develop self-understanding and self-acceptance.

Awareness can be developed and expanded through fantasy and imagery, through focusing attention on body parts, positions, and movement, through exposure to sensory experiences, and through feedback from others. Using fantasy and imagery, one is able to get in touch with thoughts and feelings which may have been hidden, either because other ideas pressed for attention or because too much discomfort would accompany their direct expression. Fantasy also makes possible the clarification of how we experience a current situation, or facilitates the emergence of inner resources and wisdom of which we were unaware.[26]

Muscle tension and limitation of motility are related to decreased self-awareness, according to Alexander Lowen.[27] In bioenergetic analysis, he attempts to integrate body function and emotions by removing the blocks to the free flow of energy. Charlotte Selver[28] emphasizes the importance of sensory awareness, which she describes as a "gradual unfolding and cultivation of sensibility, of a greater range and delicacy of feeling, which brings about concurrently the awakening and freeing of our innate energies." She believes it is necessary to restore the smooth and effective functioning of our body to allow those natural responses which have been covered over to be reawakened. Bernard Gunther[29,30] has developed a series of exercises as part of a process called sensory awakening, which leads to heightened awareness and contact with one's world, and which removes the dulling effects of our past experiences. They involve movement, breathing, massage, and other exercises to stimulate the senses.

Gestalt Therapy

Now that we have discussed a historical perspective and some theoretical roots, let us go on to consider some specific elements of the personal growth movement in a more detailed discussion.

A good beginning is the career, thought, and influence of F. S. "Fritz"

Perls. As a medical doctor in Germany, prior to World War II, Perls had been an assistant to Kurt Goldstein. As a psychoanalyst, he had been in training with Wilhelm Reich and under the supervision of Otto Fenichel and Karen Horney. Perls escaped Germany in 1933 and, with the help of Ernest Jones, took a position as a training analyst in South Africa the following year.

In 1942 Perls published *Ego, Hunger, and Aggression: A Revision of Freud's Theory and Method.*[31] In this work, Perls started to develop a theory that would move past psychoanalysis, a theory that would integrate many influences on his life and thought. Among these were gestalt psychology, existentialism, Reich's attention to the body, and elements from Eastern philosophical systems.

In 1946 Perls came to the United States, and settled in a number of communities across the country during the 1950s and 1960s. His work in New York City had a strong influence on Paul Goodman. Similar residences in Miami and Cleveland left trained practitioners in gestalt therapy like Marty Fromm and Erving and Miriam Polster.

But it was in California that Perls' influence was most astounding. In 1964 Perls came to Esalen Institute at Big Sur, one of the first centers of the personal growth movement. He stayed on as a psychiatrist in residence, and as the popularity and recognition for Esalen grew, so did the acknowledgements of Fritz Perls and gestalt therapy.

Gestalt therapy usually takes place in a group setting, and is conducted on a one-to-one basis, with the therapist and the client encountering each other in an I-Thou situation. Perls would work with one client at a time while the other members of the group listened and, hopefully, did their own silent self-therapy. After a client finished some therapeutic work, other members might then be invited to share their own self-recognitions with the rest of the group.

The theoretical basis of gestalt therapy begins with the situation of the organism as a being in relationship with a constantly changing and emerging environment. The organism is constantly striving to complete situations and to maintain a balance, or homeostasis, with its context in the environment. Perls paid particular attention to helping the client (the organism) come to awareness of how he was functioning in relationship to his environment. Perls noted that the client attempted to manipulate the environment for support. Perls' definition of maturity was the transition from environmental support to self-support, when the client would take full and complete responsibility for all of his actions and behavior.

Among the many ways that the client would experience himself and his environment, Perls noted that transactions might be projections: the client's attempt to attribute his own thoughts or feelings to another (person or thing or situation) in the environment; introjections: the client's attempt to make something outside him his own; and retroflections: the things the environment bent back to the client after the client had directed that same

thing outward—for example, the narcissist, a person who instead of direct-
ing his love outward to an object falls in love with himself.[32]

Some of Perls' most exciting work came out of therapeutic investiga-
tion of dreams. He believed that a client's dream was an existential message of the client's life situation experientially, at the time of the dream. In
order to work on the dream, Perls would direct the client to act out, in
psychodrama form, each element of the dream: all of the characters,
objects, and occurrences in the dream. In this way, the client would come
to experience the fact that he was the whole dream, rather than just one
character or symbol in the dream.

An important element of Perls' theoretical viewpoint was that a client
cannot *get well* without becoming whole. The basic road to wholeness in
gestalt therapy is through the integration of the disowned parts of the self.
Perls would have the client experiment with a dialogue so that the dispa-
rate elements of the self could encounter each other.

Perls found that these elements of the self often grouped themselves
into two distinct characters. Perls named these characters *top dog* and
under dog. Top dog is authoritarian, impatient, proper, rigid, and often
uses the expression "you should" when barking his commands at under
dog. Under dog is apologetic, manipulative, and usually wins most arguments in the top dog/under dog dialogue through deviousness and subter-
fuge. Under dog often says: "I know, I should have. I'm sorry. I'll do
better tomorrow."

A good deal of the effectiveness of the gestalt therapy approach is
found in its reliance on an intensive dynamic in the relationship between
therapist and clients, which involves a process relationship that evolves
over time. This duration allows the insights and awarenesses that occur
during the course of the therapy to be integrated into the life style of the
individual client.

Though Perls gave demonstrations and one-day workshops, the bulk of
the work that goes under the name gestalt therapy takes place in an intensive group atmosphere. Groups extend in time for a year or longer and the
client is making a commitment to a process that will involve him in such a
group experience that will aid him in new awareness, new recognitions,
and new life possibilities.

Perls perceived living as a series of situations, or *gestalten,* in process
from being incomplete to being completed. When a situation has been
completed, another situation that was in the background will move into
prominence to become figure and demand attention for completion. This
never-ending series of situations applies to the therapeutic encounter as
well. As Perls wrote in *The Gestalt Approach:*[33]

> Self-support is very different from self-sufficiency. When the patient is dis-
> charged from therapy he will not lose his need for other people. On the con-
> trary, he will for the first time derive real satisfactions from his contact with
> them.

At the same time that Perls and Esalen were coming to national promi- nence, another Esalen-enhanced technique was gaining adherents: en- counter. Kurt Back cites August 1946 as the birth date of the encounter movement.[34] Others point to encounter as an outgrowth of the sensitivity training laboratories at NTL in Bethel, Maine. No matter what its real origins, encounter has changed the face of contemporary psychotherapy, with particular reference to the intensive small group experience.

Group Experience

The intensive small group—sometimes called encounter group, sensitivity training group, or human interaction laboratory—can provide a unique opportunity to facilitate personal growth by stimulating the development of awareness of how we feel, how we perceive and react to others, and how others perceive and react to us. It also affords us the chance to make a fundamental connectedness with others, to express feelings openly and honestly, to experiment with new behavior, and to experience others un- encumbered by our usual role restrictions. Most such groups are not designed to solve problems directly, but to develop skills and an approach to deal with such problems. Jack Gibb believes that "there is no substi- tute currently available for the intimate personal group experience as a medium . . . for creating the capacity to produce an enhancing and facilitative interpersonal environment."[35] He says that "those who com- mit themselves to group experience can grow significantly," and for them "the small group experience means growth."[36] William Schutz writes that such groups are oriented toward the development of the full potential of their members, involving the physical, emotional, intellectual, social, and spiritual aspects of each.[37] According to Sidney Jourard, these groups are "places and times for each who is present to disclose himself as he now is, and for each to respond, truly respond to what has thus been revealed."[38] Clark Moustakas points out that the intensive group experience provides an opportunity to share joy and pain, happiness and sorrow, anger and excitement.[39]

Expressing Feelings

The expression of feelings in the group involves a sequence of awareness, decision, action, awareness, decision, and reaction. Figure 3.1 shows this with just two persons involved. Beginning with an awareness of how I feel about you or how I feel about myself, an action may follow. This leads to additional feelings about myself or stimulates feelings in you about me or about yourself. Another action may follow and begin the sequence over again. If either of us is concerned only with our own feelings, our involvement with each other may be terminated, as we drift into a smaller cycle with only ourselves, depicted on the right side of the diagram (a1,a2; b1,b2).

FIGURE 3.1.   A Two-Person Interaction

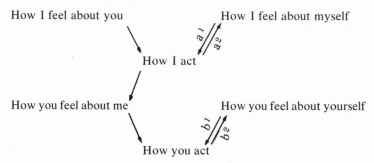

If another person reacts to my action toward you, our involvement with each other may be interrupted, and multiple interactions may quickly follow. The complexity of involvements in a group situation is illustrated in the following excerpt from one group of eight members. The episode involved four of the members and lasted about one minute.

> Betty has been speaking to Frank at length, telling him how he should behave in the group. Warren gets impatient and says to her:
>
> *Warren* (to Betty): Stop lecturing to him.
> *Jill* (to Warren): Don't be so critical all the time.
> *Betty* (to Jill): Thanks for defending me.
> *Jill* (to Betty): I didn't really defend you. I got scared.
> *Frank* (to Warren): Well, anyway, I appreciate your taking my side.
> *Warren* (to Frank): I wasn't taking your side; I was getting very impatient.

Since an interaction between two members can quickly involve others, chaos could replace communication, if everyone were to express all their thoughts or feelings all the time. To avoid this, the concept of a threshold and of making choices becomes useful. This would involve a person expressing a feeling when the need or wish to do so is greater than the need or wish not to. Sometimes one may decide not to express a feeling when there is another feeling that interferes; that is, not expressing anger because of fear of retaliation, or not expressing hurt feelings because of intense embarrassment.

Expressing a feeling fully primarily serves the needs of the person who has the feeling, and not necessarily the one to whom it is expressed. Feedback, on the other hand, can serve the needs of the person to whom it is expressed, by providing useful information which can be the basis for new learning. To attempt both at the same time rarely accomplishes either purpose adequately: either the feelings are not fully expressed, or the ideas communicated are contaminated by the affective message. Making a choice to do one or the other will lead to a more satisfying expression of feelings or a clearer communication of ideas.

In an attempt to improve a relationship, it may also be useful for each person to make clear what they want or need from each other. This kind of communication is different from either expressing a feeling or providing feedback, yet is an essential component in developing an authentic relationship.

Encounter

By providing a setting for obtaining feedback and expressing feelings, the encounter group became an opportunity where new kinds of behavior could be tested, and where participants might have an intensive group experience.

Back[40] traces three distinct theoretical foundations to the encounter movement: training laboratories, personal growth centers, and the English (Tavistock) model. The training lab aims at using the group to facilitate the experience of change. In this model change is of paramount importance, as is the group as a whole rather than the individual.

The growth center paradigm is much more concerned with the individual and his ability to function more fully, more toward the limits of his potential. The English groups, mainly those known under the Tavistock name, are concerned with the group, with much more emphasis on the relation of the individual to authority, involving a heavy psychoanalytic orientation.

Here we are most concerned with the personal growth approach to encounter techniques. One of the most wide-ranging definitions of encounter comes from Schutz:[41]

> Encounter is a method of human relating based on openness and honesty, self-awareness, self-responsibility, awareness of the body, attention to feelings and an emphasis on the here-and-now. . . . Encounter is therapy insofar as it focuses on removing blocks to better functioning. Encounter is education and recreation in that it attempts to create conditions leading to the most satisfying use of personal capacities.

Gerald Haigh considers encounter to be the antidote to alienation. He sees encounter occurring when the blocks to self-disclosure have been removed from a therapeutic relationship.[42] Carl Rogers notes that the removal of such blocks may make the first expressions of significant feelings, within the encounter process, negative expressions directed at the group leader or other members of the group.[43]

In a typical encounter group, emphasis is given to the *here and now*, to experiential learning, and to participants' feelings. By here and now is meant the experiences, relationships, and feelings occurring during the course of the group, rather than the narration of outside or past events. Experiential learning is that which occurs during the process of doing, rather than by merely talking about doing. Frequently, it is nonverbal and involves use of the body as well as of the mind. Feelings occurring in a group member or between members are given priority over ideational or cognitive material. Further, the gestalt therapy principles of making statements instead of asking questions, changing generalities to personal comments, and confronting someone directly rather than talking about them also facilitate a more intensive experience.

The encounter group leader has in mind the goals of increasing awareness and encouraging new behavior (*risk taking*). He may make interventions by modeling behavior of group members, providing feedback to others, disclosing something about himself, being open and honest, offering acceptance or support, or encouraging others to do so. He may also invite a group member to carry out a structured exercise or experiment as a way of assisting that member to "stretch his boundaries," that is, to go beyond the restrictions he usually places upon himself.

To be effective, such experiments must be specific for the person, time, and situation, and frequently modified to meet individual needs. Routine exercises, mechanically administered, do not facilitate growth, and often decrease a leader's effectiveness. When considering which particular experiment would be most useful, a leader will evaluate whether to use the group as a whole to focus on an interpersonal issue—that is, clarifying feelings or improving communication—or to concentrate on working with a single group member. He must also take into account what is possible and appropriate in the particular setting, the readiness and willingness of the individual, the readiness of the group to tolerate the intensity of the experience, and whether a better resolution might be attained with no intervention at all. He must also know when to encourage a member to go further and when to stop. To do these, he must have a thorough understanding of individual and group dynamics; with these skills, the encounter group leader can significantly enhance the intensity of the group experience.

Encounter groups have been linked to a variety of other theories, techniques, and methods. Rosenfeld[44] describes 252 ways of altering consciousness without drugs, with almost one hundred of the techniques in some way related to the personal growth movement.

Growth Approaches

In *A Catalog of the Ways People Grow*, Severin Peterson describes more than forty ways people can pursue their personal growth.[45] He says,

"Each person is his own way of growth," and emphasizes that personal involvement is basic, commitment and perseverance essential. The various processes listed are considered auxiliary. Any of them may lead to growth by extending one's boundaries beyond the limits previously established. If we can learn to use our senses more acutely, increase the range of our feelings, develop more understanding of ourselves and of others, stimulate our bodies to feel more alive, or mobilize our inner energies, then we can expand the space in which we live and broaden our experience—we can grow. In his directory of ways people grow, eight major categories are listed, according to the predominant element in the approach described: physical functioning, feelings and relationships, action and behavior, motivation and willing, suggestion and altered states, imagination and symbols, spiritual concerns, and environment. Examples of two of the major categories are:

> *Physical Functioning and Sensing:* Alexander technique, bioenergetic analysis, body awareness, breathing therapy, hatha yoga, massage, movement, sensory awareness, structural integration, tai chi ch'uan, etc.
> *Feelings and Relationships to Others:* Client-centered therapy, encounter group, gestalt therapy, logotherapy, psychoanalysis, psychodrama, psychotherapy, sensitivity training, theater games, etc.

Since many approaches overlap any single category, no classification is completely satisfactory. Some methods which emphasize physical functioning also involve feelings; some which focus on feelings and relationships also deal with action and behavior; spiritual approaches may involve altered states of consciousness or physical functioning; and so on. Whatever the approach, virtually all utilize the concept of energy flow, most recognize the importance of understanding body messages, and many emphasize our oneness with the universe. We believe that the greater the diversity of methods available, the better is the opportunity to find an approach useful for each person. William Schutz[46] states, "The fact that no one method works well for everyone creates a need for a multiplicity of methods. By having a wide variety of approaches, it is more likely that each person can find one or more techniques that he can work with profitably." As indicated above, the intensive small group experiences creates a particularly effective setting in which personal growth can occur.

Questions have been raised about how one can hope to achieve authenticity with the use of *techniques*.[47] Such techniques do not *produce* authenticity; they facilitate its emergence. By assisting a person to enter the space behind the façade which has been defensively erected, they enable an individual to avoid the habitual response. What may often appear as a *spontaneous* reaction may be a stereotyped pattern of functioning which prevents intimacy and authenticity. The usual response in a new situation is to repeat what is familiar, rather than risk a new and perhaps threatening behavior. Maslow describes the choice one has: either to go back toward safety or forward toward growth.[48] Encounter "gimmicks," if offered to fit individual needs and situations, can reveal the "phony" ways of relating to others, and allow the authentic self to emerge and an authentic relationship to develop. Soren Kierkegaard wrote, "Sometimes when you have scrutinized a face long and persistently, you seem to discover a second face hidden behind the one you see. This is generally an unmistakable sign that his soul harbors an emigrant who has withdrawn from the world . . . and the path for the investigator is . . . that he must penetrate within if he wishes to discover anything."[49]

It is not only important to have several approaches available, it is also useful to offer different opportunities for personal growth. Given the objectives and characteristics of the growth process, the intensive small group experience may be modified as to duration, frequency, and length of session, as well as content. The full range varies from those which meet regularly, usually weekly, for 1½ to 3 hours, to marathons which last 15 to 48 hours (the longer ones breaking only for eating and sleeping), to those which meet daily for 5 to 7 days or longer. Weekly groups may continue for a specified number of sessions or be open-ended, with new members entering as others leave.

Whatever structure is utilized, we would emphasize the importance of repeated experiences, since originally established patterns of behavior and ways of relating to others tend to return. Elizabeth Mintz[50] has suggested that marathons can be useful in conjunction with therapy. We agree, and further believe that the combination of an intensive short-term experience and a continuing opportunity to integrate affective and cognitive input in an ongoing group is more effective than either alone. The gains achieved in a marathon frequently require reinforcement for those whose behavior patterns have been dysfunctional for prolonged periods; and the work done in an ongoing group can often be enhanced by the more intense experience of the marathon.

Sensory Awareness

Aside from marathons, and the other approaches referred to above, many theories, methods, and techniques are deserving of a more complete treatment for better understanding of their place in the personal growth movement.

Sensory awareness is often used as an adjunct to the personal growth experience. Sensory awareness has been almost singlehandedly introduced to the American public by Charlotte Selver. She in turn traces the roots of her theories and her work back to the early twentieth-century efforts of Elsa Gindler in Berlin and Heinrich Jacoby in Zurich.[51] Sensory awareness concerns the reeducation of sensory usage so that sensitivity to both internal and external stimuli is enriched.

> In general the work may be described as the gradual unfolding and cultivation of sensibility, of greater range and delicacy of feeling, which brings about concurrently the awakening and freeing of our innate energies. This we practice through the *activity of sensing*.[52]

Selver has developed a group of exercises and experiments that allow the client to use his senses in a new, focused way. The simple process of concentration on sensory input can reveal a myriad of details often overlooked in the ebb and flow of daily existence. Often colors are enhanced, sounds seem richer and deeper, and complex inner emotions are encountered in a different light.[53]

The commitment of the client to sensory awareness work in an intensive group experience can lead to new, rich material for consideration.

Body Work

Encounter, sensory awareness, and gestalt therapy all share a common attitude that the human is more than just a mind; that humans are whole systems composed of minds *and* bodies. Many group leaders in the personal growth movement share the perception that we do not *have* bodies, but we *are* our bodies.[54]

With this new set of perceptions, a variety of new approaches to human functioning have begun to receive increasingly serious attention in the psychological community. These approaches include rolfing (structural integration), the Alexander technique, the Feldenkrais method, and bioenergetics.

Central to all of these approaches is the perception that the treatment of a client's problems or disorders must include awareness and treatment of the client's physical structure. As Ida Rolf observes:

> Behavior bears witness to a given structure. Structure, here, means relationship in space. And structure (relationship in space) on another plane, in another dimension, is behavior.[55]

Ida Rolf developed structural integration, now commonly known as *rolfing,* in order to free habitual patterns deeply ingrained in physical structure. Rolfing is a system of deep muscle manipulation and realignment. The nature of the manipulation is based on the way the rolfer *reads* the structure of the client's body in its relationship to the environment.

Particular attention is paid to the relationship between gravity and the body. Rolfing emphasizes that the client's body is a mirror of past experience. Emotional as well as physical trauma leave deep impressions in physical structure. A perfect example is fear.

When a child is scared and becomes anxious, he depresses his breathing, collapses his diaphragm, and foreshortens the muscles in the upper chest. Repeated experiences of fear perpetuate this habit and the muscular response that accompanies it. Eventually the physical condition cannot be corrected simply by standing up straight, as the child's parents are wont to tell him.

The foreshortened muscles include the fascia or sheathing that enclose the muscles. Rolf believes that only through manipulation of these fascia can (potential) restructuring be achieved. A rolfer will realign the muscle fascia so that the client has the potential for a new structural response and true structural integration.

In order that some of the potential for new structural alignment can be achieved, Judith Ashton, working with Dr. Rolf, developed a series of exercises to facilitate the changes that rolfing makes possible. Called *structural patterning,* the Ashton exercises can be used in conjunction with rolfing to keep the client's body from reverting to old patterns and habits.

Rolfing involves deep muscular manipulation of the client by the practitioner. By contrast, the practitioners in the Alexander technique touch their clients softly, if at all. Any deep muscle work that is done is an adjunct to the technique rather than part of the method itself.

F. M. Alexander was an orator at the end of the nineteenth century. One day he lost his voice, which was the equivalent of losing his livelihood. He went from doctor to doctor and was continually told that if he stopped speaking his voice would return. He tried this several times only to find that after returning his voice would once again disappear.

Rather than consulting more physicians, Alexander decided to try to cure himself. He spent long hours in front of a mirror studying *what* he did when he spoke. From this awareness he was eventually able to cure himself, after he noted a three-part process that preceded his every attempt at speech. As he began to talk, Alexander would throw his head back, gasp a breath, and depress his larynx.

However, before he was actually able to cure his loss of voice, Alexander made a variety of discoveries on the relationship between awareness and change, and on the relationship between head and neck. What developed from his new awareness was the knowledge that his loss of voice was a problem that included his entire body and not just his throat.

After Alexander regained his voice, he continued his work as a recitationist. He worked on the development of his method for curing his own problem for over ten years. His work on the stage drew many who were amazed at his control of his breathing. He became known as the "breathing man" and many would come to see him on stage.

This led to Alexander teaching a number of students the method he had developed for what he called the conscious control of the human organism. His teaching and writing on the technique brought more and more students and many famous people to study with him, including G. B. Shaw, John Dewey, and Aldous Huxley.

The Alexander technique is not a series of exercises or a talk therapy. It is a systemic approach to good and appropriate use of the body through conscious control.[56] Alexander developed a threefold pattern to implement his findings:

1. Let the neck be free (which means merely to see that you do not increase the muscle tension in any act).
2. Let the head go forward and up—forward of the neck, that is, not forward in space (which means merely to see that you do not tense the neck muscles by pulling the head back or down in any act).
3. Let the torso lengthen and widen out (which means merely to see that you do not shorten and narrow the back by arching the spine).[57]

Though these instructions sound deceptively simple, in order to carry them out the client must be fully aware of how he is using his body and how he might be able to use his body in the next moment. Old habit patterns interrupt these instructions, and the client must be able to inhibit these habitual responses and *let go* before the potential for new choices becomes available.

The Alexander technique is a means whereby the client can come to a conscious change of habits and patterns, and then integrate those changes into day-to-day living. A similar technique is called the Feldenkrais method. The originator of this method, Moshe Feldenkrais, is a physicist. He, too, came upon his method through problems with his legs and knees. Unable to find relief from doctors he consulted, Feldenkrais, a black belt in judo and a student of yoga, Freud, and Gurdjieff, turned his awareness onto himself to solve his own problems.

His primary observation was that the unity of mind and body was an objective reality, that the continuity of mental functions is assured by corresponding motor functions.[58] He decided that in order to cure his knee disorder he would have to teach himself to walk anew. He studied anatomy, physiology, psychology, and anthropology in his search for clues on how to approach his problem.

Further observations led Feldenkrais to recognize the importance of gravity in human functioning:

> The bulk of stimuli arriving at the nervous system is from muscular activity constantly affected by gravity.
>
> . . . posture is one of the best clues not only to evolution but also to the activity of the brain.[59]

Feldenkrais has developed more than one thousand individual exercises that are designed to demonstrate to the client the process of movement. The exercises are not designed to be repeated continually to build up muscle tone. They are meant to be used as awareness facilitators, so that the client can come to experience the workings of his own body/mind system.

> The motor cortex is the common axis on which both the conscious and reflex reactions are hinged; and no permanently altered reaction to any environmental stimuli can rationally be expected without a rearranged muscular response.[60]

One of the first psychological thinkers to bring attention to the body was Wilhelm Reich. His study of character armor and the relationship between physical and emotional functioning is only recently being taken seriously. Of all the work growing from Reich's original insights, bioenergetics forms the most engaging expansion. Bioenergetics seeks to reintegrate the client through five basic realizations:

1. to reestablish the client's identification with his body;
2. to recognize the pleasure principle as a major basis for conscious experience;
3. to allow the client to *be* his feelings;
4. to realize that all awareness is subjective awareness;
5. to recognize ultimate human humility in the human/universe relationship.

Most of these points stem from the work of Alexander Lowen,[61] who has also developed a number of postures, positions, and exercises that he believes will facilitate the integration of such insights.

The positions include stretching backward and bending the body forward like a bow; arching the back over a stool; and hyperextension, where the back is arched and the hands reach under the body to touch the soles of the feet.

These passive positions are supplemented by a number of active movements. Lowen will often have clients strike a bed (women with a tennis racket, men with their fists). Other movements have the client lying on his back and kicking the bed with either flexed or extended legs. Often flailing arms accompany this kicking.

The point of these exercises and postures is to start the breathing and bioenergetic flow of the body so that that flow may then be translated into action. Lowen feels that such flow will bring about bodily pleasure which can serve as a vital source of emotional well-being.

Stanley Keleman, another practitioner of bioenergetics, views bodily experience as an experience in the present which gives biological form and identity to living. He sees three states of aliveness which he calls vibration, pulsation, and streaming.

The way in which we perceive the world depends fundamentally on the quality of aliveness in our tissue. Aliveness is instinctive intelligence. A person who is sensually alive is a very reality-oriented person who is able to do a great deal of work. A person who is alive is creative.[62]

Keleman works with a client in three stages. First, the client is brought to experience his inhibited aliveness. He is encouraged to express more movement through breathing or by hitting or kicking a mattress. In the second stage, the client will slow down so he can experience what the movement has brought about internally and emotionally. In the third stage, the transitional consciousness of the second stage is translated into a multiplicity of potentials for making contact with the world.

If you want to know yourself stop moving. But if you want to *be* yourself, you must move. . . . To be yourself, to express yourself, you must allow yourself to be in the act of moving and expressing, even if that expression is lying down and going to sleep. To be who you are demands that you accept the risk of not knowing.[63]

All of these approaches to the body—Rolfing, the Alexander technique, the Feldenkrais method, and bioenergetics—share an integrative orientation in the way that they facilitate human growth and development. One element of this combination is one-to-one, therapist-to-client work; the other is an intensive group experience on a continuing basis. This demands a commitment from the client to the personal growth experience. The awareness and insights generated from the body work must be fully integrated in a therapeutic situation so that optimal functioning can be achieved.

Meditation

In addition to the growing acceptance of the body, a number of other approaches to human functioning have begun to recognize the importance of meditation, fantasy, and play in connection with personal growth. Many of these ideas come from other cultures and from disciplines outside the psychological sciences.

While Western culture has traditionally paid attention to the outside world, certain elements of Eastern culture have turned their focus toward what happens internally. This internal focus is called meditation.

The practice of meditation can be traced back through more than four thousand years of history. It is an integral part of many of the world's great religious systems: Hinduism, Taoism, Buddhism, and others. Rosenfeld describes meditation in its simplest form: sitting quietly, doing nothing.[64] White describes meditation as being

> a means of growth, both personal and transpersonal. . . . meditators claim
> that the best way—indeed, the only way—for people to change is by "working
> on yourself" from within, through meditation.
>   The highest goal of meditation is enlightenment.[65]

Essentially, meditation is a way of doing something while doing nothing. The doing nothing is the sitting quietly; the doing something is the introspection, the inner awareness. One of the goals of meditation is to enable the meditator to experience better his own internal reality. The way to do this is for the meditator to sit quietly and allow his environment to *be* around him. Alan Watts describes the listening done during meditation as being comparable to the way one would listen to music.[66]

Another important aspect of the practice of meditation is the attention that the meditator pays to breathing. A common instruction given to meditators is to watch, passively, as their breath enters, circulates through, and then leaves their bodies, only to enter again and begin a new cycle.

In Zen Buddhism meditators are instructed, at the beginning of their practice, to count their inhalations and then to count their exhalations. This counting is used as a method to help the meditators focus their attention on their breathing, rather than on thoughts, fantasies, worries, or the like.

Watts sums up the goal of true meditation most succinctly:[67]

> Above all, don't look for a result, for some marvelous change of consciousness
> or *satori:* the whole essence of meditation practice is centering upon what
> is—not what should or might be.

Psychosynthesis

Meditation has had great effects on a number of different therapeutic approaches within the personal growth movement. The practice and approach called psychosynthesis incorporates many meditational techniques into its form of psychotherapy. Psychosynthesis was formulated through the work of Roberto Assagioli beginning as early as 1910. Assagioli trained people in his method from his home in Italy.

Psychosynthesis is both a psychological and educational approach to the human being as a creature oriented toward growth. A major addition to psychosynthesis, often lacking in the theoretical foundations of other psychotherapeutic approaches, is its inclusion of the spiritual side of human nature. Psychosynthesis integrates concepts like the will, the soul, and the imagination with standard psychological ideas such as libido, instinctual drives, and the like.

This emphasis on the spiritual nature of human beings also contributes to a basic tenet of psychosynthesis: that we can transcend our personal identities to make contact with our *overself*. As Weide observes:

> Assagioli is a leader among the relatively few modern psychotherapists who work systematically with people in a detailed program of first developing, then transcending, their personal selves.[68]

Psychosynthesis uses a variety of techniques and methods. These include guided imagery, role playing, meditation, movement, journal keeping, symbolic art work and its interpretation, will training techniques, and self-identification work.

Psychosynthesis theorizes that the client has continuous but limited contact with a set of subpersonalities, inner voices, and motivations that can be examined and brought under the focus of *willful* consciousness. To do this it incorporates and synthesizes techniques from psychodrama and gestalt therapy. Often these subpersonalities involve body feelings and are worked with through the utilization of various postures and movements.

Assagioli, through psychosynthesis, has attempted to set out a detailed map of the self. His approach utilizes and integrates material from a variety of personal growth approaches under one unitized system. Other approaches that utilize many techniques and methods are much more eclectic and are known under the common name of *growth games*.

Growth Games

Lewis and Streitfeld[69] have gathered together more than two hundred different approaches to enhancing personal growth. Most of these games come out of the personal growth movement. They describe games to take responsibility, to expand sensory sensitivity, to alter consciousness, and to enliven the body, as well as games for developing warmth and trust and for breaking through personal blocks.

Other approaches to growth games incorporate gestalt therapy,[70] sensory awareness, and encounter.[71] Many of the games are designed to allow clients to experiment with therapeutic concepts outside of the therapeutic environment. Stevens sums this up, telling the client that his approach to growth games

> does provide you with tools that you can use to explore your life, simplify and clarify your problems and confusions, and help you discover *your* answers—what *you* want to do.[72]

A specialized kind of game is the theater game. Theater games are a mix of personal growth techniques, elements of psychodrama, and improvisational methods taken from theatrical training. Spolin describes the interplay between the theater and personal growth thus:

> Acting can be taught to the "average" as well as the "talented" if the teaching process is oriented towards making the theater techniques so intuitive that they become the students' own. A way is needed to get to intuitive knowledge. It requires an environment in which experiencing can take place, a person free to experience, and an activity that brings about spontaneity.[73]

Growth games, theater games, meditation, and psychosynthesis all share a common boundary with more formal approaches to the intensive group experience. The *sesshin* in the practice of Zen Buddhism is an example of this boundary. *Sesshin* is a week-long meditation where a group of people gather together under the guidance of a leader (usually a Zen master or head monk) to meditate for up to twenty hours a day. Even though the members of the group remain silent for most of the week, the intensive nature of this shared experience is most powerful.

The other techniques referred to above can operate in a variety of modalities, but the intensive group model tends to facilitate personal growth and the realization of individual potentialities. This makes it the mode of favor for implementing many of the approaches to improved human functioning.

Perspectives

Are these approaches, methods, and techniques of any value? Detractors and critics of the personal growth movement would say no, for a variety of reasons. Material in the *Congressional Review* and that brought out in hearings before the California State Legislature object to the personal growth movement because it tends to support life styles that conflict with traditional social standards. Other testimony compared personal growth techniques to brainwashing.[74]

Other critics have noted that only charismatic leaders of personal growth groups seem to get good results (but also casualties). They maintain that the method or technique employed in the group is secondary to the strength of the group leader's personality.[75] It has been noted in the political sphere that charismatic persons exert great power in many groups.[76]

Still others note that the aims of the personal growth movement negate any attempt to make long-range plans or to identify goals because of their *here-and-now* philosophical orientation. It has also been maintained that personal growth results are too ephemeral, too utopian, and thus escapist at their very core.

When, however, personal growth is viewed as making connections, so that something is created which did not exist before, and when process itself is considered fundamental, then such growth becomes the essence of existence. In this perspective, what are usually considered "results" can be seen as by-products of the process.

The general philosophy of the personal growth movement seeks to correct what are a variety of, essentially, epistemological errors through the increase of individual and group awareness. This process-oriented approach emphasizes that such errors must be acknowledged and experienced before any behavior change can take place, if such a change is desired and warranted.

Such a fundamental and basic reexamination of the nature of human behavior and experience might be criticized as being too unrealistic. Its very challenge to socially accepted norms is enough to threaten certain cherished culturally approved behaviors (e.g., the suppression of any show of aggression except war).

Certainly many people who have participated in some of the personal growth techniques have had escapist experiences or derived escapist results. Others show a decidedly different picture of the results of such contact.[77] As a young movement, personal growth will be affirmed or denied by the culture of the future.

Future Directions

Of the many future frontiers to be investigated by the practitioners of personal growth methods, the synthesis of a variety of approaches is certainly one of the most exciting developments. Psychosynthesis, which has been described above, is part of this mold and sets a high standard through its integration of fantasy, work on the will, meditation, and spiritual dimensions.

Other exciting developments occur where techniques are combined to form an expanded, holistic view of human functioning. Combinations like transactional analysis (TA)/primal therapy, TA/gestalt,[78] and gestalt/bioenergetic are new examples of such theoretical expansion.

TA is basically an intellectual and behavioral approach, and is well complemented by the deep emotional work done in primal therapy, by gestalt therapy's emphasis on a holistic approach to organismic functioning, or by body work. Bioenergetics' use of body work, physical structure, and exercises offers fresh new material to the gestalt therapist, especially in group work.

In the combination of gestalt/TA, semantic analysis is extended to new broader limits within the scope of psychotherapy. Gestalt has always aimed at correcting basic self-perceptual errors as they are manifested in the client's language. (E.g., "I can't talk to my mother" can be changed and restated as "I won't talk to my mother." This change introduces the notion of the client's inevitable responsibility for his own actions by a simple semantic adjustment.)

TA uses such words as *parent, adult, child, game, script, stamp,* and *racket* to identify psychological activities, behaviors, and relationships that the client is experiencing. The advantage of this is that these words can be used by both the therapist *and* the client. By using such terms, the therapist can better share his insights with the client through the use of this common language.

> Given the choice between the arcane and the open, between overcomplication and simplicity, I have thrown in with the "people" tossing in a big word now and then as sort of a hamburger to distract the watchdogs of the academies, while I slip in through the basement doors and say Hello to my friends.[79]

These semantic changes and identifications allow both the client and the therapist to reexamine human behavior with full perception of the construction of personal mythologies. Stories are always being told on an internal level to justify, explain, and place behavior in an acceptable context. These stories or myths can be made conscious and even discussed in therapy.

In the group situation, such use of personal mythology and combinational synthesis of psychotherapeutic approaches yields a new perspective for the growth model of human functioning.

This becomes even clearer when comparing the *growth* model with the *medical* model.[80]

Growth Models

Our position is that *treatment* in the medical model can be considered one of many pathways to growth, which differs in some ways from others. It is of particular value for those whose personal and interpersonal functioning is impaired or those who have significant, persistent disturbances in feeling, thinking, or behavior. The approaches in both models share the goals of seeking to increase self-awareness, to improve one's relationships with others, and to increase effectiveness in functioning. The differences are largely in emphasis.

The growth approach tends to focus on developing one's potential: awareness, sensing, and feelings are highlighted; risk-taking behavior is encouraged; here-and-now experience is given prominence; significance is given to making choices and decisions; work with the body is often included; and the leader often shares his own feelings and experiences, providing a model for self-disclosure and feedback.

In the medical model, correction or removal of a defect or illness by a therapist who maintains relative distance is predominant; understanding, thinking, and talking are emphasized; repetitive patterns, past history, defenses, and resistances are examined; analyzing causes and making interpretations represent significant aspects of the treatment.

The growth approach has been described by Ernest Rossi[81] as being more humanistic, subjective, and personal, rather than the more scientific, objective, and impersonal aspects in the medical model. Our experience in recent years suggests an increasing overlap between the two, a trend which we believe will benefit both models. Many encounter group leaders have come to recognize the importance of supplementing a peak emotional experience with understanding its significance in the individual's life pattern. This can be done by connecting the here-and-now experience to other situations and behavior involving conflict, and increasing one's awareness of alternatives available for their resolution. In turn, many psychotherapists have come to value some of the newer growth approaches as useful adjuncts to their own treatment methods, either incorporating them into their own work or referring patients or clients to weekend marathon workshops to supplement ongoing therapy. We hope that the differences between these two approaches, and among those who practice both, will be used creatively to enhance each.[82]

In this chapter we have reviewed and discussed the elements and approaches to personal growth. Somewhat like the spokes of a wheel, there are many paths to the center and each person can select which ones are most appropriate to his individual growth.

Chapter 4. Intentional Groups with a Specific Problem Orientation Focus

David Hays and Yael Danieli

THE SPONTANEOUS PHENOMENON of reaching out to others when one faces problems in living is not a new one. Even when alone, without actual people around us, we may find ourselves doing it through substitutes such as animals, objects, or fantasies. In our fantasies we experience ourselves discussing, arguing, consulting the imagined other. Even when physically alone, we rarely tolerate psychological isolation. This is also true when the unseen group that we all carry in our heads is not a pleasant one. In fact, some studies have found that when faced with misery we prefer to be with people who are miserable rather than with any other company.[1] It is with people whose problems are similar to ours that we feel most accepted, comforted, best known, and understood. The mere realization that others have feelings or problems akin to ours may help in rekindling the sense of belongingness to the human race.

Often we find ourselves believing that our deeds, reactions, feelings, fantasies, or thoughts are negatively unique, that they are so very shameful and unmanageable, so unacceptable and objectionable, that we should at least hide them, if not do away with them altogether. When we do not succeed in doing so, we may be labeled as "crazy" and resort to feeling isolated and alienated, even though we may try to paint the isolation with an aura of superiority. Finding people with whom we can share our feelings and concerns, people who will not necessarily judge, punish, reject, or retaliate, yet who will respond to us seriously and honestly, is in itself a relief and a *corrective emotional experience*.[2] Indeed, it is that mutual open sharing that enables us to explore, comprehend, learn, and reevaluate options other than the automatic old ones that we have used in coping with our difficulties. Such sharing allows for and admits the possibility of being useful to each other, thereby enhancing our mutual sense of trust, worth, and significance. It further enables us to give and receive the support needed to maintain hope and courage, to find nondefeating ways of living, and to resolve immediate, troubling situations.

History provides us with ample examples, and we do not need to go far back in time for them. The esprit de corps and camaraderie experienced by people during wartime have been documented not only by those who are on the battlefields, but also by those on the home front. During World War I the Gold Star Mothers got together, and so did POW wives during the Vietnam war. Tornadoes, blackouts, economic difficulties, even getting stuck in an elevator together will draw strangers across barriers that usually keep them apart. The same understanding led captors to separate prisoners of war from their comrades and create mistrust among them so that they would reveal important information. Still, we do not need extremes and catastrophes as examples. We all have memories of studying for examinations with others, brainstorming a problem with others, mourning, raging, and rejoicing with others, and feeling better for doing so, even if it merely involved having our experience shared or consensually validated.

Within the present psychological orientation we find the same phenomena conceptualized and applied systematically to problems that are seen as internally determined. These are viewed as internally determined even though they may have had their origins in interaction with psychosocial (external) reality, and therefore given to modification in such a reality. Since these conceptualizations originated in psychiatry as a treating discipline, psychotherapy started by following the medical *individual* patient-doctor helping modality.

Extending the psychological treatment of people to the *group* modality is usually seen by historians of the mental health field as accelerating during World War II, when the urgent need for an expedient method of treating the large number of psychiatric casualties did not find enough mental health practitioners available to do the job. Nevertheless, this factor does not seem sufficient to account for the subsequent massive proliferation of the intensive group modality, both in the mental health field and as used outside the profession by *self-help* groups that have mushroomed as a parallel phenomenon to group therapy: Alcoholics Anonymous, Synanon, sensitivity groups, encounter groups, and the like. The group movement, rather, seems to reflect the growth line inherent in human psychosocial development; that is, the movement from child-adult dependency to adult-adult interdependence, characterized by mutual sharing of living of two or more independent parties. Along these lines, individual therapy, by the very nature of the social contract, that is, the helpee-helper relationship, resembles the child-adult (authority) growth line, whereas the group modality capitalizes more on the peer dimension. This holds true for the stated goal and process of a therapist-led group, namely, to gradually shift the group members' reliance on the therapist to intermember reliance; and it certainly holds true for self-help groups without formal leaders such as women's consciousness raising.

One of the dimensions along which groups vary is in the definition of the change agent; that is, the nature of the leadership. The two major considerations in regard to this dimension are whether there is a formal group leader or not and, when the group is formally led, what is the role and quality of the leadership.

When the group is formally led—namely, when it is set into motion by a mental health professional or a related person—it is usually the leader's task to do the following: (1) preselect the members; (2) compose the group; (3) prepare the potential members for it; and (4) institute the ground rules for its optimal operation (for example, good attendance, confidentiality). Above and beyond being a "social engineer,"[3] especially at the beginning of the group life, the leader is responsible for establishing its stability (i.e., prevention of member attrition) and, most important, for creating a therapeutic atmosphere and building the group culture. As both a model and a participant in the group, his experience and skills, his attitudes and behavior, are of prime importance at the beginning phases and throughout the group life. It is in this context that his philosophical view of the nature of man is of the essence, since it is his image of man that will underlie his conception of what is wrong (psychopathology), what brought it about (causes, dynamics), what the goals of the group should be and how to go about achieving these goals (techniques, therapeutic agents, roles assigned to the therapist, the optimal nature of the therapeutic relationship, etc.).

Thus therapists who basically see man as a complex mechanism built mostly in response to his environment, believe that his difficulties in living stem from faulty or absent learning. As a result, they view the group as an optimal environment for defining the behaviors or lack of behaviors that produce the difficulties, unlearning the maladaptive ones, and/or learning new, more adaptive ones. They will use a directive-didactic approach in order to achieve their stated goal. Within the mental health field, although presented in barest outline, the latter represent the behavior therapy school. Others, who belong to the psychoanalytic schools, view difficulties in living as manifestations of maladaptive and unsuccessful resolutions of instinctual conflicts which were made by the person during childhood and then pushed out of awareness (i.e., repressed). Being unconscious of them, the person is incapable of comprehending the meanings of his behavior and is thereby unable to choose resolutions other than his childhood ones. Awareness, then, is the goal that follows this definition. The therapeutic climate sought by the therapist to achieve that goal is a nonjudgmental, nondefensive, accepting, uncensored, free, yet observing and interpreting interaction that will allow the group members to honestly disclose themselves and examine the meanings of their behavior and its origins. Since awareness will, according to the theory, lead to the restructuring of the patient's personality through the gradual unfolding of his unconscious childhood assumptions of living, this approach is often termed *regressive-reconstructive*. There are, by one count, as many as forty "schools" of psychotherapy, many of which are derivatives of the two major ones described above. Included among these are some which have systematic applications to group therapy: psychodrama, gestalt therapy, and transactional analysis are some of the more popular ones.

On the opposite end of the leadership continuum are the self-help or formally leaderless groups. They are built around voluntary membership on the basis of sharing and attempting to combat a common problem (i.e., alcoholism, obesity, etc.), and tend to utilize the repressive-inspirational approach while encouraging interdependence among the members and members' responsibility toward the social community. A descriptive discussion of the functioning of some of these groups will be presented in the body of the chapter, and in some instances a comparison will be made with therapist-led groups focusing on the same problem. This comparison will serve to explore the leadership dimension as it affects the group experience.

In addition to leadership, a second important variable along which groups vary is the nature of the setting in which they are held (i.e., various institutions or outside of them). The effects of the setting upon both the group leader and the group members will be given special elaboration in our section on group work in the prison system. A third line of differentiation is whether the group members share a common problem (symptom, syndrome, situation) or whether each faces a different one. This chapter will focus on the functioning of specific problem-oriented groups, namely, groups which are homogeneous with respect to the manifest problems or symptoms presented by the members. Notwithstanding the differences, a crucial factor common to all groups is the members' motivation for work and change, without which no positive or constructive change is possible. While motivation obviously relates to and interacts with the aforementioned variables, its weight is also independent of them and cannot be overemphasized. Its role will be evident throughout our chapter.

The above delineation of the variables along which groups vary and of the variety of treatment approaches is to alert the reader to the complexities involved in this field. Moreover, it also serves to give the reader some appreciation of the manifold problems confronting researchers in their attempts to develop and test hypotheses about the functioning of groups in general, and about specific populations in particular.

The Criminal

An examination of the history of group psychotherapeutic interventions with this particular population reveals its beginning in Vienna where Moreno used psychodrama with groups of prostitutes who were arrested as criminals.[4] What followed was a wide variety of application of treatment approaches attempted throughout the Western world (i.e., "guided group interaction," psychoanalysis, behavior therapy, transactional analysis, and so forth).[5] In itself the spectrum of group therapeutic attempts and methods utilized in the treatment of criminals is more reflective of the general work picture of the mental health field than of its specific work with the antisocial individual. What is significant with this particular population is that therapy itself has been taking place in prisons, a fact attesting to the slowly growing change of attitudes toward the offender, which in turn points in the direction of redefinition of the role and meaning of the correctional system. Based upon the recognition of the complex social interaction involved in the antisocial individual's development as well as in his *correction,* the European *total process* approach was first to include community participation in the criminal's rehabilitation.[6] Indeed, today the offenders are viewed as one of the populations within the field of social or community psychiatry.

Working with groups in a prison setting, Taylor emphasized the difference in value systems between the correctional world and the "outside" world as one of the therapist's prime concerns.[7] The creation of a dual role for the psychiatrist—namely, that of *director of the institution* and of *group therapist*—is an attempt in the direction of bridging the value-schism gap.[8] The model prison at Chino within the California correctional system and the Draper Correctional Center in Elmone, Alabama, follow this ideological route. While discarding the traditional, isolationist, punitive treatment of prisoners, in addition to their group therapeutic programs, they provide the inmates both with jobs and vocational training and with regular education. In fact, reports from Draper suggest that 25 percent of the students voluntarily postponed their parole in order to finish their education. In working with ex-prisoners on an outpatient basis, Hays emphasized the necessity of a close liaison between parole officers and the professional doing group therapy.[9] This notion laid the groundwork for the development of his program in the New York State Division of Parole in which parole officers themselves are trained to be change agents and to utilize group counseling techniques as one of their tools with the offender.

While these few examples point in a direction of attitudinal change, the reality of the correctional system is still generally grim and, as such, adds to the obstacles that stand in the way of doing constructive group therapy with the offender. Before we go into a discussion of the more formal-conceptual and technical aspects of intensive group work with this specific population, let us start with Hays' description of a full group life cycle which he led at Sing Sing.

The *forgery group* in the Sing Sing prison project was initiated with eight men. The age range was from 29 to 45 with the candidates including two men rated as *poor* for a group experience (on a rating scale from 1 to 4), four given a 2 rating, and two given a rating of 3. Diagnostically, using the 1957 psychiatric classification, three were psychopathic personalities with amoral trends, evidencing hostility, rationalization, projection, and denial as defenses, manifesting superego defects, manipulative and dependent attitudes, with minimal anxiety. Two were diagnosed as passive-aggressive reactions with antisocial tendencies. One was diagnosed as a character neurosis with moderate anxiety, passive-dependent, limited in his ability to verbalize, and the last one was given the diagnosis of schizoid personality with psychopathic-like trends, narcissistic, with a rigid defense system. All experienced intense feelings of inadequacy.

The group started its life in April 1957, and lived a total of 72 sessions. The first stage of the group development saw the "drafting" of two members, one of whom was active, provocative, and a rather central figure in his bid to take over as an auxiliary therapist. This happened during the first three months, when the group was struggling for its life, and members evidenced feelings of anger toward authority which were beyond the members' capacity to deal with at the time. Threatening the development of group cohesiveness, this drafting left a membership of six within a setting of feeling out a new therapist-authority, while ventilating suspicions about another possibly related system that had "bum-rapped" them. During the fifth month a third member (J.W.) resigned. The latter had to do with breaching of group confidentiality through leakage of material to the outside, relating to anger and hostility toward the institution and the Blacks in the institution. One could identify a general resistance against therapy, against looking at themselves and what was going on between them; trust and sharing were indeed issues fraught with questions.

The group as a whole evidenced intense scapegoating of the Blacks in the institution. This was intimately related to their anger against the authorities in the system whom they could not attack directly. The same attitude appeared toward the therapist. Whereas this is not an uncommon phenomenon in groups in general, in the forgery group it appeared at regular intervals throughout the life of the group as an ever present resistance factor.

While interaction was prominent at the outset and abated after nine or ten sessions, interestingly enough, it reawakened following J.W.'s "resignation." The essential themes of the group in the first five months related to dependency, the anger linked up with dependency and hostility against the authorities in the system.

The turning point of the group at its "half-life" (36th session) involved around parole board appearances of three of the group members, which naturally colored their productions and involvement. While two of them "made it," the third did not, and responded with much hostility against the authorities. One segment of the group attacked their own member who had made the parole board, identifying him with the punitive authority. While punishing him verbally, they very clearly manifested dependency, withholding, and defensive projections. This was indeed the period when withholding of love appeared as a group strategy. Involvement of the members beyond the 36th session was not too unlike a regular private practice group. The only manifest difference was that anger was much closer to the surface. The group discussed the meanings of the forgery acts, and how the masochistic aspects of these acts are inextricably bound-up with their poor self-concept. Sexual material emerged at session 43. Themes of intimacy, closeness, the group experience as reflective of ties with the original family, dream material which was oral and oedipal in nature, constituted the work of the group until its composition shifted around the 53rd session when only four members were left. From that point, adaptation to change, loss, separation, and the relationship to authority constituted the main themes. Although two members were added at session 61, its life as the original forgery group had taken on a very different shape. The group was formally terminated at its 72nd session with another of its original members paroled, thereby having two out of its eight original members remaining.

From the therapeutic standpoint, Hays used the transactional analysis orientation. Both individual and group process comments were used. He reports that his theoretical orientation with this group did not differ significantly from the one he uses with groups he carries privately. The importance of patience, flexibility and support, however, were more paramount, as was sensitivity to the resistance forces.

We will now turn to the more formal, conceptual, and technical discussion of the issues involved in treating this specific population. As is evident from the diagnostic composition of the group, presented at the outset of Hays' description, despite the group homogeneity along the forgery (symptom) line, the range of diagnoses which the members presented was highly heterogeneous, running from personality disorders to the psychotic and schizophrenic reactions, thus belying the stock term *offender* or *sociopath*. Indeed, the term *psychopathic*, once embracing all the criminal population, has lessened in usage, simply because of lack of serious study. Those individuals who fit into the diagnosis of *primary psychopathy*, established by Benjamin Karpman, are few and far between. Most others who are currently placed in this category display as much variety of clinical pictures as can be found in patients in other diagnostic categories.[10] In most cases we can discern common denominators of characteriological makeup and patterns of functioning, with the subleties and complexities of psychopathy notable. The latter notwithstanding, what seems directly relevant to working with this population is caution against the tendency to pigeonhole all offenders and toss them into one wastebasket, since that will render the therapist unable to set up a treatment plan based on the varying, unique needs of each individual.

Moreover, the therapist's flexibility which, in part, is a function of experience, is also important in establishing patients' *suitability* for the group experience. It seems that the more comfortable and experienced the therapist is in working with groups, and the more flexible, the greater is the number of candidates he will deem suitable for the group experience. Thus the issue changes from a general one—namely, that of *suitability for group therapy* as a treatment modality—to that of planful matching of group members to ensure subsequent group effectiveness, on the one hand, and creative choice of technique, on the other hand.

Hays and Wisotsky attempted to define the selection bias of therapists working with this population in determining patients' suitability for the group experience. Out of a population of 400 parolees, 40 controlled patients were reviewed. Fourteen were found to be suitable for group and 26 were rejected. The researchers studied 17 possible factors operative in the selection process. In their discussion they referred to suitability as related to a "safe bet" (making for success in treatment) and the exclusion of certain categories, types, classes, and situations (advanced age, organic problems). Selection was influenced by factors associated with higher or more positive motivation for treatment (educational background, occupational status, family status, etc.). They felt that a preferential pattern was operating in the selection process (similar to bias) such as higher education and intellect, which strongly disfavors minorities, older persons, and divorced or separated parolees.[11]

A second most important factor which has an enormous impact on any therapeutic work with the offender is the nature of the institutional setting. Much has been written about it by workers in the field. Schmideberg emphasized the primary motivational difficulties in the *captive client*.[12] Obviously, joining a group is not a voluntary matter in most prison settings. Also, even when prisoners choose to participate, their motivation may have little to do with therapy. Rather, they will often join to get good records. Hays reviewed a number of resistance elements which are directly related to the setting, such as confinement, restriction, and administration. Relevant to the secondary gain nature of motivation, he noted the issues of no fee and the link between doing time and parole board evaluation.[13]

Resembling the outside world, prisons form their own culture, where populations tend *naturally* to group on the basis of the offense, with in-out, *we-they* patterns creating segregated sub-groups, the epitome of which are the sex offenders. In this microcosm other prisoners continually emphasize the "craziness" of those involved in group therapy, specifically since most penal environments are not therapeutic milieus. This is also evident in the common, mixed attitudes of guards and prison officials toward instinctual expression. Jacobson pointed out the elements of gratification obtained by prison guards, albeit vicariously, through association and identification with prisoners who do the *forbidden* deeds while they alleviate their own guilt feelings by humiliating, denouncing, and punishing.[14]

Another institutional factor that poses a difficult obstacle to stable group work is "the drafting of inmates to other institutions," experienced by the group described above. This phenomenon, highly typical in the prison setting, is threatening to group cohesiveness. No sooner does a group achieve some cohesiveness when it may lose a member. When working with an open-ended group, members do get replaced and the group frequently struggles with both feelings of loss and with feelings related to the insensitivity of the system that shifts people from one environment to another, thereby furthering their sense of impotence. Encouraging new members to *twin* themselves with older members of the group with whom they share certain characteristics or experiences is a technical step used to enhance their moviation and neutralize initial resistances through identification with involved members.

The therapist working within the prison system faces the strong possibility of being identified with the jailers. This is a twofold problem. On the one hand, certainly at the outset of the group, members view him—almost as a *universal phenomenon* within the antisocial population—as a "representative of the authoritarian penal system."[15] One of his earliest goals, indeed, is to help them separate him from it. On the other hand, although his has a therapeutic rather than a punitive role, unconsciously the contrast between his value system and that of the correctional personnel may not be as sharp as he thinks. As he moves into closer involvement with his group, these schisms of values intensify the complex working through of the hostile-dependent elements so characteristic of the antisocial group.

Criminal acting out originally emerges as a major defense against feelings of inadequacy and is expressive of anger about unmet dependency needs the individual has experienced. Other key dynamic issues are the masochistic elements in such behavior and basic mistrust resulting in projected hostility seen in these individuals. As did the forgery group, offenders' groups may react very strongly to their perception of the therapist as manipulative, and do so with *contagious* aggression.[16] The therapist's activity and ingenuity become vital in working through these conflicts. His activity can hardly be overemphasized. Unsuccessful treatment of offenders by new therapists has occurred largely because of their passivity.[17] Based on these dynamic understandings, the therapist must be prepared to actively help inmates explore their inherent problems with authority. In fact, the forgery group spent 24 out of 72 sessions working on authority-related themes. In Kanter's description of therapists working with characterologically homogeneous groups in a relatively stable prison environment, it was noted that the individuals, as portrayed, were strikingly *normal* dynamically according to most parameters except for *attitude toward authority*. It was in relation to this dimension that the antisocial characteristics took on crystal-clear form. Interestingly, and highly significant technically, blind spots of the therapists manifested themselves in sympathetic counter-identification with the patients against the prison authorities.[18] This reflects the other end of the spectrum of the therapist's identification within the system.

The challenge to the therapist posed by the provocative and antiauthoritarian testing behavior is much greater in the prison setting than in any other. Hays recalls *frightening* some of the forgery group members when he openly told them that they had as important an impact on his growth as he had on theirs. He noted that making these statements while going through an *existential phase* in his own growth as a beginning therapist tended to block the patients' ability to ventilate and share their hostility, a factor that could be disastrous to the development of this therapy group. Resoile and Peters also stress the importance of the expression of hostile-aggressive feelings as a key dynamic issue in working with this population—in this case, pedophiles. They emphasize that when hate and aggression can be ventilated, the group becomes an *absorptive* entity, thus allowing for a shift in the basic defense operations, for freeing of energies, and for developing and strengthening inner controls.[19] A crucial part of the issue at hand is dealing with aggression through verbal rather than physical interchange.[20]

In fact, Roether and Peters, in one study, compared hostility and cohesiveness in relation to outcome of a 40-week group therapy with probationed sex offenders. Analysis of the data showed that exposure to hostility during the group process is positively related to outcome, whereas cohesiveness appears to be unrelated to it. Successful treatment cases (97%) were those who attended group sessions in which hostility to outside others was expressed. The authors state that perhaps this clue could be used to encourage specific group discussions to focus on interpersonal problems in the offender's life.[21] Looking at parole and probation settings, Hays examined the main themes appearing in a group run in the New York State parole system over a year's time.[22] Here, too, expression of anger was prominent. The three major trends at the manifest level were (1) resentment against the parole setting, correctional or other authorities in the penal system; (2) ventilation of resentment related to earlier life experiences; and (3) preoccupation with specific, current reality problems of the individual group members as related to shared historical material around such problems.

Research studies to assess the effectiveness of group psychotherapy approaches with the antisocial individual have been limited in number. Furthermore, it is difficult to make any meaningful, conclusive statements about outcome since different authors define *improvement* or *results* differently. Thus, Hartman spoke of characterological changes in all seven members of his pedophiles' group as evidenced by their social functioning in addition to symptomatic recovery in six of them.[23] Similarly, Taylor emphasized "lesser acting-out, greater reflection, group values of a different nature brought to bear in the setting to resolve problems around and with group members involved in acting-out and the sharing of information around outside criminal activities which were not previously known."[24] However, Ernst defined results in terms of attendance.[25] Recidivism has been utilized as one of the important criteria for improvement by Hein[26] and as a single criterion for improvement by the California Medical Facility at Vacaville.[27] Still, Haskell, in the setting of Riker's Island Penitentiary, viewed effectiveness in terms of change in social values in the direction of conformity to socially acceptable values and demonstrated it as related to the group process.[28]

In conclusion, we will describe the Peters et al. study of a "clinical measure of enforced psychotherapy."[29] Positive attitudes about the treatment were correlated with treatment failures. Patients who said that the group was helpful were rearrested more often than those who complained about it. In addition, the examining psychiatrist was significantly less successful in predicting future criminal behavior than was the psychiatrist who had treated the offender in a group. Inferences the authors made about the results were that the need to "con" the examining psychiatrist appeared to continue as an adaptive technique with treatment failures. Patients who fail may not sufficiently have freed themselves to express critical or negative attitudes toward the examining authority. On the other hand, patients who succeed may have learned during group therapy interactions how to handle hostility and can be openly critical of the examiner during retesting. The authors also make the point that the group evaluation method offers a more reliable prognostic indicator than a single interview, and recommended that pre-sentence evaluations include a series of group psychotherapy sessions, enforced if necessary. The authors found that variables descriptive of the socialization process in the group were the most important indicators of patient advance from one phase of the group process to the next, with variables related to leadership in the therapy group at the very top. Although the authors argued that in group therapy psychiatrists' ratings of patients' progress should be highly related to outcome, they found that the rank ordering of the change variables as indicators of patient advancement during therapy was unrelated to outcome. The *resocialization* theory of group therapy, as defined in the context of their clinic by the psychiatrists' ratings of patients' advancement during therapy, was unconfirmed since correlation with outcome was negligible and tended to become negative over time. Thus the authors inferred that the psychiatrists' perspective for evaluating patients' progress during therapy was restricted to the immediacy of the group therapy situation itself. From this they concluded that the validity of group therapy in the therapist's judgment was not so much related to the stated purpose of the clinic in terms of *outcome*, but to patients' involvement in the group experience itself in terms of *participation*.

They posed an interesting question which bears on us all in the light of increasing crime statistics and violence in our society. That is, why does our culture seem to be producing antisocial personality disorders when in Freud's age neurotic symptoms emerged? One of their speculations has to do with the higher socioeconomic status of Freud's subjects. However, they go on to ask: "Or did a Victorian society present clearer cultural norms which remained stable long enough to offer fixed guidelines to the development of an individual for introjection and identification? Does a clearly defined cultural norm structure straight-jacket superego-ego problems into neurotic symptoms? By contrast, does a fast-changing culture with fluid social norms channel expressions of the same imbalances into nonconforming anti-social behavior?" If so, they point up, "Anti-social behavior may be the contemporary manifestation of superego tyranny, which in the past produced psychoneurosis. If valid, this hypothesis would encourage establishing clearer cultural and social guidelines. However, one might be trading socially acceptable behavior for neurosis." According to Freud, they conclude, "The malaise of civilization upon the psychic structure of man is universal."

The Fortune Society

Instituted in 1967 as the first ex-convicts' self-help organization in New York City, the Fortune Society aims at both prison reform and responding to the variety of needs of the individuals who apply for assistance, with emphasis on employment. The society was founded following the production of the play *Fortune and Men's Eyes* which documented prison life and had ex-prisoners as actors. The ensuing discussion between the actors and the audience set the wheels in motion to follow organizations such as the John Howard in Illinois and Seven Steps in California. Since then thirty additional organizations were formed in the New York City area alone.

The society's weekly "rap" sessions, portrayed in its own publication *Fortune News* as *not* an *encounter* format, is a fairly recent development. Participation in the group program is voluntary and the sessions may be leaderless or run by staff members. Strictly nonprofessional, the *leaders* or *counselors* are assigned by virtue of their *life style* or better adjustment. As stated, group discussions are realistically geared with stress on sharing of *outside* adjustment problems experienced currently as well as in the past. Thus, catharsis is primary and identifying feelings such as loneliness, rejection, and inadequacy is of high importance.

Future shock, best equated with a type of post-traumatic neurosis originally related to a combat situation, is a central theme. It is an example of unconscious determinants reinforcing repetitive acting out and resulting reincarceration. The group is viewed as helping to neutralize the process. Consequently, group leaders focus on dependency strivings closely allied with the frequently found masochistic self-punishment so characteristic of these individuals which results in antisocial behavior and a return to the "haven" of prison. Group members usually attend their group for about six months and get help. To what extent? "We don't know." Why? "Because we don't deal with statistics."

The Alcoholic

Like Moreno's psychodrama with prostitutes, so did group consultation with alcoholics begin in Vienna in 1927. The counseling centers initiated by the Vienna police involved a collaborated work of medical police officers with the Good Templar's Temperance Lodge. In the United States it was the establishment of a Department for Special Studies on Alcoholism in the Laboratory of Applied Physiology at Yale University in 1930 that marked the beginning change of approach toward the problem in the direction of research and treatment substituting for contempt and punishment. A very important phase in the approach and treatment of alcoholism came about through the efforts of alcoholics themselves, namely, the formation of Alcoholics Anonymous (AA) in 1934. This spontaneous self-help group phenomenon originated approximately at the same time group therapy was taking root as a new psychotherapeutic technique.

McCarthy reported on group therapy in progress at the Yale Plan Clinic, where each group met for approximately six months. Attendance was voluntary and the atmosphere informal. Three objectives were stressed at the meetings: (1) neutralizing the alcoholic's isolation; (2) facilitating an intellectual grasp of the dynamic meanings underlying the behavior patterns leading to the excessive use of alcohol; and (3) gaining emotional release through group participation.[30] Stewart described work with alcoholics at a mental hospital in Scotland, where they were housed separately from other patients. While individual therapy was readily available, group therapy has proven equally effective, if not superior. In analyzing this finding, he emphasized the importance of empathy which exists in the group relationship and saw the identification of group members with each other as a basic healing element. This identification was more pronounced among group members than in face-to-face therapy with the psychiatrist, whose major function was perceived to be teaching the patient how to understand himself.[31] Pfeffer et al., stressing homogeneity in personality structure as well as in symptom, treated small groups (5–6) of same-sex neurotic alcoholics. They also emphasized the specific value of group therapy with alcoholics in that it allows for transference elements tolerable to the patient and provides mutual support in maintaining sobriety.[32] Much ingenuity is reflected in Martensen-Larsen's review of work with alcoholics in Denmark. In conjunction with Antabuse (a drug commonly used with alcoholics), patients are accepted into the group even when they are intoxicated, and attendance by relatives and wives is encouraged. The role of emotional expression, clarification, and insight in addition to change in drinking habits is emphasized, yet it is felt that the most important elements leading to the above are group acceptance, encouragement, and support. They use a technique similar to *twinning,* referred to in the offenders' section of this chapter. Here a new patient passing through a crisis is confronted with another who went through a similar stage in a two-person group that usually precedes the larger group meeting. Severely regressed patients are given extensive individual therapy before they join the group. They also attempt to extend the group's activity beyond the confines of the clinic and encourage social get-togethers.[33]

Allison, working in a state hospital, used a nondirective approach. This created an atmosphere which allowed for the patient's own initiative and individuality to come to the fore, on the one hand, and for a more objective viewing of group defense mechanisms, on the other. In citing the disadvantages of applying this technique, especially in the hospital setting, he pointed to the lack of group cohesion and integration due to the rapid influx of new patients and to the diagnostic heterogeneity of the alcoholic population.[34] In a similar vein, Mechanic, focusing on group atmosphere and attitudes as important for rehabilitation, questioned the advantage of mixing a small number of institutionalized volunteer patients with a large number of committed patients in the institution.[35] The factor of heterogeneity, in terms of diagnosis as well as motivation, was also brought up to account for the generally low and variable effectiveness of group therapy with alcoholics in Veterans Administration installations.[36]

Mullan and Sangiuliano's approach[37] presents a systematic attempt to deal with these variables. They work in an outpatient department where staff members operate in teams. Formulating their intensive group therapy with alcoholics within the existential framework, they see the group as offering the individual a "milieu in which to risk new behavior." Their initial focus is on the unique challenge posed by the resistance forces specific to this population—namely, the pervasive use of denial and regressive acting out—and on the patient's readiness for the "total emotional involvement of group interaction" that they offer. Thus a patient who is preoccupied with his and others' alcoholism only is viewed as not yet ready. After the staff decides on an individual patient's entry into a group, a didactic (rather than therapeutic) orientation is given him by someone other than the group therapist. In selecting and preparing a patient for a group, the staff has to (1) establish a psychiatric diagnosis besides that of alcoholism and determine whether this patient will be able to enter a particular treatment group in the future; (2) establish a treatment relationship with the patient; (3) confront the patient either with the fact that he is to go into a therapy group after preparatory hours, or that he is not ready for group preparation so that he is going to be referred elsewhere; (4) convince the patient that he is much more than an alcoholic; and (5) establish the patient's understanding of his responsibility in the group and of what he may expect in the early group sessions. An important consideration here is the tendency, on the part of alcoholic patients, to abandon the group soon after joining one or immediately after they have achieved sobriety.

In their selection process, they list the following as indicators for a patient's inclusion in a group: (1) seeks group psychotherapy in addition to AA and acknowledges that he needs a *deeper* or different experience than the one provided by AA; (2) has had previous individual or group therapy; (3) has accepted other forms of rehabilitation—AA, Antabuse treatment, physical help, or pastoral counseling; (4) shows some degree of insight, dynamic activity, and/or commitment to appointment hours; (5) shows a high level of anxiety and affect, and at the same time attempts to remain sober; (6) accepts the agency or the clinic and realizes that the staff is there to help; (7) accepts orientation meetings; (8) shows change during orientation or individual sessions of preparation. Counterindications are (1) expression of overt psychotic behavior; (2) inability to form any kind of relationship with the admission workers, therapist, or any other staff member; (3) severe psychopathic behavior; and (4) severe physical impairment.

The authors' discussion of actual group work clearly delineates early antitherapeutic trends, quasi-group cohesion versus authentic cohesion, and acting out as important considerations for the therapist. They bring up the *treatment paradox* in regard to acting out: that is, on the one hand, the patient acts out because he cannot accept his inner struggle; on the other, the group psychotherapist must accept and focus on the patient's inner conflicts and his ability to work on them in the interpersonal group context.

At the same time that so much consideration is given to heterogeneity by some therapists, others have reported success with groups that involved not only psychopaths but also schizophrenic alcoholics as well as alcoholics with other severe character disorders.[38] The notion of an initial desire to be cured as necessary for success with the alcoholic was also challenged. In this context, Brunner-Orne and associates[39] established an experimental clinic run on court premises holding weekly group therapy meetings. Patients were referred by the court after having made a choice of attending clinic instead of serving sentence. Using the now regularly preferred *team approach* to investigate medical, environmental, and social problems in addition to psychological factors, the clinic offered group therapy to every referred patient. The authors found that although patients first attended sessions under coercion, their genuine interest in the group gradually emerged and was followed by active participation. This led them to conclude that it is not always necessary for the alcoholic to enter a treatment program voluntarily in order to render it helpful. Elsewhere the Ornes[40] emphasize the value of short-term hospitalization in making the alcoholic patient available for psychotherapy. They view such a hospitalization as offering the patient a comprehensive treatment within a compassionate atmosphere that will allow him to admit to his problem, whereas doing so was usually unacceptable to him before. They stress the use of Antabuse as an adjunct to therapy. It is seen as preferable to conditioned reflex methods in that it takes a few days to wear off, thereby preventing a momentary impulse from initiating a new "binge," while retaining the patient's sense of control. Within a permissive setting the Ornes view group therapy as an integral part of treatment programs for alcoholics. Their approach is directive, and they focus on two major variables: namely, reaching abstinence, and giving patients security and substitutive emotional satisfaction. The following is an example of their actual group work.[41]

In proposing a topic for the day, the therapist may raise the question "What function does alcohol serve?" or "What does alcohol do for the individual who drinks?" He explains that obviously anything we do has a reason, so if people drink alcohol there must be something that it does for them. The therapist encourages group members to answer such questions as "What does one get out of drinking?" and "What's the point of it? Why?" Responses to these questions vary. A salesman, for instance, may say: "When I take a couple of drinks before I go on the road, I don't get embarrassed beating strangers or having to barge in on them." Another patient may say: "I don't get along with my mother-in-law and I have a fight with my wife about it. So I go out and get drunk. Then I don't care."

From a housewife: "I stay home alone all day long, with my housework. A few drinks make me feel better and then I feel up to it."

The group leader comments as little as possible at this time; rather, he encourages free discussion of the topic. The responses are interpreted either by the therapist or by other members of the group, not so much in terms of dynamics but in terms of function. Thus the group leader may point out to the salesman that alcohol, in his case, increases his self-confidence. For the husband it releases tension and anger. The housewife might be told by a group member that she is using alcohol to escape boredom and loneliness. While the leader actively encourages discussion, he also tries to keep the group goal oriented and to prevent any patient from monopolizing it by telling the full story of his life in the exhibitionistic, masochistic, self-recriminatory story-telling fashion which is so characteristic of the alcoholic. Letting the patient do it is unhelpful to him and causes the rest of the group to lose interest and leave the field. After summarizing the major factors raised by the patients, the therapist will raise a question such as "If alcohol does so many things for people, why should we attempt to stop drinking?" In other words: "Why are we here?" The group members are quick to point out reasons such as "When I get drunk I get awful nasty. My wife won't have me in the house as long as I keep drinking"; "I can't keep a job and I can't go on like this." It is interesting to note that most of the reasons given represent external pressures and are put passively, even when the statements are about the patient's own body. The group helps in internalizing these externally seen pressures. The therapist will then comment: "If alcohol serves as many functions as we have discussed, and if we can't keep on drinking, what about things it did for us? It must have done some very important things for us or we wouldn't have become compulsive drinkers. Now we can't drink any more. What can we do to make this easier? Giving it up isn't just a question of staying away from the bottle. If we can't find other things to take the place of alcohol we will never be able to give it up." With such an introduction the leader has directed the group's effort toward finding substitutive behavior patterns. This, then, becomes the task of the day.

Members of the group quickly begin to realize that no one substitute will do the many things alcohol did, and they start to split up the functions. A typical example of this is the social problem which many alcoholic patients encounter. They go to a party and everybody drinks. What can they do about it? As the specialist, the therapist presents in rough outline experiments done on the effects of drugs on college students where it was found that the same amount of alcohol, which did not effect people very strongly when given intravenously without their knowledge, would get them quite "high" if taken orally. Further, they would get quite high on grape juice if they believed it contained alcohol. Thus one sees that the effect of the drug in amounts usually consumed is to a great extent the result of the individual's belief that he is drinking. The ensuing discussion enables many of the patients to become "the life of the party" on ginger ale or any soft drink.

Another topic invariably encountered is the problem of boredom. Many alcoholics spend several hours a day drinking. When they become abstinent they suddenly have time on their hands and do not know what to do with it. Many solutions are proposed by different members, and through an interchange of ideas workable suggestions of practical help to the individual are brought up.

The release of tension, certainly a major problem, is also explored. Here suggestions from the group include going down to the Y for a work-out, changing jobs, acquiring hobbies, or going to church. Again, not all solutions fit all patients, but most get valuable suggestions from these discussions. In addition, the discussions themselves release tension. The leader may add *autogenous training* to the group sessions. This is a graduated set of exercises for relaxation which is of particular value for those alcoholics who suffer from tension states and for those with a tendency toward autonomic crises. When the time is up, the group leader briefly summarizes the conclusions arrived at by the group and emphasizes the important points which were brought up.

The Ornes' policy is to encourage group members to bring spouses and relatives to the sessions to help the nonalcoholic in his or her understanding and handling of the alcoholic with whom he or she is living. They also explain to the patient and family that relapses do not mean that all efforts were in vain; rather, that they may serve to bring to the surface areas that were not revealed before. Aside from the sessions themselves, "waiting room" discussions are highly valuable. Not only do they provide for spontaneous working through of what the patients had learned during sessions, but often patients find peers' help far more acceptable than that of a doctor and tend to use it well. In this sense they serve as spontaneous *alternate sessions*.

While believing the total effect of this process to be therapeutic in that it is effective in helping the alcoholic accept his problem, achieve and often maintain sobriety, and reduce his feelings of isolation, the Ornes view their approach as a problem-solving *work group* rather than as a therapy group. Maintaining that sobriety is a prerequisite to the psychoanalytically oriented treatment of the underlying personality problems of etiological significance, they view their work as preparatory both in the sense of clearing the road for personality growth and of making therapy acceptable to the patient. In comparing their work to that of AA, they acknowledge the similarity of the directive-supportive approach, yet see it as complementary and different in its focus on searching for the meaning of the individual's excessive drinking rather than on his *conversion cure.*[42]

Working therapeutically, in the technical sense of the term, Fox reports utilizing a combined traditional psychoanalytic group approach with psychodramatic techniques in working with this population. She added the latter to promote an almost immediate emotional reaction within the group, which is usually a challenging task with the alcoholic.[43]

Whereas the variety of functions alcohol serves and their relative significance for different individuals do not pose any specific difficulty for psychoanalytic group therapy with the alcoholic, the problem does lie in the working requirements that this treatment method demands of the patient. In every form of insight psychotherapy it is required of the patient to tolerate a certain amount of anxiety. A uniform regressive characteristic that is related to the prolonged use of alcohol and its psychological impact is the availability of a ready pseudosolution for any conflict that arises which makes it possible for the patient to avoid to a large extent any strong feelings of anxiety and to deny that any problem exists. Also, the blackout phenomena, with consequent social fears and the alcoholic's tendency to live in the temporal present, create extraordinary difficulties for the therapist in finding a common ground with this population.[44]

The alcoholic symptom is described as having both individual and interpersonal significance. Egocentric dependency needs, passivity, unreasonable demands for attention, recognition, and affection, with an underlying serious lack of self-esteem, are seen as primary.[45] Related to these are rage reactions followed by guilt and cruel self-punishment. At the same time, drinking functions as retaliatory hostile acting out against significant people in the environment in particular and society in general. On another level, unresolved oedipal conflicts make for strong competitiveness which further endangers the gratification of the core need for dependency.

Group therapy is seen as better suited for the alcoholic than individual therapy alone. It dilutes transferences (both positive and negative), makes it more tolerable for the patient to express "dangerous" feelings, and is often seen as less punitive, producing less resistance than individual therapy. For example, in a closed setting, Moore and Buchman noted that whereas individual treatment tapped hostility mostly, the team approach was valuable in terms of diffusing rage.[46]

In terms of effectiveness of group therapy, Haberman, researching "Factors Related to Increased Sobriety in Group Psychotherapy with Alcoholics" in conjunction with Antabuse, found the length of treatment as well as attendance and motivation to be related. He concluded that once-a-week group therapy under two years is unlikely to produce anything close to full recovery.[47] A recent study emphasized that examining the natural history of alcoholism has to be done before evaluating the curative value of group methods with alcoholics.[48] The authors also stress the importance of providing a *range* of facilities for alcoholics with less favorable prognostic attributes rather than placing a major emphasis on a single-treatment approach such as group therapy. They report negative results with patients manifesting *psychopathic* qualities. Their positive results were associated with patients who maintained stable interpersonal relationships and persistence in employment.

Pattison, in his "Critique of Alcoholism Treatment Concepts with Special Reference to Abstinence," calls not only for a clearer definition of the relationship between abstinence and therapy, but also for meaninful criteria for successful treatment. He points out the lack of knowledge of the differential effects of the various treatment methods utilized with these patients as related to the need for modifications of the models employed in defining and evaluating the treatment of alcoholics.[49] Finally, the most recent critical review specifically relating to group therapy of alcoholics states that presently the effectiveness of this modality is not assessable both because it is usually used in combination with other methods of treatment and because of the paucity of follow-up studies.[50]

The attitudes of therapists and patients toward group treatment with alcoholics, with their implications for success and failure, were first brought to the fore by Glatt.[51] It was in 1958 that he commented on the relatively little experience psychiatric clinics and psychiatrists in general had with this population. An examination of the literature of the succeeding years does not seem to point up significant improvement. What refinements in group psychotherapy with the alcoholic will take place following the establishment of the National Institute on Alcoholic Abuse and Alcoholism in the early nineteen-seventies remains to be seen.

Alcoholics Anonymous

Compared to the skeptical note with which we concluded our discussion of group therapy with the alcoholic, AA's melody sounds refreshingly hopeful and optimistic. "Our case histories prove that if a person definitely decides to get rid of his drinking problem, and if he is not mentally impaired, no failure is possible—provided he honestly and energetically follows the twelve suggested steps of the program. With continued sincerity of purpose, half your battle is won. Without it, neither A.A. nor anyone else can help you."[52] Having mushroomed all over the country since its inception in 1934, this self-help organization reports helping about three fourths of those who join[53] and seems fairly certain of both its definitions and its methods. AA's fundamental doctrines have varied very little since it was founded by two alcoholics: an engineer, Bill W., and a surgeon who underwent a "spiritual revelation" after having found a "common language" he could use with Bill W., the "first living human being with whom I had ever talked who knew what he was talking about in regard to alcoholism from actual experience." Indeed, this movement is run solely by and for alcoholics. As alcoholics are comfortable only with each other, they tend to congregate in bars, where their drinking habits are reinforced. The groups of AA afford them the same type of companionship in a group whose standards support total abstinence. In addition to the groups, the organization offers a sponsorship system that provides the members with immediately available individual support beyond the group when necessary, and "each new member is strongly urged to attend as many meetings as possible, and to circulate freely at meetings and elsewhere with other members."[54]

AA's approach represents a cooperative meeting ground for the concepts of medicine and religion and its recovery program is based on twelve steps:

1. "We admitted we were powerless over alcohol—that our lives had become unmanageable."
2. "Came to believe that a Power greater than ourselves could restore us to sanity."
3. "Made a decision to turn our will and our lives over to the care of God, *as we understand Him.*"
4. "Made a searching and fearless moral inventory of ourselves."
5. "Admitted to God, to ourselves and to another human being the exact nature of our wrongs."
6. "Were entirely ready to have God remove all these defects of character."
7. "Humbly asked Him to remove our shortcomings."
8. "Made a list of all persons we had harmed, and became willing to make amends to them all."
9. "Made direct amends to such people wherever possible, except when to do so would injure them or others."
10. "Continued to take personal inventory and when we were wrong promptly admitted it."
11. "Sought through prayer and meditation to improve our conscious contact with God, *as we understood Him,* praying only for knowledge of His will for us and the power to carry that out."
12. "Having had a spiritual awakening as a result of these steps, we tried to carry this message to alcoholics, and to practice these principles in all our affairs."[55]

Thus the method addresses itself to combat effectively the fundamental unrealistic omnipotent narcissism of the alcoholic, to counteract his demoralizing feelings of guilt and remorse and help restore his self-respect. The requirement to help other alcoholics not only strengthens their self-esteem but reminds them vividly of the fate in store for them if they resume drinking. Group meetings are devoted almost entirely to inspirational testimonials by members who describe the horrors of life as an alcoholic and tell how much better things are since they stopped drinking. Leadership is carried by members on a rotating basis.

Their *open meeting* started with Bob M. focusing on his recent "slip." He was obviously a person who had been in AA for some years. Strong in his delivery, articulate and freely sharing his limitations with a group of fifteen, he introduced a "renewal group for slips" to which an individual could turn in addition to the regular closed meeting. He finished his ten-minute talk by stating that "AA has the tools for all of us. No matter what the experience, there is a group for you." The diversity of groups is indeed an important aspect of what AA has to offer, especially for a beginning member. In this context, Hays recalls a patient, Phila A., a middle-aged divorced woman who had been in one of his private groups for four months. She finally left because of her inability to talk about her real problems and her strong dependency needs, while not getting the amount of support that she needed in a "reconstructive, here-and-now" therapeutic group approach. Instead, he referred her to AA, where she was placed in a *highly intellectual* group, near her home, which was more commensurate with her academic background and character structure, and was assigned to a sponsor who was a sister Radcliffian.

The *open meeting* continued, featuring Bob C., a visitor from a nearby town. He had been in this town's AA group for ninety days and was reviewing his history. His drinking started at 13 and he was now 31. "I know there was something wrong in the conduct of my current life which brought me to throwing in the towel." The ninety days he was just celebrating had been lived *one day at a time,* a central concept in the AA approach.

Fran was the guest moderator for the *closed meeting* of the same group. She started the session and then responded with comments following each person's sharing of experiences in the group's *go around.* This session focused on the *second step:* "I came to believe that a Power greater than ourselves could restore us to sanity." There were 19 members present, eight women and eleven men, the majority in their fifties and early sixties, five in their thirties. Only one woman did not speak that evening. For the rest, Hays was told after the meeting that the emerging material was more detailed than usual, partly because of his attendance.

The focal figure of the evening was John who shared the critical point at which he found himself that very day, the first day without tranquilizers. (After the session John told Hays that AA was a relatively new experience for him, following a number of hospitalizations.) He was quick to tell his group about the "rage" he felt that day, stating that he was "bringing it up as a catharsis, not as a problem." The moderator picked up John's request for help and asked the larger group to respond on the basis of "having drugs as a problem." John's sponsor provided him with tools such as *thinking* and *sobriety prayers*. Ernie, an old-timer, stressed "accepting the things you can't change." Ginger, an attractive dark-haired woman (who before the meeting asked Hays if he knew her local psychiatrist), referred John to the second-step prayer. Fran commented to both John and the rest of the group, which was rather animated at this point, that it was more important for them to be *sounding boards* than to give advice.

Joe was next. He spoke of "using the power of the group," which is the first part of power as defined in the second step. He had just returned from a slip and the important thing was to be truthful so that the group could help him. Honesty, truth, sincerity were key words repeated throughout the go-around. Bob tried everything—"psychiatry, the whole works"—but the next step was *honesty*. During the go-around and the exchange involving the acting leader, John got some clarification of his dilemma: He had a "good boy" feeling that day, yet he "was all set-up for feeling angry." Dick, dressed in a Madison Avenue fashion, spoke of his "confusion about the multitude of problems I haven't licked" and, like John, he spoke of the magic expected of AA and being let down. The moderator addressed herself to the expectations of AA and the importance of recognizing that AA had no specific expectations around the movement from one step to another. Bill passed with a few words about "belief in God." Jim, one of the young people, talked about becoming an alcoholic on beer only. Jack came to AA for the "wrong reasons." His problem was not his wife, but his "biggest character defect," namely anger.

Charlotte had been to Schizophrenics Anonymous, whose twelve steps are fashioned after AA. She had an experience in "insanity" and now had a "combination disease." It was not until she changed psychiatrists and started AA that she was receiving the "right care." Her brother was an active schizophrenic who went to AA, was taken off medication, and returned to his psychosis. What she was sharing with the group was "heresy." Could AA and psychiatry work side by side? She was "working on my insanity" in the program and was responded to by the group with compassion and understanding. George, a bearded young man, sitting next to Charlotte, had just returned from Florida. He was atypically inarticulate but spoke briefly of his need for AA. Midge, a stunning blonde, beautifully dressed, "Klondike Annie" character, in her sixties, had just slipped. She told about a *blackout,* a rather familiar tale among alcoholics. She had dried out in a nearby hospital and now she returned only to retrace "these steps," since her period of sobriety had extended over twenty-one months.

Mary spoke of her fear of God as a child and, relating to the group, stated that this was a "different kind of spirituality." Ed was next. He was Swedish in origin and a long-time drinker. Ginger was told about AA the "first day of my therapy" and for her AA represented the "teaching of honesty." Another Mary had given up her church, yet the substance of her short message to the group was "admitting you're an alcoholic and turning yourself over to another kind of power."

For the members it was an intense group experience, available to anybody and everybody, "even the poor of Mexico," as Ernie put it while describing his visit to an AA chapter in that country. "It's the identification, the ability to take what you want." It is the kind of experience which the Pole, who attended one of their recent meetings and could not speak English, could be a part of and he was understood by the group despite the language barrier. Although Hays saw it as an alien experience in many ways, other people in the field look at it as a philosophy of living which is compatible with the alcoholic and his family: an absorbing faith in himself which comes only after he has learned to understand himself through this intensive group experience, in close association with others whose experiences parallel his own. The organization also provides groups for children of alcoholics (Al-A-Teen) as well as for their wives (Al-Anon).

There are those who feel that the sponsorship system of AA represents a *rescue* operation and thus serves as an ego defense in a never-ending attempt to solve the alcoholic's conflicts.[56] This operation was likened to Anna Freud's *altruism,* a mechanism of identification first introduced by her in 1936.[52] In group psychotherapy, where such a defense system is not part of most approaches, the alcoholic has a better setting to work through his hostility. And, in general, the significant number of taboos in AA limit its effectiveness to working through in depth.[58]

Gamblers Anonymous

GA was founded in California in 1957 and modeled its recovery program after AA. Strongly believing that "it takes one to know one, it takes one to help one," this organization holds the desire to stop gambling as its only requirement for membership. Here, too, total abstinence is viewed as the only way to arrest the psychological addiction of the compulsive gambler and, to the devaluation of asking *why* the person keeps acting out his magical fantasies in this fashion, they utilize the same twelve-step program to combat the gambler's inability and unwillingness to accept reality, his emotional insecurity and narcissistic immaturity.

Their group meetings consist mostly of confessionals starting with the standard "My name is _____ and I'm a compulsive gambler" and ending with testimonials for GA. While telling their stories, the members stress the negative aspects of their behavior and the defects of their character. Ten individuals attended the *open group* meeting in a community constituting the hub of Westchester County and New York State. The group's chairperson, Bill C., referred to the experience as *therapy*. He told of a long antisocial history and confessed to being *fresh* (not gambling) only three months. His affiliation with the organization extended back eleven years. In the following go-around, Seymour focused on the misery he produced in his family. Frank shared the "real trouble" he was currently experiencing while his car was in the process of being taken away. His "confusion" spoke for itself. Compared to the rest of the group he was strikingly unable to express himself. Louis, a gangland-type character, narrated a story which, as it unfolded, sounded like a movie script for *The Godfather*. He ended his confessional by praising his children for how good they were in contrast to him. Joe, a flashy dresser, had just bought a new home; he had been in jail and was just beginning to see the light. Frank, a bearded young man, while emphasizing his brightness, told of how he "screwed up" and how he realized that there was *no cure* for his gambling. Arthur, an old-timer who had been "out of it" for only a short time despite his eleven years in GA—thus resembling the chairperson—focused on the active fantasy life he had within the context of his gambling. Vince, another young member, told about "screwing up" in college while deceiving an old aunt about an insurance policy. His story revealed an intense involvement in gambling on sports events, ending with "how much do they really mean?" Joe had just come back from Paris where he went with money given him by his brother. He did not attend group for three weeks and was on the spot. He told the group about his relationship with an alcoholic friend who had just died and commented on the close similarity between the alcoholic, the drug addict, and the compulsive gambler. The leader was articulate, smooth, and polished. He spoke about "relating," "being able to identify with another human being," and the importance of ventilating past and current wrongdoings, as well as mutual support. The meeting ended with the ritualistic reciting of the prayer: "God, grant me the serenity to accept the things I cannot change, courage to change the things I can and the wisdom to know the difference."

Despite the heterogeneity of the group in terms of age and educational, cultural, and economic background, the members emerged with a rather homogeneous character structure, the salient features of which were impulsive acting out, dependency, and narcissism. As in AA, GA members use each other to curb their acting out by telephoning upon the emergence of the impulse to gamble. *Unity* is emphasized and the rotating leaders are seen as *trusted servants,* equal to everybody else. The organization insists of nonprofessionalism and self-support, stressing mutual help rather than just getting help. In addition, Carl M., who has been off gambling for the last twelve and a half years, claims that "we are the professionals" in the sense of knowing "what makes us tick" and being able to see through the "con merchants" manipulativeness that can fool everybody else, including professionals. He sees the role of professionals as valuable *after* the compulsive gambler had stopped gambling, aiming at characterological change. His belief corroborates that of Dr. Robert L. Custer, a national authority in the field.[59] GA veterans rarely leave the organization. They stay not only to help newcomers, but the horror stories recounted by new members seem to provide the most effective therapeutic deterrent in their own struggle.

Referring to Gam-Anon, the sister organization for wives of compulsive gamblers, and to Gam-A-Teen, the one for their children (age groups of 9–12 and 13–18), Carl M. characterized GA as a "family project." These groups hold their meetings at the same time and place as GA but in different rooms.

Interestingly enough, in contrast to the dreamy, magical tone of the compulsive gambler while in action, when GA members talk of recovery and success in combating the addiction they are highly cautious and realistic. Reporting only 5 percent full recovery, they will refrain from using the word *cure* in favor of a daily struggle for *arrest,* even when they refer to fifteen years of total abstinence, never risking the dangerous illusion of "normal gambling."

Recovery, Inc.

This organization was founded in Chicago in 1937 by a psychiatrist, Dr. Abraham A. Low, who conducted groups of ex–hospitalized patients. His goal was to provide them with "A Systematic Method of Self-Help Aftercare" aiming at training them in self-leadership. After Low's death the movement continued autonomously as a self-help Association of Nervous and Former Mental Patients, thus extending membership to include all types of mental patients who are able to function in the community. Toward the purpose of preventing relapses in former patients and forestalling chronicity in nervous patients, they are still using his Recovery Method, with his text *Mental Health Through Will Training*[60] as their group's bible.

Recovery's guiding principle is that the mentally ill can develop their will power, and that through exercising the tools of "spotting, transparency, muscle control, processing, and objectivity" they can establish *endorsement* of themselves.[61] Endorsement is analogous to self-approval stemming from methodically practicing and carrying out these particular techniques. Their group approach is directive. Meetings start with a reading from Dr. Low's book and key phrases from the text constitute the communication medium among the members while they give their testimonials in a go-around fashion. The repeated affirmation of common values and the use of a common language fosters group solidarity and encourages a hopeful outlook. The group process provides mutual sharing, and identification with peers who become role models through setting examples for each other. Peers also share the responsibility for change. Verbally active, they are judgmental and supportive; they urge appropriate behaviors and reject disruptive ones. The emphasis is on day-to-day victories (another day without panic). Recovery, Inc. group leaders are experienced members who receive leadership training in the Recovery Method and volunteer their guidance at the weekly group meetings. As professionals are welcome to attend meetings, yet not to participate in them, Hays was not permitted to take any notes. The meeting he attended had an influx of new members whose position in the group was quite clearly secondary to that of the "old-timers." Jean A., the leader's wife and assistant, has apparently been caught in the past in ritualistic, obsessive-compulsive behavior. She was highly structured and very much to the point when she addressed the group at her husband's request. Her husband, Bill A., an old-time leader, started the session with the first paragraph of the chapter "Will, Beliefs, and Muscles" and had the old-timers follow him up in covering its material. Bill A. related his most recent experience at the office which was associated with his old train phobia. He told of his nervousness and tension and the reflected minimal tendency to *process*. He shared his attempts at using *spotting* and objectivity and was reinforced by the older members to tackle the experience with these specific techniques. Ruth, Mary, and Ethel were old-timers. Ruth, looking like an affluent suburban housewife, with her horn-rimmed glasses perched on her head, told the group of an encounter with her adolescent son. She reported utilizing *will* not to repeat reviewing his old behavior in response to an incident that was troubling her the night before. She was able to *objectify* and *spot* the experience and consequently got endorsement.

Vince, one of the "youngsters" in the group, came in late. Initially, he followed Bill A. by relating an encounter with a salesman at Macy's during which he used objectifying and "excusing, not accusing" as his primary tools. The leader, quietly yet consistently, stressed his recent absences and the importance of attendance, making it quite difficult for Vince to get off the hook. Pete, an alcoholic, kept raising his hand constantly throughout the meeting to comment about what he thought was going on with others. His own example related to serving food at a

Christmas affair and his focus was on *transparency*. Jack, in his twenties, sitting next to Hays, intermittently kept asking him questions, in a rather inappropriate fashion, about his service background and about other psychiatrists in a small local private mental hospital. He was responded to by the leader, who recognized his current struggle, with much softness. Edith was articulate and bright yet confused about her association with AA and now with Recovery. Ed, a newcomer, spoke of "all these terms" which he did not understand. The leader acknowledged his anxiety around the communication gap and pointed out to him that it takes time to learn the meaning of the group's language. Ethel was the last to recount a recent incident. She told of purchasing a gift for her sister and feeling badly about it until "I lowered my expectations" and "objectified."

New members were anxious to speak but were kept in line by Bill A. They were finally given a chance to share problems and ask questions in the last fifteen minutes. John, the oldest member of the group (in his late sixties), remained silent throughout. He looked depressed. The leader asked him to read a small section at the beginning of the session. He also referred to him later, yet John never responded. However, when he left the meeting while refreshments were served he was smiling warmly, which was startling but quite pleasant.

Recovery was truly *practiced*. In a group of thirteen, which was heterogeneous from every point of view—age, symptomatology, capacity to verbalize, appearance, and period of belongingness to it—the structure was firm. There was no confusion about leadership and the techniques were pointed out in a clear-cut fashion. Mutual aid through examples is inherent in the process. Since objectifying is a mainstay of the approach "gut-level" experiences are minimal. The latter are also discouraged by the highlighting of willpower, self-control, and fate. The *common problem* is having a problem. What seems to be of much significance and comfort is sharing a structure-providing method, which was developed by a charismatic leader and is teachable so that it can be passed down from the teacher to and through peers.

Because of its emphasis on words and on mastery of concepts, the value of Recovery, Inc. in helping the socioculturally deprived population has been questioned. Nonetheless, a significant change occurred in the attitude of the medical profession toward this method.[62] Whereas originally it viewed Recovery, Inc. as archaic, "naïve, unorthodox, and authoritarian, it has now moved to embrace it as an important supportive and reeducational self-help approach which does have a place in the mental health movement. On its part, the association is quite clear in stating that "Recovery does not supplant the physician, offer diagnosis, treatment, advice or counseling, or make professional referrals. Each member is expected to follow the authority of his physician or other professional person. . . . It provides self-help aftercare only."[63]

Self-Help Group Approaches Related to Obesity (Weight Watchers and Diet Watchers)

These related organizations are rooted in a larger group format compared to the other self-help groups we presented. They also have a rather simple advantage over the others. The problem they address themselves to is concrete and manifest, namely, weight and appearance. About thirteen years of age, Weight Watchers is the older of the two organizations. It was founded by Jean Niditch, a charismatic woman, whose book *The Story of Weight Watchers* was published in 1970.[64] In the book she reviews the history of an organization which has grown phenomenally to encompass approximately 170 centers and 8,500 "classes" a week, each of which has forty to fifty members. Originally, the groups were homogeneous sex-wise, with coed composition since 1966. As in Recovery, Inc., the pivotal figure is the *lecturer* or leader. This person has achieved his or her goal weight-wise, and has gone through a training program or *workshop* of nine weeks with three-week stages which enables him to run the classes.

The Guide for Diet Watchers, written by its founder, Ann Gold, in collaboration with Sarah Wells Briller,[65] refers to their group approach as *group therapy* and presents it as the "cornerstone of the Diet Watchers program." *Buddy systems* and "getting by the moment of impulse" are stressed in both organizations. There is a distinct ritualistic quality to both approaches: weight cards, go-arounds, questions and answers, and *discussion periods* all belong within their framework. Weight Watchers focuses more on the self-help than on the confessional aspect. Guilt-provoking operations as well as rewards (pins and certificates), ventilation, catharsis, mutual support, and identification are prominent. Conscious control, a "new way of life, learning to be open and honest with one another," and guidelines for how to eat properly are some of the main elements focused on in class. "The reward of self-respect" is a key theme. Diets, use of scales, and a magazine are other aspects of their programs which have grown rapidly.

The Weight Watchers night session Hays attended at a local church in a suburban New York town was a large group scene of great excitement, animation, and activity. There were 100 who attended that evening, ranging in age from 12 to several older women in their seventies, with 18 new registering members and 82 "old guard," each paying three dollars. Paying for what you get is an important aspect of the experience. This is one of the *rules* of the group and by contrast to other self-help groups it is proud of its unique character: namely, that it represented a franchise, was directed by an entrepreneur, and was profit making. Special arrangements were worked out for Hays' attendance since another rule is that visitors and guests are not permitted to attend meetings. The feeling tone of the meeting was in sharp contrast to that in other self-help groups. This may have been related to the personality of their lecturer Howard F., who has been their regular leader over the past two and one half years. Howard, a local dentist, had gone through the program *weighing in* at 233 and emerging at 183, and is a confirmed believer in the group process. The manager of that area, an attractive woman in her forties, Mrs. M., told Hays that a person like Howard either "got it or don't got it" as a lecturer and that he had been a natural although he went to their training center.

While the rituals of weighing in, recording, and registering were going on Howard spoke to Hays about the individuals in their heterogeneous group. All sizes, all shapes, but approximately 95 percent female, they were talking to one another before and after his lecture and referred to it as "group therapy." To him, this was the most important part of the experience. After almost an hour of *warmup,* he lectured on marriage, citing two people at the beginning for the *weight differential* they had maintained over an extended period of time and passing out "after" pictures of one member in the large group in a bikini. His lecture started out with Romeo and Juliet and Juliet's fat nurse, the need for mothers and grandmothers to produce fat babies with "grabbable parts," moved on to the symbolism of food, cultural differences between American women and Italian women that are changing with the times as spaghetti has been seen more and more as breaking up marriages, to "protein being in and starch out," based on a recent article in *Cosmopolitan*. He spoke of the many dropouts among the few teenagers coming into the group and then did a beautiful "rolling-in-the-aisles" satire on a wedding announcement from the local newspaper. His bit had everybody bursting with laughter. The vogue and myth of plumpness and fitness had been effectively destroyed one more night by this fun-making, formerly fat dentist. As the session moved on to his announcements of 25-pound weight losses, then of individuals well-known in the group struggling over many weeks with weight who had lost only half a pound, there was clapping and great support. Martha had lost 4½ pounds that week and was "on the road again"; Vivian had gone for eighteen weeks and never gained. Richard, "one of our male contingent," had done beautifully as he pushed the men's greater ability to make it. It was a large group scene. It was not group therapy in the technical sense, yet it was definitely an intense group experience.

Narcotic Addiction

The spectrum of group approaches with this population has been strikingly broad, particularly when one considers that the reported history of group work with the drug addict started in 1951.[66] Approaches have ranged from emphasis on the cognitive and intellectual, with the therapist being an active force in choosing topics for group discussions, to the *bull-type sessions* where a gut-level approach of group interaction is of the essence. The range of leaders has moved from psychiatrists to lay individuals and ex-addicts. The *settings* where drug addicts have been treated have also been diverse, ranging from institutions (prisons, hospitals, clinics) to neighborhood centers.

Because self-help groups have been the most prevalent intensive group modality with this population we will describe Synanon, one of the first of these organizations, founded in California in 1958. Originally starting as a self-help exploratory group club by Chuck Dederich, an alcoholic, Synanon developed into a philosophy, presenting itself as an alternative life style,[67] and expanded to be the largest and most successful commune in the United States. For the addict, it not only offers a philosophy as a substitute for drugs and other stimulants, but a way of actively and responsibly implementing it in living. As such, Synanon is an intensive group living experience, using a variety of group modalities and pressures to school the addict to become a valuable member of the community.

Synanon's philosophy is well reflected in the following prayer:

> Please let me first and always examine myself.
> Let me be honest and truthful.
> Let me seek and assume responsibility.
> Let me understand rather than be understood.
> Let me have trust and faith in myself and my fellow man.
> Let me love rather than be loved.
> Let me give rather than receive.[68]

Yet it is not verbalization of this that is demanded of the addict in return for free clothes and room and board. Chuck Dederich believed that "the addicts knew more about addiction than the specialists who tried to examine them. Psychologically I knew the addict was emotionally immature, a child. I assumed they were like children and treated them as such." And, less flatteringly, "There is only one thing the dope fiend knows, and that is how to shoot dope. . . . I never bothered asking the why or what; they don't know. I tell them how. I show them how to live, one step at a time. They don't know what is right and wrong. I just tell them what the rules are: (1) no drugs or alcohol of any kind, and (2) no physical violence. And what to do—start working on the dishpan—and if they don't like it, they can leave any time."[69] These are the first two cardinal rules of living at Synanon house, and the demand to kick the habit "cold turkey" and undergo the agony of withdrawal is a crucial test for the addict's genuine motivation to work.

Structurally, there are three major ways in which Synanon differs from usual institutional treatment operations: (1) In Synanon the addict has to carry on a realistic job (in contrast to basket weaving, etc.). This could be in serving the community or, if he works on the outside, he brings the salary he earns to the community. (2) Hierarchically, here he is equal to everybody else, and his position or rank is determined by his character. (3) Conquering the habit, although highly praised, is just the first step toward accomplishing Synanon's goal of self-cultivation. The optimal minimum length of stay is two years, and the decision about *graduating* is a communal one. Although the addict is free to leave at any time prior to it, the organization views premature leaving as a failure.

All forms of group interaction at Synanon are geared toward implementing their philosophy. The most important one is the Synanon game, in which everybody must participate several times a week. A game involves group sessions of ten to fifteen people and may last up to three hours. The participants act as mirrors for each other, reflecting to the individual the way others see him. Each person's involvement in the game is a fight for his own self-image and dignity during which he learns his impact on others and others' impact on him. In addition to teaching interpersonal responsibility, the games are regulators of members' behavior within the community, since it is there that their actions are exposed.

"The group sessions do not have any official leader. They are autonomous; however, leaders emerge in each session in a natural fashion. The emergent leader tells much about himself in his questioning of another. Because he is intensely involved with the subject or the problem in a particular session he begins to direct, he is in a natural fashion the 'most qualified' session leader for that time and place. In short, the expert of the moment may be emotionally crippled in many personal areas, but in the session where he is permitted by the group to take therapeutic command, he may be the most qualified therapeutic agent."[70]

A second group tool used at Synanon is a public speaking lesson, where one member at a time gives an impromptu speech in front of a small group and gets their constructive criticism on it. The *verbal haircut* is a much more extreme version of the latter. Here the person is strongly reprimanded and verbally torn apart for his behavior. The encounters, which take about 8 to 12 hours, are also used extensively. Here, too, each member takes a turn being challenged, grilled, and criticized for his faults, emotional weaknesses, suspect motives, and behavior at Synanon. The rationale behind the vicious cross-examination and brutal verbal exposures used in both group formats is that the fundamental causes for becoming and remaining a drug addict are emotional, covered up by a variety of subterfuges and defenses that should be broken through. They believe that only after this will the person be able to stop avoiding looking at his behavior and realize how weak, insecure, irresponsible, immature, unrealistic, and dependent he is. Gut-level catharsis is obviously an important mechanism in this process. Synanon members see this kind of interaction as manifesting responsible concern and, while being administered by a basically loving "family," leading to the establishment of self-control and identity. Marathons are second only to the games in terms of importance in Synanon. Often lasting up to 36 straight hours, they further enable the members to work through defenses and gain insights into core characterological problems.

More than half the members who enter the therapeutic community stay for at least six months. Of those that have stayed past three months, 90 percent are drug-free. In addition to the original community in Santa Monica, today Synanon has branches in Reno, Nevada, Westport, Connecticut, and Oakland and San Diego, California. Membership in these total somewhere in the thousands. An east coast offspring of Synanon, which is very similar to it both in terms of its philosophy and in its modes of operation, was established by Casriel in 1963. Standing for Drug Addicts Treated on Probation, the organization is called Daytop Village.[71] Here, too, the optimal length of stay is for about two years and much of its success is attributed to accepting addicts who genuinely want it to work not only in the direction of detoxification but in terms of interpersonal education toward productive adulthood.

Conclusion

As we have seen, both group psychotherapy and self-help groups have become a major reparative force in the lives of many thousands of individuals with specific problems. Identification with "their group," initially based on the manifest symptom alone, has started them on the road to change. Then, as Foulkes surmises: "The deepest reason why these patients . . . can reinforce each other's normal reactions and wear down and correct each other's neurotic reactions, is that *collectively they constitute the very Norm, from which, individually, they deviate*" (author's italics and capitalization).[72]

The ways in which the establishment and maintenance of these norms take place are quite similar and the mechanisms involved are limited in number across groups. Yalom, for instance, lists ten such mechanisms, which he terms *curative factors*. Although operating in every type of helping group, "they assume a differential importance depending on the goals and composition of the specific group; factors which are minor or implicit in one group approach may be major or explicit in another. Furthermore, patients in the same group may be benefited by widely differing clusters of curative factors." These are (1) imparting of information; (2) instilling of hope; (3) universality; (4) altruism; (5) the corrective recapitulation of the primary family group; (6) development of socializing techniques; (7) imitative behaviors; (8) interpersonal learning; (9) group cohesiveness; and (10) catharsis.[73] Obviously they are arbitrary and interdependent, and attempt to be descriptive of the process of change and its conditions. The reader may realize that, according to this list of factors, AA and GA, for instance, rely very heavily on 2, 3, 4, and 10 of the above and that self-help groups in general follow ideologies much more clearly and directly than do therapy groups. Some therapy groups rely quite heavily on 1, 5, 6, 8, and 10, when 9 represents a condition for change.

Whether one chooses to look at different group approaches through the aforementioned set of variables or not, it is clear that the stated differences in goals are quite important, that is, most therapy groups aim at general personality independence and growth rather than at independence from specific symptoms alone. We speculate that the long-term group dependency seen in most self-help groups is related to this difference, as well as to their modes of operation, that is, the encouragement of dependency on the group, the organization, or the specific ideology. On the surface, this may seem paradoxical when one remembers the emphasis *self*-help groups put on active mutual help in contrast to the initial focus on being helped found in therapy groups. It may be that the most crucial asset of self-help groups is in providing a human and philosophical substitute for the original dependency reflected in the symptomatic behavior, especially when the latter was indeed embedded in social isolation which is often reinforced by societal attitudes and legislation. Cross-fertilization, however, has been taking place among the two camps. The oldest formal self-help group, AA, has shown some movement toward a *group therapy orientation* following the tendency for more introspection on the part of the growing number of younger members.[74] Similarly, in the midst of a rapidly changing world, with resulting problems for which there exist a rather limited core of trained mental health professionals, who themselves do not have readymade answers, there is a growing recognition on their part of the value of self-help groups.

The comments Peters et al. made concerning the lack of clear cultural and social norms and the results in present-day society are relevant.[75] It seems that part of the attraction and success of self-help groups can be attributed to the fact that in their curative attempts they fill some of this gap. Thus, although technically they differ from group therapies, even if the latter address themselves more forcefully to the ability to live and grow in a changing world, there are some very basic human needs which are gratified by the self-help groups. The sociologist Parsons has formulated the view that modern life (industry, technology, etc.) has profoundly affected the family institution. In particular, he described the movement from the extended to the nuclear family unit.[76] Within this framework, the current interest in groups in general and in self-help and communal groups in particular can be viewed as representing a reaction to the current dissatisfaction with the dysfunctional, isolated nuclear family and an attempt to reestablish the extended family.

Whatever the analysis and the speculation, the reality is that both group therapies and self-help groups exist side by side in their attempts to help specific problem populations. We have described some of the group work done with some of them and raised many questions. It is clear to us that much research has to be done in order to try to answer these questions.

Chapter 5.   The Romance of Community: Intentional Communities as Intensive Group Experiences

Rosabeth Moss Kanter

THE ROMANCE OF COMMUNITY captured the American imagination in the late 1960s and early 1970s. More and more people began to experiment with ways of living more closely with others. The city, the country, and increasingly the suburbs were dotted with new communal groups. Magazine articles described the crisis of the nuclear family and wondered whether communes were the wave of the future. When people at parties learned of my research on communes, it was almost impossible to turn the conversation to anything else.[1] In the 1840s Ralph Waldo Emerson had remarked that every other person carried in his vest pocket a plan for the perfect society; we witnessed the same phenomenon in the late 1960's. Walking down the street in Cambridge, Massachusetts, or Berkeley, California, on the right day in 1970, you might have run into someone handing out leaflets with plans for a new community or schemes for social improvement. You could have picked up an underground newspaper and seen the ads placed by communes looking for members, people looking for communes, or people just looking for each other.

What was happening? What were the dimensions of the movement to create and form new kinds of communities? What were the historical roots of this movement—its expression of recurrent themes—and what was unique about it? What concepts can help us understand the dynamics of togetherness? What are the principles and mechanisms by which such communities operated? What are their advantages and limitations? These are the questions I'll try to answer as I consider what kind of group experience intentional communities of various kinds seek and find.

A good working definition of an intentional community is a group of over six unrelated adults sharing space and an economy for the express purpose of creating a whole way of life. Beyond this minimal definition, however, could be found groups of diverse sizes, all holding singular views on the content of their *whole way of life*. Some examples:

In Cambridge, Massachusetts, a ten-person urban commune celebrated its fifth anniversary in the summer of 1974. Babies were just born to two of the married couples in the house. One of nearly 200 such groups identifiable in the Boston area alone, most of them more transient, this commune developed its own rituals (such as grace before dinner with hands held) and celebrated its own holidays (such as Omega Day in the spring, a combination of Easter and Passover that also coincided with an important event in the house's history—the time the men in the original group turned in their draft cards).

In the desert of New Mexico, thirty-five people, from infants to grandmothers in their sixties, former members of the Bahai church in Indiana, lived and worked around an old factory building they took over thirteen years ago. They broke with their church because they felt that it did not practice what it preached; they wanted to live out religious ideals every moment of their lives. Their attempt to infuse daily life with values led to the creation of their own free school, which conducts classes in the large open kitchen and dining room. They cooperated with neighboring groups that also have free schools. One nearby community consisted of dropouts from college teaching, interested in humanistic psychology and the personal growth movement, who hoped to start a human potential institute on their land. But first they were learning to farm, raise animals, clear land, build their own cabins, and survive the tough New Mexico winters.

In Moundsville, West Virginia, on September 4, 1972, members of the Hare Krishna sect gathered at their central farm to chant in celebration of the birth of Lord Krishna nearly five thousand years ago. Over one thousand devotees lived together in city houses serving as temples. Clothed in saffron robes and carrying simple instruments, they gathered on street corners to chant Hare Krishna and spread the message. Their faith was demanding: they ate no fish, meat, and eggs, engaged in sex only under strictly regulated marital conditions, and turned over all of their worldly goods to the sect. They believed that purity of mind and body is the path to spiritual awakening.

In Somerville, Massachusetts, twelve members of an urban commune thought of themselves as the *professional commune* because the lawyers, architects, and social workers in the house leave every morning carrying attaché cases like any other commuters. This house met in an encounter group, extended their experience together by renting a summer camp for intense encounter weekends, and then decided to live together in the city. Two of the members bought the house, and the group remodeled it from attic to bathrooms.

The number of young professionals making similar decisions in the early 1970's was so great that even such publications as *the Wall Street Journal* commented on the cooperative housing boom. In places as diverse as New Orleans, Berkeley, Newton, Massachusetts, and Cleveland Heights, Ohio, several couples, or groups of professional friends, or divorced parents who did not want to raise their children alone, were buying or renting large houses together, sometimes in exclusive neighborhoods. Projects in these cities often helped people find one another and share the lessons and experiences of other groups. Communication techniques were commonly taught.

It is virtually impossible to catalogue the types and expressions of intentional community of the early 1970s. There were Zen meditation centers, macrobiotic houses, political collectives, traditional Christian communities (such as the three-community Bruderhof in the East or Reba Place Fellowship in Chicago), new messianic Christian groups (like the Brotherhood of the Spirit), service communities to help drug addicts (like Synanon) or the handicapped (like Camphill Village), and even groups inspired by *Walden Two,* B. F. Skinner's fictional utopia portraying a scientifically planned community providing happiness via behavioral psychology.

There were hundreds of nameless rural farm groups that consisted of a few friends and only vague plans, and perhaps greater numbers of urban groups with shifting membership, named by their address. Behind these specific communities was an even greater population of migrants who meander from place to place. Some observers used the tribal metaphor of the migratory band. As Benjamin Zablocki puts it, "What we define as communes may be nothing more than temporary encampments of large migratory tribes."[2] This statement was supported by interviews with urban commune members, many of whom face the dissolution of their immediate group, yet all of whom predicted they would continue to live in communal groups. And even further behind the formation of specific communities was a more general culture of spiritual, therapeutic, and communal seekership in the United States, creating a demand for short-term personal growth experiences in temporary communities.

Communal Imagery

The communal love story revolves around three images: spiritual, familial, and pastoral. On the spiritual level *community* promises salvation and therapy, an end to alienation; on the familial level it promises intimacy, a solution to crises of loneliness and marital breakdown; on the pastoral level it promises closer harmony with nature, an escape from the urban wasteland. These are the promises and lures; not all of them, of course, are fulfilled.

Many people see intentional communities as an opportunity to contact the spiritual roots of their existence, to learn about themselves, to reach out to God or to unknown, mystical forces beyond our level of rational understanding. They seek to rediscover the unity of mind and body and reinfuse daily life with the spiritual and emotional. Most communes in the past have had some sort of religious thrust; modern communities stressed a personal growth orientation. But a common bond links past and present communes: the attempt to deal with psychological estrangement, to bring people into closer touch with themselves, to reunite mind and body, spirit and flesh, work and growth. Where religion talks about saving souls, the current therapeutic rhetoric talks about curing sicknesses caused by living in a sick society. Side by side, the 1960's and 1970's witnessed astrology cults, the I Ching, the Jesus movement, and encounter groups. Thus some communes can be compared to religious groups (like monasteries), while others resemble personal growth institutes, certain rehabilitation centers, and therapeutic communities (Synanon, for example). Uniting all of these different groups is a belief in human perfectibility: that if social institutions are structured in close loving ways, close loving human beings will be produced.

Many groups sought to define themselves as *families,* use images of brother and sister in describing the relationships among members and sometimes take a single family name. Their goals, they said, were simply to live together as one family. Writers on the contemporary commune movement often took the family image at face value and described the forming of communes as an attempt to recreate the romanticized extended family of nostalgia. Some communes actually succeeded at becoming a family together in the traditional sense of multiple generations. This image probably described the movement's hopes better than its reality, however. The majority of communes clearly resembled peer groups or college fraternities more than they did families; they encompassed a small age range, had no shared history or shared future vision, tended to back away from the responsibilities of parenthood, and limited the financial or emotional demands members can legitimately make on one another. Commitment was varied and turnover was high. Despite these differences, however, the family myth persisted, and was often invoked when members wanted more commitment or intimacy from each other.

The final image is pastoral, a romance with the land and all that is considered *natural.* Rural communes, staking out their territories in the woods or the mountains or the fields, were only one part of the land craze that swept certain parts of the country in the late 1960's, driving up land prices in such diverse areas as New Mexico and Vermont. For communes many themes come together in the ideal of a return to the land. Members come closer to nature and the natural order and return to a simpler life more concerned with the fundamentals of existence. The kinds of jobs to be done around the land often require no special skills and provide an opportunity for everyone to do some kind of work. The products are visible and can be consumed by the community; members together can truly and directly appreciate the "fruits" of their joint labor. A number of tasks, such as the harvest, lend themselves in particular to communal work efforts with all members participating. The physical labor required by a land-based way of life is vital to integrating the body and the mind. The land also provides the community with its own means of livelihood and direct access to its own natural resources.

Even urban communes on dingy city streets showed their pastoral orientation. Often their interiors had the feel of a country commune: crafts hung on the walls, kitchens walled with old barn boards, big mason jars filled with grains sitting on open shelves, herbs hanging to dry, green plants and animals underfoot. Many urban groups talked about getting land someday, and a few even owned or shared country places. The encounter group, too, had its version of the pastoral and natural, not only in the beautiful isolated settings many personal growth groups chose but also in nudity, a reminder of the Garden of Eden.

It should be clear, then, that the recent intentional community movement in the United States drew on and implemented romantic longings prevailing the culture. But these longings are not unique. An excursion into history will demonstrate the ties between common past and present communal movements.

Historical Background

Western history has always had its life style revolutionaries, religious seekers, dropout "freaks," and lonely souls looking for new ways to unite meaningfully with the human and natural community. The recent dramatic, visible proliferation of socially oriented life style movements—hippie flower children, rural and urban, communes, Jesus freaks and satanic cults, meditation centers and Krishna devotees, new psychotherapies, and human potential institutes offering transcendent experiences and greater levels of awareness—these were contemporary manifestations of a centuries-old quest. Whenever social institutions have become so big, so impersonally powerful, or so complicated that they threaten to separate certain people from basic human experiences, whenever social change has disrupted social ties and loyalties, radical groups have banded together to seek a simpler, more integrated, value-based communal existence. The three major historical threads I will discuss are monasticism, millennialism, and utopianism.

MONASTICISM

Beginning in the third, fourth, and fifth centuries, early Christians formed monastic communities as a radical alternative to the established church, as peaceful enclaves where a minimally material, contemplative life could be lived. They gave up worldly property and pursuits in order to devote themselves to spiritual growth. Wrote a Church historian:

> The desire for prayer and self-discipline leads to solitude as inevitable as the desire to preach leads to congregations. When the worldliness of any society is felt to reach a certain point beyond which the ideals of the spiritual life cannot be maintained, the moment has come for flight. Already in the first half of the third century, sent out by the combined force of worldliness and Gnosticism in the cities, Christian men and women migrated to the desert. The Church was beginning to yield not to persecution from without but to the dissolvent pressures within.[3]

Not only religious professionals began to live communally. From the eleventh century on, in the more developed and populous parts of Europe, groups of laymen started living in communes with a quasi-monastic flavor, holding all property in common—occasionally without the sanction of the Church.[4]

Contemporary versions of traditional monastic orders strikingly resembled the communal counterculture in values, goals, and the order of life. This is not surprising, for the well-known Trappist monk, Thomas Merton, wrote in *Mystics and Zen Masters* of the common themes in Catholic monasticism, Eastern spiritualism, and old American communes like the Shakers.[5] A Benedictine monastery of women in the Northeast, for example, follows the rules St. Benedict wrote in 530–543 A.D. This monastery was founded after World War II by several Europeans who gave up promising careers in medicine and teaching to move to the United States and join the Order. They purchased an old farm with an abandoned factory on the site, renovated the building, and developed the land. Out in the fields the sisters wore their own version of the ubiquitous counterculture blue jeans: blue denim habits. Their history resembled that of most communities: a series of trial-and-error experiments. The monastery's order of life was dictated by the intertwining of the spiritual and the pastoral: prayers seven times a day mixed with labor in the fields and in the animal barns. The nuns expressed profound awareness of the rhythm of days and the rhythm of seasons, and they describe an organic wholeness to their life. Said one sister, "Every part of life has a relation to every other." Everyone worked in the garden on rotation and had two jobs, one manual, one intellectual. Each served the community and did something creative and self-expressive. One sister drew fancy lettering in addition to sewing and mending community clothes; another grew and experimented with herbs besides cleaning the houses.

The monastery was very much a self-contained community, encompassing all life functions except sexuality and procreation, and the Benedictine nuns, in particular, emphasized their separation from the world with a physical enclosure—a barrier that always came between the sisters and society. Despite this separation, the monastery became a spiritual center for a number of young people who formed their own weekend community in the monastery's guest houses so they could work on their own growth and experience close relationships. For these youth the monastery offered peace, order, and the joy of getting back to nature. One said, "It represents something spiritual that is being lived out. It has intensity. We are grounded in a centuries-old tradition. We need its limits and its grounding to free us."

MILLENNIALISM

The monastic tradition is one historical communal thread; millennial movements are another. Norman Cohn defines millennial (or millenarian) movements as sects which picture salvation as:

1. collective, in the sense that it will be enjoyed by the faithful as a collectivity;
2. terrestrial, in the sense that it will be realized on this earth, not in some other worldly heaven;
2. imminent, in the sense that it will come both soon and suddenly;
4. total, in the sense that it will utterly transform life on earth, so that the new society will be no mere improvement on the present but perfection itself;
5. miraculous, in the sense that it will be accomplished by, or with the help of, supernatural agencies.[6]

Taking their cue, then, from the Christian belief that after his second coming Christ would establish a golden age on earth of one thousand years, millennial movements include any group with messianic overtones that devotes itself to ushering in the New Age. Throughout world history, such groups have developed among both rich and poor, although primarily among the dispossessed. (A large literature in anthropology explains millennial movements in the so-called primitive societies as part of their response to colonialism and modernization.) But there were also affluent dropouts, then as now. The Franciscan spirituals of thirteenth-century Italy came from noble and merchant families, yet renounced property to live like beggars, dedicating themselves to fostering an age of the Spirit, "when all mankind would be united in prayer, mystical contemplation, and voluntary poverty."[7] An important millennial theme is the reversal of status and equalization of wealth that the movement will bring about. Most millennial movements are guided by messiahs or prophets around whose teachings the movement coalesces; often believing and belonging results in the formation of a new community with a fixed physical location, or the gathering of the faithful into migratory cells which carry the message outward.

Norman Cohn's *The Pursuit of the Millennium* described a large number of millennial groups in Europe from the thirteenth to the sixteenth centuries, ranging from bands of flagellants to social crusaders who formed new towns. One of the most interesting for present purposes is the Brotherhood of the Free Spirit, a movement that took root in the twelfth century and lasted over one hundred years. This sect is remarkable for its resemblances to the hippie movement of the 1960s. Like more orthodox Christian mysticism, it desired immediate communion with God and stressed the importance of intuitive, ecstatic experiences. (Interestingly, the movement developed a theory of the seven stages of the progress of the soul, culminating in deification, a doctrine almost directly paralleling the seven-stage theory of the contemporary Brotherhood of the Spirit, a 300-member Massachusetts commune.) The sect's heresy lay in its total amoralism: the belief that the person was perfect as is, and therefore had the right to do that which society and the Church forbade. Conscience or remorse were unnecessary, as these sayings illustrate: "He who is free in spirit escapes from [the Devil,] Hell, and Purgatory." "I belong to the Liberty of Nature, and all that my nature desires I satisfy . . . I am a natural man."[8] The hallmarks of the movement were promiscuity and poverty. Promiscuity was taken as a sign of spiritual emancipation, and while Cohn says that reports of sexual orgies were probably exaggerated, the group did engage in ritual nakedness, recapturing the innocence of Adam and Eve in the Garden of Eden. And there were more similarities to the hippies: this cult of voluntary poverty was peopled from among the mobile, restless intelligentsia. It operated underground, and itinerant "holy beggars" of both sexes wandered from town to town, wearing colorful and shabby costumes. (There were also more settled free spirits, notably women, who lived together in one house or a group of houses.) Like the hippies, the brotherhood was not a single movement but a number of like-minded groups, each with its own rites and practices. And like many other groups throughout Western history, this sect also wanted to return to the romanticized egalitarian state of nature, in which exploitation and oppression disappear and are replaced by brotherly love, community of property, and even sharing of spouses. The movement flourished in the thirteenth century; a hundred years later, followers had retreated into self-indulgence and luxury.[9]

Communities continue to be founded around millennial ideals, some optimistic, heralding the New Age, others pessimistic. An example of the latter is the *doomsday cult* in northern California described by John Lofland.[10] This group was organized by a woman from Korea who brought the message to the United States that the messiah was living in South Korea. Part of the message was that the world would end in 1967. Gradually, followers gathered who lived together communally in one house and attempted to put into practice the teachings of the messiah and prepare for the end of the world. This group has now gained adherents throughout the country.

Millennialism has also bought us a large number of utopian groups important in America's communal history, from the Hutterites to the Shakers. The Hutterites are the oldest communal group in the world and second only to the Israeli kibbutzim in population and settlements; in 1965, 17,800 Hutterites lived in 164 colonies in the Great Plains of the United States and Canada. They were founded in 1533 by Jacob Hutter in Moravia. Originally one of a number of Anabaptist sects that broke away from the established Church, the Hutterites believed in adult baptism, self-help, avoidance of worldly affairs, and return to direct use of the Bible as a source of inspiration. They were also unique in their adoption of full communalism: the establishment of villages in which work, goods, and services were fully shared. Their long history, as told by John Bennett and John Hostetler, is one of numerous ups and downs. By the late sixteenth century over 20,000 members lived in 90 villages in Moravia. Forced out in 1622 because of conflict with the Church and government officials, the remnants of these settlers gradually abandoned communalism, though maintaining a distinctive dress and form of worship. Some Hutterites settled in Russia in 1770 and reinstated community of goods, but by the nineteenth century land was again divided and held by individual nuclear families. In the 1870s some hard-core revivalist Hutterites migrated to the United States when the czar of Russia withdrew his protection from the communities; in the United States they found both freedom of worship and large parcels of land. Three branches of the group settled in the Great Plains, reestablishing communal living. Each branch has its own Council of Elders and marries only within its own ranks, but some joint affairs are conducted.[11] Hutterite colonies are rarely larger than 150 people, and when a settlement gets too large a new one is begun. The Hutterites maintain an austere life style and strict sexual and moral code yet they have also gradually incorporated bits and pieces of modern agricultural technology (as distinguished from the Amish, who abandoned communalism but refuse to use any of the fruits of modern technology). Due to their peaceful, simple life, the Hutterites have acquired a reputation for excellent mental health, a reputation only partially confirmed in Joseph Eaton and Robert Weil's study in the early 1950s, *Culture and Mental Disorders.* [12] Eaton and Weil found that, while their rates of psychosis were just as high as other populations, the Hutterites were free of some of the traumatic consequences of American life, such as alcoholism and migraine headaches. As the sick were cared for at home by the colony, many of the secondary consequences of mental illness were reduced, but as the Hutterites came into more contact with the outside and as their own rates of social change increased, they too were subject to the stresses of modern life and the inevitable strains of a close-knit community. [13]

UTOPIANISM

The Shakers, Oneida, the Harmony Society, Amana, and Zoar are among the well-known nineteenth-century American utopian communities founded by religious sectarians. These groups add the search for a perfect society to their shared belief in the millennium. Again, people who were radicals for their time broke away from the established Church and society in order to create an intense, self-governed community living out of ideals of brotherhood and equality. The Shakers were originally a group of dissident English Quakers whose founder, Ann Lee, was jailed for a time. Believing her to represent the Second Coming of Christ, the female half of the Godhead, the Shakers came with Mother Ann to the United States. More and more people joined the sect and, after Ann Lee's death, around the 1780s, members settled in communal villages. By the 1840s they numbered in the thousands; today there are remnants of two Shaker villages in the North-east. The Shakers are noted for their celibacy and strict separation of the sexes, the quality of their crafts and products (Shaker inventions include the clothespin and the flatbroom) and their ritual: an ecstatic, physically active set of dances and exercises, rivaling any modern encounter group in intensity of activity and feeling. The ritual first gave them their name: Shaking Quakers, later shortened to Shakers.

The Oneida community also had radical origins. Started by John Humphrey Noyes (a dropout from Yale Divinity School), growing out of a Bible class held in the early 1840s in his Vermont home, the group moved to Oneida, New York, in 1848, where they prospered under communalism for thirty-three years. Two of Oneida's practices are particularly relevant today. The first was complex marriage, in which every member of the community (at one time over two hundred people) was considered married to every other. Sex was to be widely shared and fidelity was frowned upon, for exclusive attachments were considered antithetical to the spirit of community. The second practice was mutual criticism, a kind of encounter and feedback session in which individuals were both praised and criticized and the internal life of the community examined.

Since the time of Plato people have been writing about Utopia, but it was not until the nineteenth century in the United States that many people actually tried to establish communities based on utopian visions. (Over one hundred nineteenth-century communities have left historical records.) Such visions were social, economic, and political, rather than primarily religious. In the small socialist community many people saw a refuge from the dehumanization and exploitation of the Industrial Revolution. With the sharing of property and appropriate educational institutions, such men as the British industrialist Robert Owen believed that a new kind of human being in a new order of society would emerge. The community blueprints of the "secular utopians" tended to be rational and well organized, but most of the communes they founded did not work out. New Harmony (1825–1827), Owen's famous experiment, was a disaster, ending in strife and disharmony after only two years. In the 1840s over forty socialist communes were founded on the Fourierite model, a set of plans developed by the French utopian theorist, Charles Fourier. But most of them failed early in their history. Other strictly socialist communes, economically rather than spiritually animated, have appeared from time to time (there was another wave of experiments during the Depression, notably around cooperative farming), but most of these have lived and died in obscurity. Economic goals do not seem to result in viable communities and, for the most part, American socialist or politically animated movements have stayed aloof from the communal movement.

There have been many historical precedents for the founding of intentional communities—based on monastic, millennial, and utopian traditions. Movements of the past, like movements of the 1960's and 1970's, have swung between the ascetic and the ecstatic, the totally amoral and the rigidly moral, but they have all shared the romantic dream of a closer, more fulfilling human community and have risked disapproval by breaking from the establishment to implement the dream.

The Special Flavor of Contemporary Communes

Contemporary communes built on the older traditions but also were shaped by two phenomena unique in scope to the twentieth century: the invention of psychotherapy and development of mental health and personal growth movements, and the widespread availability of psychedelic drugs.

Important for understanding the modern pursuit of community is the invention of psychotherapy and human relations technology, and the increasing psychologization of American life; in John Seeley's words: "the intellectual centralization of self-analysis as a collective and personal preoccupation."[14] As many people have observed, psychotherapy in many respects is the new American religion. Many books deal with the history of psychotherapy, the invention of T-groups and encounter groups, and the vast proliferation of therapeutic techniques; we will consider them only briefly here.

Around the turn of the century the work and thought of Sigmund Freud became known in the United States, but was gradually transformed from a pessimistic and radical theory of the relationship of human beings and society (because of the assumed inevitability of conflict between the id and the ego) to a more positive view of the possibilities for *working on* social relationships in order to alleviate psychic distress. Somewhat later in the century the concept of group therapy was developed; in 1947 the first T-group (T for training, as in laboratory training, but later popularly called *sensitivity training*) was held in Bethel, Maine, to "try out new methods for re-educating human behavior and social relationships";[15] and by the early 1960s—with the appearance of Esalen Institute in Big Sur, California, the encounter group, and a variety of awareness techniques promising to enhance the joys of living and relating—the human potential movement was born. Common to all of these is the notion that personal growth—the psychic version of salvation—occurs through intense, intimate confrontations with others, in which people are *open* and *honest* about their true and immediate feelings.

John Seeley has brilliantly described the emergence of the *mental health movement* in *The Americanization of the Unconscious*. He explains how and why psychotherapy has gained preeminence and how the mental health movement functions as a secular church. He finds the roots of widespread acceptance of the movement in our affluence, brought about by a technological revolution which has diminished suffering from natural disaster, famine, or the want of material objects. He says:

> Lightning rods, ever-normal granaries and the mass production of goods *permits* us to pay some increased attention to the inner life. The mental health movement *encourages* us to do so; the nature of present-day life virtually *forces* it upon us; and the disappearance of the formerly accepted and accredited ways of so doing inclines us to the trial and adoption of new methods. So we move from the "cure of souls" . . . to "psychotherapy" and "mental hygiene"; from preoccupation with salvation to preoccupation with adjustment or peace of mind; from the attack upon evil to the war against anxiety. . . .
>
> That the general shape and form of the resultant movement should in many vital particulars resemble those of any other church ought to occasion no great

astonishment. Like the early church, the mental health movement unites and addresses itself to "all sorts and conditions of men," so only they be "for" mental health as they were formerly for virtue. . . . Like the church, it consists of a body of laymen and specialists, with the latter having as their special charge the psychological welfare of the former, to be worked out, however, by both together. Like the church, there is a "fellowship of all believers" that transcends great variety of belief, but differentiates from the unbelievers. . . . But much more important than these incidental analogies is the fact that the movement occupies or seeks to occupy the heartland of the old territory. The protagonists and practitioners of mental health are increasingly called upon to pronounce on what used to be called moral questions.[16]

Other research confirms this analysis. One such study finds many parallels between today's encounter groups and nineteenth-century religious revivals.[17]

The mental health movement or its daughter branch, the human potential movement, led naturally to a development of intentional communities—communities that try to apply the lessons of the movement into everyday life, to promote healthy, growing environments. Whether or not they succeeded is another question, but the utopian images of spiritual development, attention to immediate feelings, and good honest relating pervading much of the counter-culture were intertwined with the human potential movement.

The recent romance with community also benefited from the widespread availability of psychedelic drugs. Drugs and drug culture have received extensive treatment elsewhere, and I do not want to suggest that new communities and drug use were synonymous. While some communes of the hippie era, notably the crash-pad type, were heavily "into drugs," the vast majority of communes were not. However, the appearance and availability of psychedelics had a wider impact on the whole culture in a way particularly relevant for communes. Consciousness-expanding drugs made it possible for many people to enjoy ecstatic experiences formerly associated with spiritualistic, revivalistic religions. They provided an experience of breaking and transcending limits. They stimulated intimate, collective rituals to which young people who rejected the rituals of established religion could relate ("tripping," passing the joint, etc.). These phenomena opened up new possibilities for many people (whether or not they adopted regular drug use). Among these possibilities for youth and the middle-aged alike: dropping out of the institutionalized routines of the established society and seeking further ecstatic and communal experiences. (I am not suggesting, however, that the use of psychedelics was functional for communal life; the opposite is probably likely true.)

Contemporary communalism, including the great group revival, had several distinct features. Historical traditions remained: monasticism in both Western and Eastern forms; militantly millennial groups coalesced around prophets; old-style religious groups with a strict order of life; and the utopian socialists seeking larger social change. But the overwhelming emphasis in the contemporary movement was a concern with individual fulfillment and relations in a small group.

Contemporary groups used family images more often than community images. By and large, contemporary communes encompassed fewer visions of social reconstruction, fewer hopes for permanence, fewer people, fewer demands on those people, and fewer institutions (most communes do not have their own means of support and depend on outside incomes) than did communal movements of the past. Related to the limiting of scope was the rise of groups without serious ideologies or plans for social reform that banded together in search for relationships. The vast majority of urban communes and many rural communes fell into the latter category. As I described these communes in *Commitment and Community:*

> They develop from friendships rather than groups welded together by shared ideology; their basis is solidarity. Composed primarily of seventeen-to-thirty-year-olds, they may be temporary ways of "making do" for a particular phase in a person's life, rather than permanent settlements oriented toward the future. The language of the counter-culture signals this: "into," "trip," "scene." These terms all convey an episodic quality, a temporary contact that one dips "into," then soon and easily moves "out of." In these communes, lacking a highly developed utopian or transcendent vision, the personal and the intuitive substitute to define the quality of life; e.g., how good are the "vibes," how many "uppers" can a person have. For this reason, personal fulfillment rather than strength or endurance of the group are measures of success for these communes, even though often the first is not possible without the latter.[18]

From "Communitas" to Community: Some Concepts

While the modern romance with community had a unique ambience of its own, the excursion into history we have just completed should also make clear that what we witnessed in the recent past was only one in a series of periodic outbursts of communal fever. Not only do organized communal movements with marked similarity to today's recur throughout Western history, but every period also contains special institutions (like the nineteenth-century revival or the encounter group) which offer the feeling of community without the picking up of stakes. What I wish to suggest is that *communion* or *communitas* (to use two of the many terms for this phenomenon), the immediate, ecstatic experience of oneness with other people, is a recurrent human longing. It is a special experience, set apart from the ordinary, run-of-the-mill, routine, emotionless way in which we conduct the ongoing business of society. Every society, both *primitive* and modern, operates two modes of relating side by side: organized, orderly stable relationships of role and position, caste, class, and rank—what the anthropologist Victor Turner calls *structure*—and spontaneous, emotionally charged, class-less, role-less, and definition-less experiences of common humanity and belonging together—what Turner terms *communitas*. Both modes of relating appear to be necessary to make social life possible.

In *The Ritual Process*, Turner proposes a set of dichotomies to make clear the distinction between communitas and structure:

transition/state
totality/partiality
homogeneity/heterogeneity
equality/inequality
anonymity/systems of nomenclature
absence of property/property
absence of status/status
nakedness or uniform clothing/distinctions of clothing
sexual continence/sexuality
minimization of sex distinctions/maximization of them
absence of rank/distinctions of rank
humility/just pride of position
disregard for personal appearance/care for it
no distinctions of wealth/distinctions of wealth
unselfishness/selfishness
total obedience/obedience only to superior rank
sacredness/secularity
sacred instruction/technical knowledge
silence/speech
suspension of kinship rights, obligations/acknowledgement of them
continuous reference to mystical powers/intermittent reference
foolishness/sagacity
simplicity/complexity
acceptance of pain and suffering/avoidance of them
heteronomy/degrees of autonomy[19]

The coincidence of elements in communitas are those found alongside communal movements of all times and places: a concern with equality and sharing, extending to equal rights for women; rejection of property and private ownership, including the deliberate embrace of poverty; criticism and often rejection of marriage and family ties, expressed in either celibacy or promiscuity; and spirituality. Historically, the strongest outbursts of communalism have occurred alongside many other movements for equality, social justice, and a return to spirituality. In the 1840s and 1850s, as well as in the 1960's and early 1970's, communalism has shared the stage with a women's movement, a black movement, and a growth of

spiritual consciousness. In another context, the list of characteristic elements of communitas could also read as a program of encounter group
values.

Turner shows, in *The Ritual Process*, that the rites and rituals of primitive societies around social transitions and life processes have the
properties of communitas. They render categories of position and social
distinction irrelevant; the group instead experiences global unity. He also
finds the elements of communitas in the hippie movement. He writes of
the hippies:

> These are the "cool" members of the adolescent and young adult
> categories—which do not have the advantages of national *rites de passage*—
> who "opt out" of the status-bound social order and acquire stigmata of the
> lowly, dressing like "bums," itinerant in their habits, "folk" in their musical
> tastes, and menial in the casual employment they undertake. They stress per-
> sonal relationships rather than social obligations, and regard sexuality as a
> polymorphic instrument of immediate communitas rather than as the basis for
> an enduring structured social tie.[20]

We can find characteristics of communitas as a transitional process not
only in social activities encouraging personal life transitions and identity
changes, but also in any movement seeking larger transitions from one
state of society to another. Thus the brotherhood of a revolutionary group
may share many features of communes and may contain frequent experiences of communitas.

Whenever structure appears to overwhelm communitas, as critics of
bureaucracy and technology say it does in modern American society,
individuals go out of their way to create new forms of communitas. If a
person is more accustomed to structure, he may gain his first taste of
communitas in a moment of ecstatic closeness with another person in
which all barriers between the two seem to disappear, and then conclude,
"This is terrific, like nothing I've ever felt before. This is the way life
should be. This is the real me. Why can't we live like this all the time?"
(Such "conversions" are commonly reported in encounter groups.) At
this point the person might attempt to eliminate all characteristics of structure and establish a community base in which communitas can become a
way of life. The resulting community is not identical with communitas in
all respects for it, too, will have business to conduct and relations to
organize in terms of roles or positions or stable expectations if it is to
survive. Communitas, then, consists of experiences which are not necessarily equivalent to concrete, specific communities. (The German social
theorist Herman Schmalenbach has said essentially the same thing, using
the term communion instead of communitas.)[21]

One example of this is the case of the Sunrise Hill commune. It was
founded in a burst of inspiration at a conference and died less than a year

later, as members failed to organize or regulate their shared life. Gordon Yaswen wrote of the initial experiences of communitas:

> The culmination of the conference came upon its last night. A huge campfire was kindled, and beer and wine were available freely. As darkness drew over the dell: a spontaneous music of voice and percussion—wordless and tuneless—began emanating from the assemblage. As more time passed the music went on, and grew until it seemed to fill the very night sky above, and spill out over the dell's rims to drift off across the countryside. This music was not only strong, but surprisingly harmonious as well, with its component parts coming in, and fading out, fluidly and sensitively. But above all else, the music was of both intense feeling and primitive power, and for this to be coming out of a group of (largely) middle-class rebels in one of the most civilized and sophisticated societies known to man, was a miracle in itself. In me, it aroused the belief that I was witnessing the evidence of a turning-point in a societal evolutionary cycle that was about 5000 years long. It seemed to me that night—that Man was upon the verge of a new Primitive Age, and that this group (at Heathcote) was among the vanguard of the descent into that new era. After this music had gone on for quite a while, many of its participants broke into a wild and spontaneous dancing, interspersed with embracings and "heap-ings" of exhausted bodies comfortably atop one another. It was plain by now that we had something on our hands that was decidedly not programmed, and it was anyone's guess as to where it was headed. Something awfully powerful was working its will among us, and the night soon was swept into a frenzied and ecstatic blur. . . .
>
> And so, when the Conference ended, Sun Hill stood as an extremely nebulous, though intensely exciting idea. Those further interested were to meet at the site on July 4, 1966. If later events proved the sagacity of the Sun Hill project questionable and the groundwork spindly; we who were involved must be pardoned for having partaken too heavily and unreservedly of that intoxicating "Yes" spirit that pervaded the Heathcote Conference. The found-ing of Sun Hill was mainly an act of faith; there was little of prudence in it.[22]

At the commune's end, during the next winter, he wrote:

> Somehow our inspiration had evaporated; our spirit had been drained by the months; our love for, and faith in, each other had curled up like the flowers before the frost . . . we were a handful of demoralized people standing about the wreckage of a beautiful dream.[23]

It is sad but true that most communes ended like Sunrise Hill, in the early wreckage of beautiful dreams. The ideal state of communitas re-quires hard work in order to transform it into a concrete community where the work gets done and members feel committed.

My research, reported in *Commitment and Community,* was con-cerned with what it takes to build a strong commune or intentional com-munity out of the dream of communitas. I compared stable, long-lived nineteenth-century and contemporary communes (some lasting as long as several generations) with short-lived communes that fail early in their history in order to learn about the important factors in building a strong community. How does a group operate so as to create a viable commune? I found that stable communes tend to develop social practices based on six commitment-building processes: sacrifice, investment, renunciation, communion, mortification, and transcendence.[24] The order of life in strong communities incorporates these six processes.

Social Practices of Strong Communes: Six Commitment-Building Processes

SACRIFICE

Sacrifice operates on the basis of a simple principle of cognitive consistency: the more it *costs* a person to do something, the more *valuable* he will consider it, in order to justify the psychic *expense* and remain internally consistent. For example, it has been demonstrated in a laboratory setting that when people work for very small rewards they must justify their poorly compensated efforts by belief or commitment, and they became convinced of the worth of what they are doing. In many religions, sacrifice is conceptualized as an act of consecration, bringing one closer to and making one more worthy of salvation; vow of poverty is common. The counterculture's romanticization of poverty can be viewed as a similar thrust toward purity: *poor* is equated with *pure*. In the eyes of the group and in the mind of the individual, sacrifice for a cause indeed makes it sacred and inviolable. It also represents a gesture of thrust in the group, indicating how important membership is. Martin Buber has described the role of sacrifice in building community:

> Community is the inner disposition or constitution of a life in common, which knows and embraces in itself hard "calculation," adverse "chance," the sudden access of "anxiety." It is community of tribulation and only because of that community of spirit; community of toil and only because of that community of salvation.[25]

Commune membership may involve many kinds of sacrifice, beginning with poverty and asceticism. Some kind of abstinence and austerity characterized all successful nineteenth-century communes, as I describe them in *Commitment and Community,* while unsuccessful groups made no such demands on members. Certain sacrifices were part of the general hardship of the early days of a movement (such as poor living quarters and the necessity of building from scratch, and meager food), while others were part of a spiritual discipline, such as the celibacy adopted by Harmony in 1805, or the Shakers' eventual ban on alcohol, or Oneida's occasional austere diet. The contemporary Black Muslims required resistance to worldly temptations. They insisted on "purity," and members give up drinking, smoking, and certain foods. In the late 1960's, large numbers of middle-class youth from affluent families deliberately sacrificed material comforts to move into primitive dwellings, engage in arduous physical labor, and adopt strict vegetarian, organic, or macrobiotic diets.

Some communes sacrifice respectability, deliberately choosing illegal and unconventional behavior. Many observers have pointed out that radical movements often define suffering and persecution by the establishment as an integral part of growth in the movement.[26] Members of many groups use the martyrdom of themselves or their leaders as an aid to commitment. In this sense the collective paranoia of political communes is functional: to believe one is under threat of attack by the police or neighbors lends great importance to the group. Sacrifice, then, welds members together in common suffering and common denial. What has been sacrificed for is thus hard to leave, for it is thereby invested with value.

INVESTMENT

The process of investment provides the (person) with a stake in the group's fate. Time, energy, money, property, and reputation all become bound up with the movement, so that leaving it means leaving behind all these resources. Through investment, individuals become integrated with the group since their resources have become part of its *economy*. Members have, in fact, purchased a share in the proceeds or results of the group and now have a stake in its continued good operation.

We would thus expect to find more strongly committed members in those groups which stress investment. As shown in *Commitment and Community,* this was true in nineteenth-century American utopian communities. More of the longer lasting (or successful) groups than the short-lived (unsuccessful) ones asked the following of members: no membership without full-time involvement; financial contribution and sign-over of property to the group at admission; and sign-over of property received while a member. Moreover, such investments were often irreversible; defectors were sometimes not reimbursed when they left. At Harmony the book in which original contributions were recorded was eventually burned as unneeded.[27]

Benjamin Zablocki also found that investment is an important variable in the survival of contemporary communes. Studying sixty-one groups, he distinguished three categories, on the basis of members' degree of investment in the collectivity: *transcendent communes,* or high investment, in which members "ask not what the commune can do for them but rather what they can do for the commune''; *utilitarian communes,* in which members both invest and withdraw in about equal measure; and *crash-pad communes,* in which there is a constant net drain on the resources of the commune. He found that 38 percent of the transcendent communes survived for five years or more, as compared with only 10 percent of the crash-pad type. Utilitarian communes fell in the middle, with 31 percent surviving over five years.[28]

Investment of money, resources, time, and energy then helps build commitment and ensure a strong collectivity.

RENUNCIATION

Commune membership often involves giving up any social ties that potentially compete with loyalty to the new group. Egon Bittner suggests that a common feature of radical movements is that all traditional extra-group ties be suspended: "the member owes nothing to the outside, regardless of the nature of the pre-existing bond."[29] Renunciation is a common aspect of new communities of all kinds, and generally it centers around three categories of relationships: with the outside world, within male-female couples, and with biological family. Structural arrangements which ensure that the person give up competing relationships, both outside the group and with exclusive subgroupings within the total group, help concentrate not only his or her loyalties and allegiances but also his or her emotional gratification on the group. The potential for satisfaction within the group increases as options for relationships elsewhere are decreased, and he or she must make peace with the group because, in fact, there is no place else to turn.[30]

For this reason, many communes (in particular, rural communes and intentional communities) withdraw physically from the outside world, locate in a new place, and establish separate communities in which all of life can take place. Joining involves giving up one's former home and family and moving to a new place. Such separation from the outside world in order to establish a new community was, of course, a defining feature of many nineteenth-century American utopian movements. Among those communities, the longest lived were those that strongly renounced the larger society. The successful communes were not only geographically isolated, but they were also self-contained, offering most of life's services within their own boundaries. Contemporary Black Muslims in urban areas offered many services within the large Muslim community, without recourse to the larger society, but still remained in cities. But most urban communes were too small to supply all the services necessary in a city. Successful communes of the past tended to view the outside world as evil or sinful and, in their internal arrangements, they sometimes rejected or

violated many of the rules and norms of that larger society, thus reinforcing the act of separation. They tended to adopt a unique form of dress
which would immediately distinguish members from outsiders. Often they
used their own language and terminology, as do many contemporary
communes, where members not only come to speak a similar language but
also to sound and look alike in their speech and mannerisms. Finally,
successful communities tended to ignore the traditions and celebrations of
the outer society and adopt their own instead. The average member of
successful nineteenth-century communes rarely ventured outside of the
boundaries of the community. Similarly, there were rules and guidelines
for interacting with visitors who came into the community, as there are in
many closed groups.[31]

Modern communes shared many of these signs of renunciation. There
was a special countercultural dress style brought in by the hippies and
modified by members of rural communes, who wore clothing appropriate
for farm work. Rejection of outside holidays and rituals was also common,
as was their replacement by distinctive commune celebrations. Many
rural communes also turned their collective backs on the outside by not
reading newspapers or seeking information about national or world
events. Hostility to the old order or the established society, and symbolic
or actual rejection of it are common themes in communal movements.

Some urban communes also recognized their special problem: the outside is always close and always intruding. In many groups people tried to
avoid the outside, to stay home as much as possible and bring visitors in.
When one woman living next door to an urban commune remarked to its
members that she and her boy friend always went to the commune and
they never came to her house, she was told that "energy was flowing
inward in this system, and it can't flow outward."

Communal movements also encourage renunciation of exclusive ties
or special subunits within the group, since they could result in competition
for loyalty and affection and potentially they exclude some people and
isolate members from one another. Thus members are often asked to
reduce the importance of one-to-one or family relationships in order to
gain membership in the larger community of the movement. I have noted
in *Commitment and Community* that two opposite and extreme practices
may be involved in such renunciation: celibacy or promiscuity. The two
poles are represented among nineteenth-century American communes, as
in Shaker celibacy and Oneida complex marriage. In both arrangements,
no person can have exclusive sexual or emotional intimacy with any other,
either because it is entirely prohibited, or because sexual intimacy is widespread and available to anyone in the group. In both cases, sex and
intimacy are regulated.

Recent communes also swing between celibacy and promiscuity, although a widening, rather than a restricting, of sexual experience was the

rule. Some religious communes, including the Hare Krishna sect, were highly ascetic about sex; though the Hare Krishna movement permitted marriage, the sect tried to ensure that special relationships did not come between the person and the collectivity. Married couples chanted special prayers while having intercourse, a continual reminder of their larger obligations. Early hippie and counterculture communes, on the other hand, wanted to *smash monogamy* and, by sharing sex widely, develop group rather than private relationships.

The American Shakers provide one example of further renunciation which some communal groups encourage: breaking bonds with the biological family. This renunciation is well expressed in the words of a Shaker hymn:

> Of all the relations that ever I see
> My old fleshly kindred are furthest from me.
> How ugly they look, how hateful they feel,
> To see them and hate them increases my zeal.

This hymn summarizes the social functions of renunciation: the cutting of old social ties so as to be a zealous member of the new community.

COMMUNION

The *we-feelings* of brotherhood (or sisterhood) and comradeship and the experience of communitas encompassed by communion are essential to the determination to maintain the group, even in the face of obstacles and disagreements. Communion mechanisms as defined in *Commitment and Community,* develop equality, fellowship, and group consciousness which, in the ideal case, lead to the formation of a cohesive, emotionally involving community.

Common background and shared experience help develop communion; thus it is no accident that most communal movements most successfully recruit from members of the same strata. New recruits may join because of their primary ties to other members, and most contemporary communes are based on solidarity among friends rather than on shared belief. Most stable contemporary communes begin, at least, with members of the same family or friendship net.

Though prior personal bonds may give the commune an edge, primary ties can develop among strangers if the community provides members with opportunity for shared activities that put newcomers in contact with each other more than with former friends and outside relationships. A Black Muslim reported to John Howard:

> When you start going to the temple four or five times a week and selling the newspaper you do not have time for people who are not doing these

things. . . . All the friends I have now are in the Nation. Another Brother and I get together regularly and read the Koran and other books. . . . We read and talk about the things we read. . . . I couldn't do that with my old friends.[32]

In this case, as in many others, common activity and work help solidify ties among members. Those communes, then, that have their own enterprises may create a greater sense of communion than those in which members' involvements with each other are more limited. *Careers* or jobs within the commune are thus functional beyond their task accomplishment, material proceeds, or utility in helping members renounce former lives; they also help cement the new bonds. Those communes which can and do encompass a person's whole life have a better opportunity to build communion.

Beyond shared activities and space is the experience of shared ownership, both of property and work. These emphasize joint effort over individual achievement and common identity over private ambition; members' efforts are directed toward group rather than individual ends, and they share equally in group tasks and rewards. While not always absolutely egalitarian, many communes still aim at this kind of brotherhood, represented by communal property ownership and job rotation. Private property and individual careers are not always compatible with gaining strong we-feeling.

Many groups develop a sense of communion by finding common endeavors in which all members can participate. Constructing a building seems to me to be the most important of these, for it leaves the group with a permanent monument to their shared work. The emphasis on constructing and shaping one's own environment central to the commune movement may have roots here. The end—the actual building—may not be as important for the group's identity as the means by which the building came about. I found on many communes an infectious sense of group pride in self-made buildings, which often leads to great festivity, like the gala celebration in the Connecticut Bruderhof community after the construction of new beams in the dining hall.

Shared ownership is also sometimes experienced as a subtle group tendency rather than as an explicit norm. It was explicit, of course, in the communistic groups of the last century, which held all property in common (including clothes in Oneida) and found joint ownership an important source of community feeling. Many contemporary groups shared clothes too; in one simply because it got to be too much bother to sort the laundry. In another, an urban group, members began by sharing towels, then moved to sheets, and then owned furniture collectively. Even in modern "doing your own thing" communes, where much individual ownership is maintained and demands minimized, some people still felt it important to take pride only in that which is shared. (In a rural hip commune, there was a woman, a particularly respected member of the commune, who had just finished building a very striking looking one-room, two-level redwood house, with the help of some others in the group. It was very cleverly and artistically created, with windows that were really sculptures, and framed with pieces of twisted wood found in a nearby forest. She expressed both great pride and guilt—guilt that she should have such a nice house of her own.) That collective ownership is effective in building commitment and group solidarity is borne out by the experiences of nineteenth-century American utopian movements. The longest lived of these groups usually owned everything in common down to such personal possessions as clothing, and shared work on a rotating basis.

Among the most important communion mechanisms are the very rituals which often give the commune part of its definition as a spiritual and familial happening. Through ritual, members affirm their oneness and pay homage to the ties that bind them. Ritual provides symbols by which group loyalty is elevated, celebrated, and enhanced. Here Durkheim's classic proposition that religion is the worship of the immediate social group becomes clear.

Ritual was an important part of the life of many communes of the past, especially for the Shakers. Every evening each Shaker group gathered to dance, pray, and express the togetherness of the group. As mentioned earlier, many aspects of the Shaker ceremony resemble encounter group exercises (in both fantasy, energetic body movement, and emotional outburst). After the ritual, one Shaker reported that the group felt "love enough to eat each other up." The Shakers also had a number of special ceremonies in which spiritual or imaginary events occurred. Some of these centered around spiritual fountains on nearby "magic" hills near the villages reputedly populated by angels and spirits—but spirits only Shakers could see, of course. Among the spirits were such luminaries as Napoleon, George Washington, and Queen Elizabeth.

Present-day communes often created their own rituals, some with the same special or hidden elements that only group members share. Those groups oriented around religion or mysticism found ritual an abundant source of group feeling. But even creedless communes develop ritual. One group began its *family meetings* by sitting in a circle and chanting "om." A number of communes used sensory-awakening or encounter exercises as a kind of ritual. Rituals can even be invented around mundane events like cleaning the refrigerator. In one community the group arose around six-thirty and met on a grassy lawn at seven for T'ai Chi Chuan exercises—a beautiful flowing Chinese moving meditation. For an hour they stood in rows and moved together, all following the pattern. And then they went in to breakfast.

Examples of such ceremonies are plentiful, from rituals involving nudity among the medieval Free Spirit movement to the Maori of New Zealand's communal dance around a pole invested with symbols. All involve group members in a common, emotionally charged experience in which barriers among them are broken down. It is impossible to remain separate and aloof, for example, when everyone is vulnerable.

The sharing of food and of song are both experiences which, cross-culturally, are invested with group meaning and help develop and sustain communal solidarity. Through such rituals, people have a chance to feel their togetherness in a purely emotional way. Music was particularly important in the life of many communal groups—from listening to it together to singing or playing instruments. Several communes had rock bands and cut records (Synanon, Mel Lyman's Avatar group of Fort Hill, and the Spirit in the Flesh of Brotherhood of the Spirit).

Finally, communion is also developed through shared persecution or danger. Facing a common enemy helps bind people together, as conflict theorists from Georg Simmel to Lewis Coser have pointed out.[33] Conflict outside the group also helps redirect hostilities and aggression that would otherwise be directed inward—toward other group members—as Freud noticed. Thus emotion in the group can be effectively polarized: love and affection, expressed in ritual and common ownership, toward fellow members with whom there is a common identity and in whom there is trust; and hostility and anger, expressed in actions toward the movement's enemies, toward the outside which is distrusted, feared, and perceived to be different. Plainly, then, communal movements partly achieve communion by having enemies, just as they gain activity and purpose by facing dangers and challenges from unconverted multitudes.

The anthropologist Peter Worsley suggests that emotional enthusiasm is heightened through a deliberate break with convention. This "welds the devotees together in a new fraternity of people who have deliberately flouted the most sacred rules of the old society. They are bound together by their sense of guilt. . . . They are bound together in mutual support against all those who still hold the old beliefs."[34] We can expect communion so generated to decline should the movement become legitimized and conventional; indeed, something like this may have happened to the radical political groups of the late 1960s.

All of the communion mechanisms described here help create strong affective bonds which can hold people together even when other factors threaten to tear them apart. Communities imbued with them are strong, stable, and long lived.

MORTIFICATION

An important aspect of strong commitment to a new community, I argued in *Commitment and Community,* is changing one's identity—the death of the old self and the birth of a new one. According to Benjamin

Zablocki, this phenomenon has been recognized by the Bruderhof communes:

> The only reason it is not possible to create a new society out of the materials of the old is that people will not release their death grip on the old. . . . [One might draw the lesson that] the costs of commune formation are greater than has generally been anticipated. The Bruderhof would say that the cost is nothing less than the death of the old self to make room for the birth of the new.[35]

The identity change process if variously conceptualized and symbolized by communal movements: taking a new name, as in many hippie communes and the Black Muslims; calculating a person's age from the date of joining or conversion, as in Synanon. Worsley said that "one of the most appropriate and widespread symbols of rebirth is adult baptism, which gave its very name to the Anabaptist movement."[36] Mortification processes attempt to convince the person that true meaning and worth derive from allowing his self-concept to be directed by the group. They provide a new set of criteria for evaluating the self and choosing behavior; they reduce all people to their common human denominator, distinctions erased, and transmit the message that the self becomes whole and fulfilled when the person can finally live up to the new moral standards of the new community. Even hippie communes talked of the need to "change people's heads" around.

Mortification sometimes occurs during a defined period of resocialization, after which the person is considered reborn. But it may also be an ongoing process in which humility, brotherhood, and the meaning of the group are continually held before the person, while his prideful, separate ego is continually eroded. The concept and functions of mortification are captured in lines from several Shaker songs: "That great big I, I'll mortify," "I will bow and be simple"; and in this Shaker verse:

> Whoever wants to be the highest
> Must first come down to be the lowest,
> And then ascend to be the highest
> By keeping down, to be the lowest.[37]

Systems of feedback, confession, self-criticism, and mutual criticism are one way to promote mortification. Successful nineteenth-century utopian communities often had sessions where the individual "bared his soul"—admitting weaknesses, failings, and imperfections. The individual humbled herself before the group, in actuality or imagination. No part of her life was left unexamined and uncriticized, since all of her belonged to the new community. The group probed into the most intimate matters: sex, history, personal hygiene. Such mortification practices indicated to members that even their innermost *selves* were being *watched* by others, that the group cared about their thought and character, and that the community provided standards for growth. Often the criticism was public, as in Oneida and Amana, and part of a group process remarkably like an encounter group or a Synanon *game* session today. The criticism sometimes consisted of feedback by the group to the person about his good, as well as his bad, behavior and characteristics. For members of Oneida, particularly, mutual criticism was considered purifying, cleansing, and uplifting, even though painful at the time. Mutual criticism provided a convenient form of participatory government and conflict management for the radical community, and we see many examples of it among revolutionary groups. Group encounters and feedback sessions are frequent in contemporary communes.

Public denouncements and visible mortifying sanctions for deviants within the group (as in the shaved heads of Synanon deviants) also promote mortification. One kind of mortifying sanction practiced by the Shakers was the ritual known as the *warring gift*, engaged in when a member was thought to be losing his commitment or violating community norms. A number of Shakers would approach the deviant, point at him, and shout "Woe! Woe!" or invectives in "tongues," while shaking, whirling, and trembling, supposedly under divine inspiration. The purpose was to elicit a confession before the elders. Contemporary Synanon sessions are not very different from this.

Finally, internal stratification systems, based not on the status criteria of the outer society but on the new moral and spiritual standards of the new community, can aid mortification. The new member can begin at the bottom of the spiritual ladder and earn his way up through devotion and commitment. Such systems of *spiritual differentiation*, in which, as Synanon said, "character is the only status," were frequent among successful, but not unsuccessful, nineteenth-century American utopian communities. They were found, then, in groups that build strong commitment.

Mortification helps destroy the old self, prideful and oriented to the standards and status of the outside. It paves the way for the person to gain a new sense of self and a new source of status and self-esteem. At the same time, through mortification, the new self is oriented around devotion and a loyalty to the group.

TRANSCENDENCE

Finally, commitment is built through transcendence, defined in *Commitment and Community* as the experience of higher power and meaning residing in the group, the felt connection with forces and events outside of and beyond the life of a single person. Transcendence provides the new sources of identity and meaning. It ties the group and its purpose to cosmic events, to unknown forces that impel and explain life itself. Martin Buber described transcendence as fulfilling "the need of [a person] to feel his own house as a room in some greater, all-embracing structure . . . a longing for that *rightness* which, in religious or philosophical vision, is experienced as revelation or idea, and which of its very nature cannot be realized in the individual but only in human community."[38]

Transcendence develops out of a group's ideology, its leadership practices, and its connection with tradition. It develops to the extent that a group successfully captures and promotes awe and mystery. This is the spiritual component of group life—the reaching upward into the unknown.

This *reaching upward* is expressed by a contemporary urban commune that talked about the need to have a "spirit in the center." Said one member:

> The reason you get together is the spirit, and it can be a fairly primitive spirit or it can be a highly differentiated, clearly understood spirit, and it guides you— it's an oversoul, if you will. It also has a black side, it does nasty things to you as well as give you life. It threatens you and puts you through changes and paces. You begin to realize that you have to want to do the commune thing awfully bad and to keep doing it; otherwise, it's much easier to go off and be middle America.

This group was atypical, for most urban communes lacked such religiously infused ideologies. But this partly accounted for the group's strength. It was over four years old (unusually enduring for an urban group), ran a bookstore and a craftshop, and built its life around a shared mystical world view, which was used as an explanation of all events. A house astrologer plotted members' charts; a person with a pain in his ankle might be told that it's due to astrological factors. In many respects this group resembled spiritually based rural communes such as Brotherhood of the Spirit, Jesus communes, or Eastern meditation centers, all with their transcendent ideologies.

Among transcendence-inducing characteristics are elaborate ideologies which explain the essential nature of humanity and which account both for how things became as they are and how they will be in the future. Such ideologies tend to be characteristic of successful communes, as they are of millennial movements. Millennial ideas help connect the person with great power, because he will be part of the *in-group* after the revolutionary reversal in which the powerful are toppled and the meek inherit. Echoes of this were heard throughout political radicalism and the counterculture. Explanations for the present ordering of power and a promise of sweeping change are first elements of transcendence-inspiring doctrines. The Brotherhood of the Spirit's doctrine, for example, was that people go through seven life stages: from the materialistic, to the intellectual, to a sixth level "when karmic energy uses you like the hand on a harp," and, finally, an escape from "this astral plane." They believed themselves to be the "teachers of the Aquarian Age" and expected to communicate their message to the world after a number of *earth changes,* such as civil strife, ecological disasters, and earthquakes have proven that the old order was no longer viable.

A second feature of transcendence-inspiring doctrines is the exclusiveness of the ideas or insights contained in the doctrine—that they are *secret,* revealed only to a few. To some extent, the more esoteric and unconventional the doctrine (within the often infinite limits of credibility), the better for building commitment to a defined and bounded community, for by accepting them the believer becomes special. Georg Simmel wrote brilliantly on the social functions of a secret. Regardless of content, he argued, the fact of having a secret helps weld the sharers of it into a special elect entity.[39] Perhaps for this reason, some movements only share all of their knowledge with the converted. John Lofland discovered this secretiveness in the *doomsday cult,* for example. The Shakers, as mentioned earlier, had special hills near their villages populated with spirits only believing Shakers could see.

Third, an ideological system includes transcendence if it helps tie the movement to something powerful and successful. The *inevitability* of the coming of the New Age is important for building believers' commitment; it cannot be a matter of likelihood or probability. Social movements do not coalesce around "maybes." Millennial prophets continue to predict the end of the world on specific dates even though the possibility of error is much greater when a time is specified. (Yet disconfirmation of prophecy may not be as important as *social* certainty; members may support one another in beliefs that external events prove wrong.) Many movements promote feelings of success not only by tying themselves to historical inevitability but also to people and events that have themselves been successful. Many movements ally themselves with great figures of history, the most notable, for Christian-oriented groups, Christ himself. Some groups stress his physical presence in the movement by considering the contemporary leader an incarnation, as did Harmony, the Shakers, and other groups in the last century, and Fort Hill and Brotherhood of the Spirit communes in the early 1970's. In addition, the Shakers had the convenient *capacity* to convert the dead.

Finally, ideologies that promote transcendence are comprehensive and particular. They tend to give meaning even to the most minute daily acts and include every part of a person's life under their wings. No part of life is unconnected to or unexplained by or unguided by the movement's ideas. This is true of such groups as the Shakers, where doctrine even guided such events as getting out of bed in the morning. Other religious communes, and those based on Eastern mysticism, also invoke transcendence in minute daily acts; an ex–Bahai group in New Mexico had a book of household quotes from the scriptures and a sign about the uplifting joy of sweeping. The holiness of physical work is expressed by a number of groups. The Shakers called their prayer *laboring* and their productive work was a kind of prayer in which they were doing God's work according to the standards of the angels. The Lama community, a modern Eastern spiritual center, described itself as "a retreat for those seeking self-discovery through philosophy, religion, and hard physical labor."

A movement also gains power and meaning through charismatic figures who seem to possess special magical, superhuman properties. Even if leaders did not have these traits, it is likely, in some instances, that followers would invent them. It is also important that the charisma be somewhat removed from the life of the ordinary member—be, in effect, *larger than life*. Charismatic leaders have been found throughout communal history. They are likelier in groups with a strong religious orientation. In the past there were Ann Lee of the Shakers, John Humphrey Noyes of Oneida, and George Rapp of Harmony, all godlike to their followers. Recently there were Mel Lyman of Fort Hill (the Avatar), Michael Metelica of Brotherhood of the Spirit, Charles Dederich of Synanon, and others. Many communes, especially small, highly participatory urban ones, survived without *gurus,* but in larger groups the charismatic served as catalyst, founder, teacher, model, or spiritual center.

The kinds of ideas and practices that promote transcendence provide a new source of identity, status, and esteem for the person. They imbue the community and its demands with moral necessity, for the person's own internal sense of meaning becomes wedded to the group's beliefs. Communes with features of transcendence, my research reported in *Commitment and Community* has demonstrated, last longer than groups without any such processes.

The six commitment-building processes just described give a group greater prospects of endurance and stability. It is not necessary to have all of them; indeed, no one group has all the characteristics I have mentioned. But having a number of commitment mechanisms adds to a commune's chances for success-solidarity as a group and fulfillment for individual members.

The Benefits of Communalism

The communal experience is that of a special culture, with its own language, meaning system, and interpretation of events. In this sense it is a *whole way of life,* as noted earlier in our initial definition. Intentional communities vary in their size, scope, and comprehensiveness: some have had land and territory, resembling villages, while others (the urban variety) often have leased houses on busy city blocks; some have had highly organized enterprises, from farming to production, while others have sent their members to work at outside jobs. But, despite this range of differences, all communes and communities of minimum stability have had one thing in common: members share the experience of a distinctive, separate, value-infused culture. The very fact that the lines between inside and outside are so clear is an indication. This was vividly illustrated one night at dinner at an urban commune. While others were waiting for dinner, two members walked in direct from their outside jobs. He, a social worker, was wearing a striped, button-down shirt and a tie. She, a bilingual teacher, had on high-heeled shoes, nylon stockings, and a tailored suit. They left to change, and when they reappeared for dinner they had shed the uniform of the outside and merged with all the other counterculture costumes. The transformation was complete, and they were almost unrecognizable as the occupants of "straight" jobs. He wore tattered blue jeans tied with a bright orange woven belt and no shirt. She wore a long flowing faded cotton skirt and a peasant blouse.

What gives the communal experience a special cultural flavor is not only the three values mentioned earlier (spiritualism, familialism, and pastoralism) but also the distinctive order of life it creates, as demonstrated in the preceding section. Communities have their own life rhythms, rituals, myths, legends, and heroes; their own language, dress, and food preferences. Their environments are dotted with special colors and objects. They attempt to bring communitas into their daily lives through a focus on the equality of all, rejection of material ambitions, and attention to process and growth, emphasizing the present moment and present experiencing.

The special culture contained by intentional communities has offered several psychologically important experiences. The first and most obvious is that of intimacy and belonging. Members live closer together than other members of our society and share more of life. Rather than accidentally belonging to families or to vague, shifting peer groups, they are deliberately and firmly included in a distinct, bounded group. This group may provide support of both emotional and material varieties. The longer lived and more comprehensive the community, like the large-scale intentional communities of the past and prosperous modern groups like Synanon (which became a utopian community instead of a self-help group for drug addicts), the more the member's welfare is ensured. In addition to the social welfare aspects of communal living, the sheer human contact is often exhilarating to members.

The second important experience communes provide is a sense of power and specialness. Close-knit small communities offer a person direct participation in the immediate events shaping his destiny, an experience important for psychological well-being but too often lacking in the wider society. The sense of direct participation has been cited through communal history, and control over one's environment is often cited as a motivating factor in formation of communes. Moreover, some communes enable a member to manipulate resources and events far beyond what he would have access to were he not living communally. "Where else but at Synanon," members asked, "could ex–drug addicts run a million-dollar corporation?" Similarly, at Brotherhood of the Spirit in western Massachusetts, 300 young people, virtually penniless, alone, managed, in the space of four years, to acquire and run several businesses (including a main street pool hall and coffee house) and to construct large, impressive dormitory buildings.

The pooling of resources in communes, then, often provides another kind of power: the ability to accomplish immensely more than one could alone or with a small family. A sense of potency also comes from another aspect of communal life: the members' possession of secret, shared knowledge. Community members often express the feeling that they know the truth about how people should live together, that they are the pioneers in a new revolution, that they are the vanguard of a New Age. While this feeling also makes them more vulnerable to failures, it is still a source of gratification and commune members, like the rest of us, can rationalize the failures: As a woman in a long-lived urban commune with several enterprises put it: "When I first read a commune magazine about the communes that failed, I was scared. But then I realized that the ones that work didn't have time to write anything." A classic sociopsychological study also demonstrates that the failure of a group's prophecy does not necessarily destroy the group; members can still remain welded together by their special, secret truths, even if externally demonstrated to be incorrect, because of the social support they give one another.[40]

Finally, a commune's special culture is psychologically important in the meaning and understanding it provides, in its infusion of values into every aspect of daily life. We have already seen how the order of life developed by successful or stable groups makes no aspect of life separable from values that give meaning to each activity. And, often, all parts of human life are offered their place in the group's world: work, love, prayer, and others. Most important, psychological rhythms are often taken into account, and expressive outlets for both love and hostility, activity and contemplation, may be provided. One of the most vivid examples of this rhythm is the way the Shaker communities struck a balance between asceticism and ecstasy. All day long the celibate Shakers worked in silence, but at night they burst out in ecstatic fervor in ritual dances and encounters, offering song, motion, and a great deal of physical contact. As part of the ritual, Shakers could express great love for fellow Shakers as well as criticisms each in their place; at the same time, the bulk of hostility was transferred to the outer society, which Shakers bitterly condemned. The Shakers, therefore, were not only celibate and *re*pressive, but also highly *ex*pressive. Viable communities not only channel some emotions, as all human organizations do, but they also offer meaningful outlets for the range of human feelings.

Tensions and Conflicts

Intentional communities have their problems as well as their rewards. Some of these stem from paradoxes inherent in the attempt to translate communitas into community: over time, spontaneity gives way to order. Communitas itself, the spontaneous, emotion-laden feeling of belonging together, is inherently unstable as a basis for social organization, and it must be routinized into an ongoing structure, with clear expectations, in order for any group to survive. Emotional "highs" are unpredictable and unreliable foundations for group life, especially when the group must earn a livelihood and run a household in addition to expressing the feelings of its members. Communes which hope to avoid rules, roles, positions, and all of the accouterments of structure, and count only on a brand of naïve anarchism—everyone doing his own thing—tend not to survive beyond the "honeymoon," unless they find a way to build and sustain commitment and collective solidarity. They need the structure and organization described earlier. Benjamin Zablocki wrote of the inevitable movement from spontaneity to order:

> Most communes start out with no restrictions on behavior. Everyone is allowed to do his own thing at all times. It is expected that the gentleness, love, and compassion engendered by mystical drug experiences (or in other ways) will prove adequate substitutes for the moral and legal constraints which all other societies have found necessary. The initial experiences are often encouraging and exhilarating. . . . After a while, however, the strains inherent in such situations begin to reassert themselves. Work may slow down, jealousies may arise, or people may start spending more and more time away from the commune. At the same time, as the commune grows older, it may begin to give its attention to complex tasks such as starting a school, expanding housing facilities, or developing a business enterprise. Increased strain on one hand, and more complex tasks on the other, eventually lead most communes to abandon their absolute anarchism in favor of some more restricted alternative.[41]

The tension between spontaneity and order makes communalism a somewhat unstable social form, and it takes time for groups to strike a balance between strong collective demands and routine organization, and individual freedom of expression. Without some degree of order, a commune can be nothing more than an emotional episode. But for certain people this is fine; they would prefer to see a group dissolve if it cannot live by spontaneity alone.

In the past, as I showed in *Commitment and Community,* the most enduring communes have also been the most organized, centralized, and tightly controlled. Georg Simmel, writing about secret societies, pointed to an important paradox in social life: that groups which leave the established order to be free of its restrictions often end up duplicating that very order in their new organization. Simmel called this a *ubiquitous social norm:* "structures which resist larger, encompassing structures through opposition and separation, nevertheless themselves repeat the forms of these structures." Thus, if the unorganized route leads to poor chances for survival, the highly organized route carries its own dangers: rigidity and authoritarianism. In one sense, all communes, as George Hillery pointed out, offer individuals the ultimate freedom: the choice to stay or to leave.[42] Yet throughout human history some people have always voluntarily subjected themselves to control by others. And the danger of the highly organized community is that it loses its human feeling and leaders use their power toward destructive rather than constructive ends. (Charles Manson was an example of this, although a rare one. He was accused of leading his band of devoted female followers on a campaign of violence and murder.) Most communities of the highly organized variety combine strong leadership with much democratic participation, but they still resemble formal organizations more than the Garden of Eden.

Communes also face the specter of the tyranny of group pressure for conformity. Group pressure plays a large part in the life of all communal orders, from the large, highly organized intentional community to the small, loose urban commune. The close relations of a commune make it difficult for the person to hide behavior or feelings from others, and fear of violating the standards of the group often play a large part in motivating conformity. As Joseph Eaton and Robert Weil pointed out in their analysis of the Hutterites, in place of the many symptoms of alienation and estrangement that afflict people in the wider society, members of the Hutterite colonies often suffer from acute guilt feelings when they feel they have violated group norms. John Bennett wrote:

> Hutterites may be especially vulnerable to feelings of lack of acceptance by their fellows. . . . Kaplan and Plaut discuss what they call "uncertainty of acceptance" as a general pattern among Hutterites. . . . Test protocols were interpreted as showing needs for "affiliation and comradeship" and "even greater" fears of lack of support by other human beings and rejection of the individual by the group.[43]

Such needs for acceptance mean that other people can often exert a great deal of control over the individual's behavior. In Synanon group pressure was the primary form of social control. The Synanon *games* and *stews* (their group encounters) were responsible not only for the cohesion of the community but also for the striking and dramatic changes in the former-drug-addict members. (Edgar Z. Friedenberg attacked Synanon for "brainwashing.")[44] Even in unorganized communes informal group pressure still constituted a powerful influence for conformity, and members often reported great discomfort at "letting down the group." It may be, in fact, that group pressure is more oppressive in anarchistic groups that lack formal statements of rules and understandings; in the absence of clarified standards and expectations, nearly any event is a potential source of anxiety, and those who are loudest and most aggressive may exert the most control over others.

Group pressure also arises around decision making. Most communes pride themselves on their democratic decision-making procedures in which all members supposedly have an important voice. Many modern groups attempted to make decisions only by consensus. Yet, as in most groups, some members still exerted more influence than other members; the verbally facile can beat out the shy and quiet; and challenging what appears to be the will of the majority, or the sentiment of the meeting, is very threatening and anxiety provoking for many people. Field observations of urban communes showed that the ideal of decision making by consensus may break down in reality. In one thirteen-person house, a coalition of three men nearly always got their way on issues, and anyone failing to add one's positive vote was looked upon with disapproval because "we all should agree on everything." Benjamin Zablocki noted a similar phenomenon in the Bruderhof community:

> The pressure to conform stems from the very nature of the Bruderhof decision-making system. The idea of the preexistent decision (God's will) makes it a serious matter to be caught on the wrong side of an issue. One is not merely expressing a minority opinion, but possibly showing that he is out of touch with the Holy Spirit. Furthermore, the need for absolute unanimity, far from giving power to the individual dissenter, places a great burden upon him not to dissent unless he is pretty sure that he's right. It is an interesting paradox that, at least in the highly cohesive group, making the power of dissent equivalent to the power of veto is a means of weakening rather than strengthening dissent.[45]

Dissent is even more difficult in a group that is less certain of itself and more likely to perceive conflict as a sign of breakdown.

Intentional communities experience pressures for conformity not only in overt behavior but also in feelings. One of the principles of communitas is that it represents a common bond of feeling among all members and that emotions as well as behavior are an important part of the life of the group. But many communes translate this to mean that a unanimity of sentiment must exist at all times. Such unspoken norms make it difficult for members to express challenges to the prevailing agreements or the communal ideologies and myths. It is particularly hard to say that things are not going as well as everyone is pretending. As one commune member wrote:

> Ten or more of us were able to live in the same house in the middle of a dirty, cold, alienating city by playing some pretty heavy games. The game we played most is called Peace Treaty. The object of the game is to hide your feelings enough that you don't have to deal with them, or anyone else's. You play it by being very polite and considerate toward your cohabitants—smiling at them, asking about their health, activities, etc., while avoiding any of the commitments involved in really being interested in how they're feeling or where their heads are at. You also avoid expressing your own hostilities and fears.

Even the Hutterites, at the opposite end of the communal spectrum, too, often find it convenient to avoid discussing conflict and maintaining myths of solidarity.[46]

Far from fostering honesty and openness, then, some communal situations may encourage overt support for myths about group sentiment and suppress any statements or behavior that might challenge the myths. (The same process occurs, of course, in other primary groups, such as families.) These myths can describe negative as well as positive states, as Arthur Gladstone's description of what one commune meant by "honesty" indicated:

> A couple of years ago I helped start a commune. We all felt frustrated and oppressed by conventional ways of living and wanted to work out a loving way of living together. I left after a few months, upset and discouraged about what we were doing to each other. We had developed a style of "honesty" which emphasized being able to tell someone what you thought was wrong with them. We sought freedom from the pressures and limitations of conventional relationships, such as marriage—and criticized and pressured anyone who didn't relate in ways we thought desirable. We gave up a lot of the restrictions and hypocrisies of our society—but we didn't give up the most crucial thing, the habit of attacking anyone we disagreed with. We were all very clever at spotting other people's faults and very willing to tell about them—and we had great trouble noticing our own shortcomings and were mostly unwilling to hear about them. I am still very interested in communal living and eager to do it again, but I want to be with people who feel the urgency of discovering and ending our attacks on one another.[47]

Another set of tensions in communal life stems from relationships. We have noted that successful communes value collective solidarity to such an extent that they often attempt to preclude exclusive or private relationships. The nineteenth-century Oneida community is perhaps the most dramatic example of a community that attempted to eliminate all such attachments, while still producing children and having an active sex life. Oneida practiced *complex marriage* and reared all its children together. Yet dyadic ties and mother-child attachments persisted despite community criticisms, occasional punishments such as separation, and strong norms against "sticky" relationships. Members had to work hard to ignore the special feelings engendered in them by a lover or a parent or a child. Reports from the Hutterites and Shinkyo, a Japanese commune, also indicate the difficulty with which adults put aside impulses to favor their own children or kin in decisions or distribution of supplies.[48] In the Hutterite community the persistence of parent-child favoritism is especially striking because of several centuries of communal socialization; Hutterites have never experienced life in separate isolated nuclear families. Denying or ignoring special feelings can provoke strain in communal situations, then, as well as produce the diffusion of emotional energy necessary for collective commitment.

The pressure against exclusive relationships for the individual arises both out of ideology and group *need.* Communal ethics often condemn marriage and monogamy as "capitalistic" institutions, responsible for many of the psychological ills of our society. (John Humphrey Noyes of Oneida wrote a pamphlet, *Slavery and Marriage,* in the 1800s.) More than one modern group tried to smash monogamy, but then ran afoul of the very human feeling for attachment. A few communes experienced trouble in attempting to institute group marriage. They began by saying, "We're a commune. Therefore we should all be sleeping with one another." However, they found that not only did most members not like the "freer" sex, they felt oppressed by it.

More often, communal groups contain special relationships (such as couples), but there are strong pressures against the pair not to withdraw their energy from the group. The need to centralize energy of all kinds on the group and diffuse it among members and group tasks seems to be an underlying dynamic in group life: the more radical the group, the more unstable and uncertain its future and the more sources of outside support unavailable to it, the stronger the need to collect energy. (Many social theorists have written about this phenomenon.) The tendency to *collect energy* is surprisingly universal, even in the loosest communes with the most limited programs and expectations for future existence. A member of a small, loose urban commune of students explained the situation in her house, around a couple:

> There were subtle hostilities from almost everyone being directed at their partial withdrawal from the rest of us into their own world. It came out in criticisms of their relationship by various people. . . . It's true that if you start to get into a heavier-than-usual relationship with anyone, you should have every freedom to let it develop. Living in a commune, however, carries with it a responsibility to maintain a certain amount of awareness of where everyone else is at and how what you are doing is affecting the total group.

But the group need sometimes conflicts with individual desires, leading to tensions and strain. An example of such conflict arose in another urban household. According to members of the group, they had only one expectation for a member: attention to the group, an attention which could be made up of little things. The crisis for this commune arose over the presence of a couple that met in the house and ultimately left. Their attachment to each other was extremely strong, and he, especially, was jealous of any time she spent away from him. Finally, they were confronted in a meeting about their neglect of the house and the other members. Said one person:

> We thought we had no expectations, but in fact we really did. We wanted a time commitment and attention to the house. This was difficult to acknowledge because we hadn't made it explicitly, but we could feel the strain around [the couple].

In group meetings the meaning of the terms *close, communal,* and *enough time* were discussed; a great deal of pressure was brought to bear on the couple. Finally, they announced their decision to leave before any request was made to them. It was important to the group that it happened that way, for members reported that they would have been hard pressed to expel them. The two people who left, however, said that they felt judged. They said that the group was responding not to them but to the issue of "coupleness"—it simply did not want couples.

Attachments outside of the commune are often as much a source of strain as relationships within, for they may even physically remove the member for periods of time. Conflicts frequently arise, especially in urban communes surrounded by other people, around the issue of how much time members are spending with the group.

Applications and Assessment

Communes and intentional communities respond to recurrent human longings, and romanticization of the joys of sharing a whole way of life closely and intimately with others. Like all romances, the flirtation with community gives way to demands for commitment and routinization of the relationship, to difficulties and tensions as well as magical moments. There is no perfect society. There is only *human* society. And all communities are very human societies. They have problems, but they also offer solutions to many pressing social problems; among them, the loneliness, alienation, and sense of estrangement that drive many people into therapy. Communes, then, may be not only intentional communities and sometimes religious communities, but also therapeutic communities. The definitional lines here are fine and hard to draw. Synanon began as a therapeutic community for drug addicts, then found that its way of life was so attractive to many people without drug problems that it began to emphasize its communalism rather than its therapy. (The Synanon story has received extensive treatment elsewhere.)[49] Similarly, growth and learning centers of all kinds have found they cannot do one without the other: either they cannot offer therapeutic experiences, such as encounters, without developing a whole community or, like the experience of Tale of the Tiger, a Zen center in Vermont, they cannot build the right kind of community without therapeutic attention to the psychic states of the people who come.

It is unlikely that all of us will be living in communes in the future for communes are an extreme, radical, and demanding social form. The time of social excitement over communes has already passed. However, many of us may feel the effects of communalism on our family relationships (more open and more closely connected with other families), on our community life (more attention to relationships in neighborhoods and other territories and the sharing of resources, as in food co-ops), and at work (more worker cooperatives and worker democracies and more rotation, sharing of work, and attention to values in other settings). Some may live in communes for a period of time as a personal learning experience, like going to college, to learn about handling close relationships and sharing decision making in a cooperative fashion. Many may live in communes or group situations during transitional phases in our lives—between schools, careers, jobs, or marriages—when the supportive aspects of the intense communal group are most needed.[50]

Finally, we may see mental hospitals, reform schools, and even prisons replaced by therapeutic communities with many features of a commune, even though the expectation is that most people (the *clients*) will come for only short periods of time while others (the *staff*) will make the community their career. R. D. Laing's experiments with psychiatric communes like Kingsley Hall in Britain are one example; halfway houses for mental patients are another.

In Maxwell Jones' classic description of the therapeutic community he helped found out of the Industrial Neurosis Unit at an English hospital, we see many aspects of communalism put into practice. First, the community defined *therapy* not as an isolated event but as total experience covering the entire working day and contacts with others. *Treatment* consisted primarily in fostering the normal interactions of a healthy community life. Members (*patients*) performed work of social value, attended daily community meetings in which many decisions were made and grievances expressed, and participated in groups which not only offered encounter experiences (feedback, psychodrama, etc.) but also shared dancing, music, and art. The staff attempted to break down hierarchical distinctions and interact with patients on a human level, while still retaining some of their special authority. The hospital unit was an attempt to construct a culture, a whole way of life, for it was felt that only with such integration of parts of life would therapy be possible. The success rates in this environment were very high.[51]

While the romance with community may not settle down to a permanent marriage, we still have much to learn and gain from the communal experience. Its messages encourage us to reexamine the premises on which all of our social institutions are built. Its lessons offer guidelines on the infusing of daily life with community spirit. And its failures and stresses remind us of the fallibility of too glib schemes for social perfection: declaring a *new era* does not make it so, and many tyrannies are perpetuated in the name of freedom. In both the old and the new flirtation with the idea of community lurk basic human and societal dialectics: structure and communitas, security and liberation. The communities all of us inhabit find their own, sometimes uneasy, balances.

Notes

Introduction

1. D. Bell, *The Cultural Contradictions of Capitalism* (New York: Basic Books, 1976).

Chapter 1

1. G. R. Bach and H. A. Illing, *"Historiche Perspective Zur Gruppen Psychotherapie,"* in *Z. Psychosomatic Medicine* (1956), pp. 131–147; H. Mullan and M. Rosenbaum, *Group Psychotherapy* (New York: Free Press, 1962); M. Rosenbaum and M. Berger, *Group Psychotherapy and Group Function: Selected Readings* (New York: Basic Books, rev. ed., 1975).
2. G. R. Bach, *Intensive Group Therapy* (New York: Ronald, 1954); G. R. Bach, Personal Communication (1972); R. J. Corsini, "Historic Background of Group Psychotherapy: A Critique," in *Group Psychotherapy*, vol. 8 (1955), pp. 213–219; *Ibid.*, pp. 219–255; R. J. Corsini, *Methods of Group Psychotherapy* (New York: McGraw-Hill, 1957); S. B. Hadden, "Historic Background of Group Psychotherapy," in *International Journal of Group Psychotherapy*, vol. 5 (1955), pp. 162–168; J. I. Meiers, "Origins and Developments of Group Psychotherapy," in *Sociometry,* vol. 8 (1945), pp. 499–534; Rosenbaum and Berger, *Group Psychotherapy and Group Function;* S. R. Slavson, "Pioneers in Group Therapy," in *International Journal of Group Psychotherapy*, vol. 1 (1951), pp. 95–99; G. W. Thomas, "Group Psychotherapy: A Review of the Recent Literature," in *Psychosomatic Medicine,* vol. 5 (1948), pp. 166–180.
3. Mullan and Rosenbaum, *Group Psychotherapy;* J. H. Pratt, "The Tuberculosis Class: An Experiment in Home Treatment," in *Proceedings, New York Conference on Hospital Social Service*, vol. 4 (1917), pp. 49–68.
4. E. Worcester, S. McComb, and I. H. Coriat, *Religion and Medicine* (London: Methuen, 1908).

5. Mullan and Rosenbaum, *Group Psychotherapy*.

6. J. H. Pratt, "The Use of Dejerine's Methods in the Treatment of the Common Neuroses by Group Psychotherapy," in *Bulletin of the New England Medical Center*, vol. 15 (1953), pp. 1–9.

7. J. Dejerine and E. Gauckler, *The Psychoneuroses and Their Treatment* (Philadelphia: Lippincott, 1913).

8. E. W. Lazell, "The Group Treatment of Dementia Praecox," in *Psychoanalysis Review*, vol. 8 (1921), pp. 168–179.

9. E. W. Lazell, "The Group Psychic Treatment of Dementia Praecox by Lectures in Mental Re-education," in *U.S. Veterans' Bureau Medical Bulletin*, vol. 6 (1930), pp. 733–747.

10. E. Jones, *The Life and Work of Sigmund Freud*, vol. 2 (New York: Basic Books, 1955), p. 55.

11. I. Yalom, "Review of S. Freud, Group Psychology, and the Analysis of the Ego," in *International Journal of Group Psychotherapy*, vol. 24, no. 1 (1974), pp. 67–82.

12. S. Freud, *Group Psychology and the Analysis of the Ego* (London: Hogarth Press, 1948).

13. A. Le Bon, *The Crowd* (London: Benn, 1952).

14. R. Dreikurs, "Group Psychotherapy: General Review," in *First International Congress of Psychiatry* (1950), 1952, pp. 223–237; R. Dreikurs and R. J. Corsini, "Twenty Years of Group Psychotherapy," in *American Journal of Psychiatry*, vol. 110 (1954), pp. 567–575; R. Dreikurs, "Early Experiments with Group Psychotherapy," in *American Journal of Psychotherapy*, vol. 13 (1959), pp. 882–891; R. Dreikurs, "Group Psychotherapy from the Point of View of Adlerian Psychology," in H. M. Ruitenbeck, ed., *Group Therapy Today* (New York: Atherton Press, 1969).

15. J. L. Moreno, *Die Gottheit als Komediart* (Vienna: Anzengruber Verlag, 1911); J. L. Moreno, *Who Shall Survive?* (New York: Beacon House, 1953); J. L. Moreno, *The First Book on Group Psychotherapy* (New York: Beacon House, 1957).

16. Moreno, *Die Gottheit als Komediart*.

17. J. L. Moreno, "Application of the Group Method to Classification," in *National Commission on Prisons and Prison Labor* (1932); J. L. Moreno, "Psychodrama and Group Psychotherapy," in *Sociometry*, vol. 9 (1946), pp. 249–253.

18. Moreno, *Who Shall Survive?*

19. J. L. Moreno, *Sociometry, Experimental Method, and the Science of Society* (New York: Beacon House, 1951).

20. J. L. Moreno, "The Viennese Origins of the Encounter Movement, Paving the Way for Existentialism, Group Psychotherapy, and Psychodrama," in *Group Psychotherapy*, vol. 22 (1969), pp. 7–16.

21. R. Fine, D. Daly, and L. Fine, "Psychodance: An Experiment in Psychotherapy and Training," in *Group Psychotherapy*, vol. 15, no. 3 (1962), pp. 203–223.

22. J. Facos, "Group Psychotherapy and Psychodrama in a College Classroom," in *Group Psychotherapy,* vol. 16, no. 3 (1963), pp. 173–176.

23. T. Burrow, *A Search for Man's Sanity: The Selected Letters of Trigant Burrow* (New York: Oxford University Press, 1958).

24. M. Rosenbaum, "Review of Trigant Burrow," in *Psychoanalysis and Psychoanalytic Review,* vol. 47, no. 2 (1960), pp. 118–122, originally in "The Psychoanalyst and the Community," in *Journal of the American Medical Association,* vol. 62 (1914), pp. 1876–1878.

25. *Ibid.*

26. L. C. Marsh, "Group Therapy and the Psychiatric Clinic," in *Journal of Nervous and Mental Disease,* vol. 82 (1935), pp. 381–392.

27. L. C. Marsh, "Group Therapy of the Psychoses by the Psychological Equivalent of the Revival," in *Mental Hygiene,* vol. 15 (1931), pp. 328–349.

28. L. Wender, "The Dynamics of Group Psychotherapy and its Applications," in *Journal of Nervous and Mental Disease,* vol. 84, no. 1 (1936), pp. 54–60.

29. P. Schilder, "Results and Problems of Group Psychotherapy in Severe Neurosis," *Mental Hygiene,* vol. 23 (1939), pp. 87–98; P. Schilder, "The Cure of Criminals and the Prevention of Crime," in *Journal of Criminal Psychopathology* (1940), pp. 140–161.

30. L. Lowrey et al., "Group Therapy" (special section meeting), in *American Journal of Orthopsychiatry,* vol. 13 (1943), pp. 648–690; S. R. Slavson, *An Introduction to Group Therapy* (New York: Commonwealth Fund, 1943); S. R. Slavson, *Bibliography on Group Psychotherapy* (New York: American Group Psychotherapy Association, 1950).

31. S. R. Slavson, "Treatment of Withdrawal Through Group Therapy," in *American Journal of Orthopsychiatry,* vol. 15 (1945), pp. 681–689 (p. 689).

32. Lowrey et al., "Group Therapy," pp. 648–690 (p. 656).

33. H. S. Ginott, "Play Group Psychotherapy: A Theoretical Framework," in *International Journal of Group Psychotherapy,* vol. 8, no. 4 (1958), pp. 410–418.

34. A. Wolf, "The Psychoanalysis of Groups," in *American Journal of Psychotherapy,* vol. 4 (1949), pp. 16–50; vol. 1 (1950), pp. 525–558.

35. A. Wolf and E. K. Schwartz, *Psychoanalysis in Groups* (New York: Grune and Stratton, 1962).

36. E. K. Schwartz and A. Wolf, "Psychoanalysis in Groups: The Mystique of Group Dynamics," in W. C. Hulse, ed., *Topical Problems of Psychotherapy, II, Sources of Conflict in Contemporary Group Psychotherapy* (Basel: Karger, 1960), pp. 119–154.

37. *Ibid.,* p. 126.

38. A. A. Low, *Mental Health Through Will-training* (Boston: Christopher, 1950).

39. R. J. Corsini and B. Rosenberg, "Mechanisms of Group Psychotherapy: Processes and Dynamics," in *Journal of Abnormal and Social Psychology,* vol. 15, no. 3 (1955), pp. 406–411.

40. Dreikurs, "Group Psychotherapy from the Point of View of Adlerian Psychology," in *Group Therapy Today;* S. H. Foulkes, Letter, in *International Journal of Group Psychology,* vol. 21, no. 4 (1971), p. 497; G. D. Goldman, "Some Applications of Harry Stack Sullivan's Theories to Group Psychotherapy," in *Group Therapy Today;* N. Hobbs, "Group Centered Psychotherapy," in C. Rogers, ed., *Client-centered Therapy* (Boston: Houghton Mifflin, 1951); B. Kotkov, "Bibliography of Group Therapy," in *Journal of Clinical Psychology,* vol. 6 (1950), pp. 77–91; F. Powdermaker and J. Frank, *Group Psychotherapy* (Cambridge: Harvard University Press, 1953); S. Rose, "Horney Concepts in Group Psychotherapy," in *Group Therapy Today*.

41. J. W. Klapman, *Group Therapy: Theory and Practice* (New York: Grune and Stratton, 1946); J. W. Klapman, "The Case for Didactic Group Psychotherapy," in *Disorders of the Nervous System,* vol. 11, no. 2 (1950), pp. 35–41; J. W. Klapman and W. H. Lundin, "Objective Appraisal of Textbook Mediated Group Psychotherapy with Psychotics," in *International Journal of Group Psychotherapy,* vol. 3 (1952), pp. 116–126.

42. S. Gifford and J. A. Mackenzie, "A Review of Literature on Group Treatment of Psychoses," in *Disorders of the Nervous System,* vol. 9 (1948), pp. 19–23.

43. C. Boenheim and L. O. Dillon, "Group Psychotherapy in the Mental Hospital," in *Mental Hospital* (1962), pp. 380–381; J. D. Frank, "Group Psychotherapy," in *Veterans Administration Technical Bulletin*, vol. 91, no. 10 (1953).

44. G. Saslow and J. D. Matarazzo, "A Psychiatric Service in a General Hospital: A Setting for Social Learning," in *Mental Hospital,* vol. 13 (1962), pp. 217–220.

45. J. Wolpe, *Psychotherapy by Reciprocal Inhibition* (Stanford, Calif.: Stanford University Press, 1958); J. Wolpe and A. Lazarus, *Behavior Therapy Techniques* (New York: Pergamon Press, 1968); J. Wolpe, *The Practice of Behavior Therapy* (New York: Pergamon Press, 1969).

46. A. A. Lazarus, "Group Therapy of Phobic Disorders by Systematic Desensitization," in *Journal of Abnormal and Social Psychology,* vol. 63, no. 4 (1961), pp. 504–510.

47. Wolpe, *Psychotherapy by Reciprocal Inhibition*.

48. E. Jacobson, *Progressive Relaxation* (Chicago: University of Chicago Press, 1938).

49. A. A. Lazarus, "Behavior Therapy in Groups," in G. M. Gazda, ed., *Basic Approaches to Group Psychotherapy and Group Counseling* (Springfield, Ill.: Thomas, 1968).

50. N. Hobbs, "Group-centered Psychotherapy," in C. Rogers, ed., *Client-centered Therapy* (Boston: Houghton Mifflin, 1951).

51. J. C. Bock, "Self-Orientation and Orientation to Others During Nondirective Group Psychotherapy," in *Medical Service Journal of Canada,* vol. 17, no. 2 (1961), pp. 111–117; T. Gordon, *Group-centered Leadership*

(Boston: Houghton Mifflin, 1955); L. Gorlow, E. L. Hoch, and E. F. Telschow, *The Nature of Non-directive Group Psychotherapy* (New York: Columbia University Press, 1952).

52. C. R. Rogers, "The Process of the Basic Encounter Group," in J. F. Bugental, ed., *Challenges of Humanistic Psychology* (New York: McGraw-Hill, 1967).

53. C. R. Rogers, "In Retrospect: Forty-Six Years," in *American Psychologist,* vol. 29 (1974), pp. 115–123.

54. A. E. Bergin and S. L. Garfield, eds., *Handbook of Psychotherapy and Behavior Change: An Empirical Analysis* (New York: Wiley, 1971); A. E. Bergin and H. H. Strupp, *Changing Frontiers in the Science of Psychotherapy* (Chicago: Aldine-Atherton, 1972); O. F. Kernberg, E. D. Burstein, L. Coyne, A. Appelbaum, L. Horwitz, and H. Voth, "Psychotherapy and Psychoanalysis: Final Report of the Menninger Foundation's Psychotherapy Research Project," in *Bulletin of the Menninger Clinic,* vol. 36 (1972), pp. 3–275.

55. C. R. Rogers, "The Increasing Involvement of the Psychologist in Social Problems: Some Comments, Positive and Negative," in *California State Psychologist,* vol. 9 (1968), pp. 29–31.

56. Rogers, "In Retrospect: Forty-Six Years."

57. H. F. Thomas, "Encounter—The Game of No-game," in A. Burton, ed., *Encounter* (San Francisco: Jossey-Bass, 1969), pp. 69–80.

58. Burton, *Encounter,* p. 23.

59. W. M Lifton, *Working with Groups* (New York: Wiley, 1961).

60. A. B. Smith, L. Berlin, and A. Bassin, "Problems in Client-centered Group Therapy with Adult Offenders," in *American Journal of Orthopsychiatry,* vol. 33, no. 3 (1963), pp. 550–553.

61. O. H. Mowrer, *Learning Theory and Personality Dynamics* (New York: Ronald, 1950); O. H. Mowrer, *Psychotherapy Theory and Resarch* (New York: Ronald, 1953).

62. G. Saslow and J. D. Matarazzo, "A Psychiatric Service in a General Hospital," pp. 217–220; I. F. Small, R. Matarazzo, and J. G. Small, "Total Ward Therapy Groups in Psychiatric Treatment," in *American Journal of Psychotherapy* (1963), pp. 254–265.

63. F. K. Taylor, "A History of the Group and Administrative Therapy in Great Britain," in *British Journal of Medical Psychology,* vol. 31 (1958), pp. 153–173, parts 3, 4.

64. J. Bierer, ed., *Therapeutic Social Clubs* (London: Lewia, 1948); J. Bierer, "Modern Social and Group Therapy," in N. G. Harris, ed., *Modern Trends in Psychological Medicine* (London: Hoeber, 1948); J. Bierer, "The Day Hospital: Therapy in a Guided Democracy," in *Mental Hospital,* vol. 13 (1962), pp. 246–252.

65. W. R. Bion, *Experiences in Groups* (New York: Basic Books, 1961).

66. D. Stock and H. Thelen, *Emotional Dynamics and Group Culture* (New York: New York University Press, 1958).

67. S. H. Foulkes, *An Introduction to Group-analytic Psychotherapy* (London: Heinemann, 1948); S. H. Foulkes and E. J. Anthony, *Group Psychotherapy* (London: Penguin Books, 1957); S. H. Foulkes, "Psychoanalysis, Group Psychotherapy, Group Analysis," in *Acta Psychotherapy Separatum,* vol. 7 (1959), pp. 119–131; S. H. Foulkes, Letter, in *International Journal of Group Psychotherapy,* vol. 21, no. 4 (1971), p. 497.

68. S. H. Foulkes, *Personal Communication,* 1973.

69. Foulkes, Letter.

70. Foulkes and Anthony, *Group Psychotherapy.*

71. *Ibid.*

72. H. A. Ezriel, "A Psycho-analytic Approach to the Treatment of Patients in Groups," in *Journal of Mental Science,* vol. 96 (1950), pp. 744–747.

73. Bierer, *Therapeutic Social Clubs.*

74. M. Jones, *The Therapeutic Community: A New Treatment Method in Psychiatry* (New York: Basic Books, 1953); M. Jones, "Group Psychotherapy and the Therapeutic Community," Paper read at 39th Annual Conference of American Orthopsychiatry Association, Chicago, March 1962.

75. M. Jones, Personal Communication, 1974.

76. Stock and Thelen, *Emotional Dynamics.*

77. D. S. Whitaker and M. A. Lieberman, *Psychotherapy Through the Group Process* (Englewood Cliffs, N.J.: Prentice-Hall, 1964).

78. T. M. French, *The Integration of Behavior,* vols. 1, 2 (Chicago: University of Chicago Press, 1952–1954).

79. F. Perls, *Gestalt Therapy Verbatim* (Lafayette, Calif.: Real People Press, 1969); F. Perls, *In and Out of the Garbage Pail* (Lafayette, Calif.: Real People Press, 1969).

80. F. S. Perls, R. E. Hefferline, and P. Goodman, *Gestalt Therapy* (New York: Julian Press, 1951).

81. R. L. Harman, "Goals of Gestalt Therapy," in *Professional Psychology,* vol. 5, no. 2 (1974), pp. 178–184.

82. J. Fagan and I. Shepherd, eds., *Gestalt Therapy Now: Theory, Techniques, Application* (Palo Alto, Calif.: Science and Behavior Books, 1970); A. Levitsky and F. Perls, "The Rules and Games of Gestalt Therapy," in H. M. Ruitenbeck, ed., *Group Therapy Today* (New York: Atherton Press, 1969); E. Polster and M. Polster, *Gestalt Therapy Integrated: Contours of Theory and Practice* (New York: Brunner-Mazel, 1973).

83. E. Berne, "The Nature of Intuition," in *Psychiatric Quarterly,* vol. 23 (1949), pp. 203–218; E. Berne, *Principles of Group Treatment* (New York: Oxford University Press, 1966).

84. E. Berne, *Games People Play* (New York: Grove Press, 1964).

85. W. Reich, *Character Analysis* (New York: Orgon Institute Press, 1949).

86. G. R. Bach, "The Marathon Group: Intensive Practice of Intimate Interaction," in *Psychological Reports,* vol. 18 (1966), pp. 995–1002.

87. F. H. Stoller, "Marathon Group Therapy," in G. M. Gazda, ed., *Innovations to Group Psychotherapy* (Springfield, Ill.: Thomas, 1968); F. H. Stoller, "Accelerated Interaction—A Time Limited Approach Based on the Brief Intensive Group," in *International Journal of Group Psychotherapy*, vol. 18 (1968), pp. 220–225.

88. A. Wolf, "The Psychoanalysis of Groups," in *American Journal of Psychotherapy* vol. 4 (1949), pp. 16–50; vol. 1 (1950), pp. 525–558.

89. M. Berger, ed., *Videotape Techniques in Psychiatric Training and Treatment* (New York: Brunner-Mazel, 1970).

90. I. Alger, "Audio-visual Techniques in Family Therapy," in D. Bloch, ed., *Techniques of Family Therapy* (New York: Grune and Stratton, 1973); J. B. Reckless, "Audio-visual Feedback in Group Psychotherapy," in *Canadian Psychiatric Association Journal* vol. 17 (1972), pp. 331–332.

91. C. F. Midelfort, *The Family in Psychotherapy* (New York: Blakiston, 1957).

92. N. Ackerman, *The Psychodynamics of Family Life* (New York: Basic Books, 1958).

93. M. Grotjahn, *Psychoanalysis and the Family Neurosis* (New York: Norton, 1959).

94. L. Von Bertalanffy, *General Systems Theory—Foundation, Development, Applications* (New York: Braziller, 1968).

95. S. E. Able and M. N. Jacques, "Systems Theory Approach to the Identification of Judgmental Errors in Family Treatment Decisions," in *International Journal of Social Psychiatry*, Spring-Summer 1973, pp. 110–113; H. E. Durkin, *The Group in Depth* (New York: International Universities Press, 1964).

96. R. Speck, "Psychotherapy of the Social Network of a Schizophrenic Family," in *Family Process*, vol. 6 (1967), pp. 208–219.

97. J. Bell, "Recent Advances in Family Group Therapy," in M. Rosenbaum and M. Berger, eds., *Group Psychotherapy and Group Function*, rev. ed. (New York: Basic Books, 1975).

98. M. Rosenbaum, "Co-therapy," in H. Kaplan and B. Saddock, eds., *Comprehensive Group Psychotherapy* (Baltimore: William and Wilkins, 1971); and H. H. Spitz and S. B. Kopp, "Multiple Psychotherapy," in *Psychiatric Quarterly Supplement*, vol. 31 (1957), pp. 295–331.

99. M. A. Lieberman, I. D. Yalom, and M. B. Miles, *Encounter Groups: First Facts* (New York: Basic Books, 1973).

100. M. P. Lawton, "A Group Therapeutic Approach to Giving Up Smoking," in *Applied Therapeutics*, vol. 4 (1962), pp. 1025–1028.

101. M. P. Farrell, "Transference Dynamics of Group Psychotherapy," in *Archives of General Psychiatry*, vol. 6 (1962), pp. 66–76.

102. H. E. Durkin, "Vicissitudes of the Concept of Transference in the Clinical Practice of Group Psychotherapy," in *American Journal of Orthopsychiatry*, vol. 32, no. 2 (1962), pp. 313–314; H. E. Durkin, *The Group in Depth*, p. 313.

103. Foulkes and Anthony, *Group Psychotherapy*.

104. I. Ziferstein, "Group Psychotherapy in the Soviet Union," in *American Journal of Psychiatry*, vol. 129, no. 5 (1972), pp. 595–599.

105. H. R. Teirich, *"Gruppentherapie und Dynamische Gruppenpsychotherapie in Deutschland,"* in *Heilkunst*, vol. 10 (1957), pp. 1–6.

106. M. Rosenbaum, "Resistance to Group Psychotherapy in a Community Mental Health Clinic," in *International Journal of Social Psychiatry*, vol. 9, no. 3 (1963), pp. 1–4; M. Rosenbaum, "Current Controversies in Psychoanalytic Group Psychotherapy and What They Mask," in L. D. Eron and R. Callahan, eds., *The Relation of Theory to Practice in Psychotherapy* (Chicago: Aldine, 1969), pp. 63–84; M. Rosenbaum, "The Responsibility of the Psychotherapist for a Theoretic Rationale," in *Group Process*, vol. 3 (1970), pp. 41–47; I. Yalom, *The Theory and Practice of Group Psychotherapy* (New York: Basic Books, 1970).

107. D. L. Snow and M. L. Held, "Group Psychotherapy with Obese Adolescent Females," in *Adolescence*, vol. 8, no. 31 (1973), pp. 407–414.

108. J. Henderson, "Training Groups for Public Health Nurses," in *Canada's Mental Health*, vol. 21, no. 5 (1973), pp. 12–14; A. Mattson and D. P. Agle, "Group Therapy with Parents of Hemophiliacs," in *Journal of the American Academy of Child Psychiatry*, vol. 11, no. 3 (1972), pp. 558–571.

109. L. Ormont, "The Use of Group Psychotherapy in the Training of Marriage Counselors and Family Life Educators," in *Marriage and Family Living*, vol. 24, no. 22 (1962), pp. 140–150; J. S. Perlman, "Group Therapy of Married Couples," in *International Journal of Group Psychotherapy*, vol. 10 (1959), pp. 136–142.

110. M. Siegel, "Group Psychotherapy with Gifted Underachieving College Students," Paper read at 19th Annual Conference of American Group Psychotherapy Association (mimeographed, 1962).

111. H. Holt and C. Winick, "Group Psychotherapeutic Experiences with Clergymen," in *Journal of Religious Health*, vol. 1, no. 2 (1962), pp. 113–126.

112. G. Mickow and M. Benson, "Group Therapy for Sex Offenders," in *Social Work*, vol. 18, no. 4 (1973), pp. 98–104.

113. H. M. Rosow, "Some Observations on Group Therapy with Prison Inmates," in *Archives of Criminal Psychodynamics*, vol. 1, no. 4 (1955), pp. 866–896.

114. C. C. Jew, T. L. Clanon, and A. L. Mattock, "The Effectiveness of Group Psychotherapy in a Correctional Institution," in *American Journal of Psychiatry*, vol. 129, no. 5 (1972), pp. 602–605.

115. D. G. Appley and A. E. Winder, *T-Groups and Therapy Groups in a Changing Society* (San Francisco: Jossey-Bass, 1973); K. W. Back, *Beyond Words: The Story of Sensitivity Training and the Encounter Movement* (New York: Russell Sage Foundation, 1972); R. Carkhuff, "A Human Technology for Group Helping Processes," in *Educational Technology*, vol. 13 (1973), pp. 31–38; G. M. Gazda, ed., *Basic Approaches to Group Psychotherapy and Group Counseling*, 2nd ed. (Chicago: Thomas, 1975); C. Goldberg and M. C. Goldberg, *The Human Circle: An Existential Approach to the New Group Therapies* (Chicago: Nelson-Hall, 1973); M. Lieberman, I. Yalom,

and M. Miles, *Encounter Groups: First Facts* (New York: Basic Books, 1973).

116. N. Murray, "Malunion of the Femur Treated by Group Psychotherapy and Psychodrama," in *Southern Medical Journal,* vol. 55, no. 9 (1962), pp. 926–939.

117. K. W. Back, "The Experimental Group and Society," in *Journal of Applied Behavioral Science,* vol. 9, no. 1 (1973), pp. 7–20; H. M. Levinson, "Use and Misuse of Groups," in *Social Work,* vol. 18, no. 1 (1973), pp. 66–73.

118. E. A. Locke, "Is Behavior Therapy Behavioristic," in *Psychological Bulletin,* vol. 76, no. 5 (1971), pp. 318–327; E. A. Locke, "Purpose Without Consciousness: A Contradiction," in *Psychological Reports,* vol. 25 (1969), pp. 991–1009.

119. J. A. Johnson, *Group Therapy: A Practical Approach* (New York: McGraw-Hill, 1963).

Chapter 2

1. W. Bion, *Experience in Groups* (New York: Basic Books, 1959); M. Jones, "Group Treatment with Particular Reference to Group Projection Methods," in *American Journal of Psychiatry,* vol. 101 (1944).

2. T. Burrow, "The Group Method of Analysis," in *Psychoanalytic Review,* vol. 14 (1927).

3. P. Schilder, "Results and Problems of Group Psychotherapy in Severe Neurosis," in *Mental Hygiene,* vol. 23 (1939), pp. 87–98.

4. J. Moreno, *Who Shall Survive?* (New York: Beacon House, 1953).

5. Bion, *Experience in Groups*.

6. S. H. Foulkes and E. J. Anthony, *Group Psychotherapy: The Psychoanalytic Approach* (London: Penguin, 1957).

7. C. Rogers, "The Process of the Basic Encounter Group," in J. T. Bugental, ed., *Challenges of Humanistic Psychology* (New York: McGraw-Hill, 1967).

8. D. Bakan, *The Duality of Human Existence: An Essay on Psychology and Religion* (Chicago: Rand-McNally, 1966).

9. J. Dewey, *Character and Events* (New York: Holt, 1929).

10. M. Lakin, *Interpersonal Encounter: Theory and Practice in Sensitivity Training* (New York: McGraw-Hill, 1972).

11. C. Argyris, "On the Future of Laboratory Education," in *Journal of Applied Behavioral Sciences,* vol. 3 (1967), pp. 153–183.

12. S. Koch, "The Image of Man Implicit in Encounter Group Therapy," in *Journal of Humanistic Psychology,* vol. 11, no. 2 (1971), pp. 109–128.

13. M. Lakin, "Some Ethical Issues in Sensitivity Training," in *American Psychologist,* vol. 24 (1969), pp. 923–928; Lakin, *Interpersonal Encounter: Theory and Practice*.

14. J. Sherwood, "An Introduction to Organization Development," in J. W. Pfeiffer and J. E. Jones, eds., *1972 Annual Handbook for Group Facilitators* (Iowa City: University Associates Press, 1971).

15. D. McGregor, *The Human Side of Enterprise* (New York: McGraw-Hill, 1960).

16. J. P. Campbell and M. D. Dunnette, "Effectiveness of T-Group Experiences in Managerial Training and Development," in *Psychological Bulletin,* vol. 70 (1968), pp. 73–104.

17. J. R. Gibb, "The Effects of Human Relations Training," in A. E. Bergin and S. L. Garfield, eds., *Handbook of Psychotherapy and Behavior Change* (New York: Wiley, 1971).

18. D. Stock, "A Survey of Research on T-Groups," in L. P. Bradford, J. R. Gibb, and K. D. Benne, eds., *T-Group Theory and Laboratory Method* (New York: Wiley, 1964).

19. M. Lieberman, I. Yalom, and M. Miles, *Encounter Groups: First Facts* (New York: Basic Books, 1973).

Chapter 3

1. H. M. Ruitenbeek, *The New Group Therapies* (New York: Avon, 1970), p. 22.

2. W. Sheldon, *Varieties of Delinquent Youth* (New York: Harper, 1949), quoted in W. C. Schutz, *Elements of Encounter* (Big Sur, Calif.: Joy Press, 1973), p. 6.

3. J. F. T. Bugental, *The Search for Authenticity* (New York: Holt, Rinehart, & Winston, 1965).

4. E. Shostrom, *Man the Manipulator* (Nashville, Tenn.: Abingdon Press, 1967).

5. E. Berne, *Games People Play* (New York: Grove Press, 1964).

6. R. D. Laing, *The Politics of Experience* (New York: Pantheon, 1967).

7. A. Janov, *The Primal Scream* (New York: Dell, 1970).

8. H. Prather, *Notes to Myself* (Lafayette, Calif.: Real People Press, 1970).

9. M. Buber, *I and Thou* (New York: Scribner, 1958).

10. G. Land, *Grow or Die* (New York: Random House, 1973).

11. C. R. Rogers and B. Stevens, *Person to Person* (Lafayette, Calif.: Real People Press, 1967).

12. J. Gibb, in L. N. Solomon and B. Berzon, eds., *New Perspectives on Encounter Groups* (San Francisco: Jossey-Bass, 1972).

13. J. Gibb, in H. A. Otto and J. Mann, eds., *Ways of Growth* (New York: Viking Press, 1969).

14. J. Gibb, in H. A. Otto, ed., *Human Potentialities* (St. Louis: Green, 1968).

15. W. C. Schutz and C. Seashore, in L. N. Solomon and B. Berzon, eds., *New Perspectives on Encounter Groups* (San Francisco: Jossey-Bass, 1972).

16. A. H. Maslow, *Toward a Psychology of Being* (Princeton: Van Nostrand, 1962).

17. C. Moustakas, in H. A. Otto, ed., *Human Potentialities* (St. Louis: Green, 1968).

18. S. Jourard, in H. A. Otto and J. Mann, eds., *Ways of Growth* (New York: Viking Press, 1968), p. 2.

19. S. Jourard, in L. Blank, G. B. Gottsegen, and M. D. Gottsegen, eds., *Confrontation: Encounters in Self and Interpersonal Awareness* (New York: Macmillan, 1971.)

20. C. Moustakas, in H. A. Otto, ed., *Human Potentialities* (St. Louis: Green, 1968).

21. A. Watts, *The Wisdom of Insecurity* (New York: Random House, 1951; Vintage Books).

22. F. S. Perls, in J. Fagan and I. L. Shepherd, eds., *Gestalt Therapy Now* (New York: Science and Behavior Books, 1970.)

23. F. S. Perls, R. F. Hefferline, and P. Goodman, *Gestalt Therapy* (New York: Dell, 1965).

24. F. S. Perls, *Gestalt Therapy Verbatim* (Lafayette, Calif.: Real People Press, 1969).

25. J. F. T. Bugental, ed., *Challenges of Humanistic Psychology* (New York: McGraw-Hill, 1967).

26. R. Assagioli, *Psychosynthesis* (New York: Hobbs, Dorman, 1965).

27. A. Lowen, *The Betrayal of the Body* (New York: Macmillan, 1967).

28. C. Selver and C. Brooks, in H. A. Otto, ed., *Explorations in Human Potentialities* (Springfield, Ill.: Thomas, 1966), p. 493.

29. B. Gunther, in H. A. Otto, and J. Mann, eds., *Ways of Growth* (New York: Viking Press, 1968).

30. B. Gunther, *Sense Relaxation* (New York: Macmillan, 1968).

31. F. S. Perls, *Ego, Hunger, and Aggression* (New York: Random House, 1969).

32. *Ibid.*, p. 120.

33. F. S. Perls, *The Gestalt Approach and Eye Witness to Therapy* (Ben Lomond, Calif.: Science and Behavior Books, 1973), p. 114.

34. K. W. Back, *Beyond Words* (Baltimore: Penguin, 1972), p. 6.

35. J. Gibb, in H. A. Otto, ed., *Human Potentialities*.

36. J. Gibb, in L. N. Solomon and B. Berzon, eds., *New Perspectives on Encounter Groups*.

37. W. C. Schutz, *Here Comes Everybody* (New York: Harper and Row, 1971).

38. S. Jourard, in L. Blank, G. B. Gottsegen, and M. D. Gottsegen, eds., *Confrontation: Encounters in Self and Interpersonal Awareness*.

39. C. Moustakas, in H. A. Otto, ed., *Human Potentialities*.

40. Back, *Beyond Worlds,* pp. 106–116.

41. Schutz, *Here Comes Everybody*, p. 3.

42. V. V. Haigh, "Psychotherapy as Interpersonal Encounter," in J. F. T. Bu-

gental, ed., *Challenges of Humanistic Psychology* (New York: McGraw-Hill, 1967), p. 223.

43. C. R. Rogers, "The Process of the Basic Encounter Group," in J. F. T. Bugental, ed., *Challenges of Humanistic Psychology,* p. 265.

44. E. J. Rosenfeld, *The Book of Highs* (New York: Quadrangle, New York Times Book Co., 1973).

45. S. Peterson, *A Catalog of the Ways People Grow* (New York: Ballantine Books, 1971).

46. W. C. Schutz, *Joy* (New York: Grove Press, 1967).

47. M. Lakin, *Interpersonal Encounter: Theory and Practice in Sensitivity Training* (New York: McGraw-Hill, 1972).

48. Maslow, *Toward a Psychology of Being.*

49. S. Kierkegaard, *Either/or,* vol. 1 (New York: Doubleday, 1959; Anchor Books).

50. E. E. Mintz, *Marathon Groups, Reality, and Symbol* (New York: Avon Books, 1971).

51. C. Selver and C. Brooks, "Report on Work in Sensory Awareness and Total Functioning," in H. A. Otto, ed., *Explorations in Human Potentialities,* p. 488.

52. *Ibid.,* p. 493.

53. R. Gustaitis, *Turning On* (New York: Macmillan, 1969), pp. 253–268.

54. S. Keleman, *Sexuality, Self, and Survival* (San Francisco: Lodestar Press, 1971), p. 24.

55. I. Rolf, "Structural Integration," in *Journal of the Institute for the Comparative Study of History, Philosophy, and the Sciences,* vol. 1, no. 1 (1963), p. 7.

56. I. Rubenfeld and E. J. Rosenfeld, "The Alexander Technique," in B. Aaronson, *Workshops of the Mind* (New York: Anchor Press/Doubleday, in press).

57. F. M. Alexander, *The Resurrection of the Body* (New York: Delta, 1969), p. xxvi.

58. M. Feldenkrais, "Mind and Body," in *Systematics,* vol. 1, no. 4 (1964).

59. M. Feldenkrais, in *CIBA-GEIGY Journal,* no. 1 (1971).

60. M. Feldenkrais, *Body and Mature Behavior: A Study of Anxiety, Sex, Gravitation, and Learning* (New York: International Universities Press, 1949), p. 160.

61. Lowen, *The Betrayal of the Body.*

62. S. Keleman, "The Body is All," in *The Geocentric Experience: A Bulletin* (Los Gatos, Calif.: Lamplighters Roadway Press, 1972), p. 50.

63. *Ibid.,* p. 55.

64. Rosenfeld, *The Book of Highs,* sec. 10.

65. J. White, *What Is Meditation?* (New York: Anchor Press/Doubleday, 1974), p. xi.

66. Alan Watts, "The Art of Meditation," in *ibid.*

67. *Ibid.,* p. 33.

68. T. N. Weide, "Varieties of Transpersonal Therapy," in *Journal of Transpersonal Psychology,* vol. 5, no. 1 (1973), p. 9.
69. H. R. Lewis and H. S. Streitfeld, *Growth Games* (New York: Bantam, 1970).
70. J. O. Stevens, *Awareness: Exploring, Experimenting, Experiencing* (Lafayette, Calif.: Real People Press, 1971).
71. C. Hills and R. B. Stone, *Conduct Your Own Awareness Sessions* (New York: Signet, 1970).
72. Stevens, *Awareness,* p. 3.
73. V. Spolin, *Improvisation for the Theater* (Evanston, Ill.: Northwestern University Press 1963), quoted in S. Peterson, *A Catalog of the Ways People Grow* (New York: Ballantine, 1971), p. 273.
74. Back, *Beyond Words,* pp. 231–232.
75. M. Lieberman, I. Yalom, and M. Miles, *Encounter Groups: First Facts* (New York: Basic Books, 1973).
76. E. Canetti, *Crowds and Power* (New York: Viking Press, 1960).
77. R. Gustaitis, *Turning On;* F. S. Perls, *In and Out of the Garbage Pail* (Lafayette, Calif.: Real People Press, 1969).
78. M. James and D. Jongeward, *Born to Win: Transactional Analysis with Gestalt Experiments* (Reading, Mass.: Addison-Wesley, 1971).
79. E. Berne, *What Do You Say After You Say Hello?* (New York: Bantam, 1972), pp. xv–xvi.
80. B. Satir, *Conjoint Family Therapy* (Palo Alto, Calif.: Science and Behavior Books, 1964).
81. E. L. Rossi, "Game and Growth: Two Dimensions of our Psychotherapeutic Zeitgeist," in *Journal of Humanistic Psychology,* vol. 7 (1967), pp. 139–154.
82. S. Miller and S. Miller, *First Report of the Project in Humanistic Medicine* (San Francisco: Esalen Institute, 1973).

Chapter 4

1. S. Schachter, *The Psychology of Affiliation* (Stanford, Calif.: Stanford University Press, 1959).
2. F. Alexander and T. M. French, eds., *Psychoanalytic Therapy* (New York: Ronald Press, 1946).
3. M. A. Lieberman, "The Implications of a Total Group Phenomenon: Analysis for Patients and Therapists," in *International Journal of Group Psychotherapy,* vol. 17 (1967), pp. 71–81.
4. J. L. Moreno, *The First Book on Group Psychotherapy* (New York: Beacon House, 1957).
5. F. H. Ernst, "Use of Transactional Analysis in Prison Therapy Groups," in *Corrective Psychiatry and Journal of Social Therapy,* vol. 8, no. 3 (1962), pp. 120–132; V. Hartman, "Notes on Group Psychotherapy with Pedophiles," in *Canadian Psychiatric Association Journal,* vol. 10, no. 4 (1965), pp. 283–289;

H. L. P. Resoile and J. J. Peters, "Outpatient Group Therapy with Committed Pedophiles," in *International Journal of Group Psychotherapy*, vol. 17, no. 1 (1967), pp. 151–158; P. Schilder, "Results and Problems of Group Psychotherapy in Severe Neurosis," in *Mental Hygiene*, vol. 23 (1939), pp. 87–98; A. P. Travisono and C. F. O'Neil, "Intromittive Family Therapy," in *Corrective Psychiatry and Journal of Social Therapy*, vol. 12, no. 3 (1966), pp. 229–238; H. A. Wilmer, I. Marks, and E. Pogue, "Group Treatment of Prisoners and Their Families," in *Mental Hygiene*, vol. 50, no. 3 (1966), pp. 380–389.

6. A. Hein, "Group Therapy with Criminal Psychopaths," in *Acta Psychotherapeutica*, vol. 7 (1959), pp. 6–16.

7. A. J. W. Taylor, "A Therapeutic Group in Prison," in *International Journal of Group Psychotherapy*, vol. 11, no. 2 (1961), pp. 180–187.

8. I. D. Yalom, "Group Therapy of Incarcerated Sexual Deviants," in *Journal of Nervous and Mental Diseases*, vol. 132, no. 2 (1961), pp. 158–170.

9. D. S. Hays, "Problems Involved in Organizing and Operating a Group Therapy Program in the New York State Parole Setting," *Psychiatric Quarterly*, vol. 34 (1960), pp. 623–633.

10. R. S. Kiger, "Treating the Psychopathic Patient in a Therapeutic Community," in *Hospital and Community Psychiatry*, vol. 18, no. 7 (1967), pp. 191–196.

11. D. S. Hays and M. Wisotsky, "Suitability for Group Psychotherapy in a Parole Setting," Paper presented at American Group Psychotherapy Association Annual Meeting, 1965.

12. M. Schmideberg, "Psychiatric Study and Psychotherapy of the Criminal," in J. L. Masserman and J. L. Moreno, eds., *Progress in Psychotherapy* (New York: Grune and Stratton, 1960), pp. 156–160.

13. D. S. Hays, "Resistance to Group Psychotherapy as Observed in the Correctional Setting," Paper presented at May 1960 meeting of Association for Group Psychoanalysis and Process.

14. E. Jacobson, "Observations on the Psychological Effect of Imprisonment on Female Political Prisoners," in K. R. Eissler, ed., *Searchlights on Delinquency* (New York: International Universities Press, 1949).

15. C. H. Ostby, "Conjoint Group Therapy with Prisoners and Their Families," in *Family Process*, vol. 7, no. 2 (1968), pp. 184–201.

16. F. Redl, "Resistance in Therapy Groups," in *Human Relations*, vol. 1, no. 3 (1948), pp. 307–313.

17. G. Adler and L. Shapiro, "Psychotherapy with Prisoners," in J. Masserman, ed., *Current Psychiatric Therapies*, vol. 9 (New York: Grune and Stratton, 1969), pp. 99–105.

18. S. S. Kanter et al., "A Comparison of Oral and Genital Aspects in Group Psychotherapy," in *International Journal of Group Psychotherapy*, vol. 14, no. 2 (1964), pp. 139–157.

19. Resoile and Peters, "Outpatient Group Therapy with Committed Pedophiles."

20. Hartman, "Notes on Group Psychotherapy with Pedophiles."

21. H. A. Roether and J. J. Peters, "Success and Failure of Sex Offenders," Paper read at American Association for the Advancement of Science Section of Psychology, 1971.

22. Hays, "Problems Involved in Organizing and Operating a Group Therapy Program in the New York State Parole Setting."

23. Hartman, "Notes on Group Psychotherapy with Pedophiles."

24. A. J. W. Taylor, "Therapeutic Groups Outside a Prison," in *International Journal of Group Psychotherapy*, vol. 13, no. 3 (1963), pp. 308–314.

25. Ernst, "Use of Transactional Analysis in Prison Therapy Groups."

26. Hein, "Group Therapy with Criminal Psychopaths."

27. Ernst, "Use of Transactional Analysis in Prison Therapy Groups."

28. M. R. Haskell, "Group Psychotherapy and Psychodrama in Prison," *Group Psychotherapy*, vol. 13, no. 1 (1960), pp. 22–33.

29. R. L. Sadoff, H. A. Roether, and J. J. Peters, "Clinical Measure of Enforced Group Psychotherapy," in *American Journal of Psychiatry*, vol. 128, no. 2 (1971), pp. 224–227.

30. R. G. McCarthy, "Group Therapy in an Outpatient Clinic for the Treatment of Alcoholism," in *Quarterly Journal of Studies on Alcohol*, vol. 7, no. 1 (1946), pp. 98–109.

31. D. A. Stewart, "Empathy in the Group Therapy of Alcoholics," in *Quarterly Journal of Studies on Alcohol*, vol. 15, no. 1 (1954), pp. 74–110.

32. A. Z. Pfeffer, P. Friedland, and S. B. Wortis, "Group Psychotherapy with Alcoholics: Preliminary Report," in *Quarterly Journal of Studies on Alcohol*, vol. 10, no. 2 (1949), pp. 198–216.

33. O. Martensen-Larsen, "Group Psychotherapy with Alcoholics in Private Practice," in *International Journal of Group Psychotherapy*, vol. 6, no. 1 (1956), pp. 28–37.

34. S. G. Allison, "Nondirective Group Therapy of Alcoholics in a State Hospital," in *Quarterly Journal of Studies on Alcohol*, vol. 13, no. 4 (1952), pp. 596–601.

35. D. Mechanic, "Relevance of Group Atmosphere and Attitudes for the Rehabilitation of Alcoholics," in *Quarterly Journal of Studies on Alcohol*, vol. 22, no. 4 (1961), pp. 634–645.

36. K. Wolff, "Group Therapy for Alcoholics," in *Mental Hygiene*, vol. 51, no. 4 (1967), pp. 549–551.

37. H. Mullan and I. Sangiuliano, *Alcoholism, Group Psychotherapy and Rehabilitation* (Springfield, Ill.: Thomas, 1966).

38. A. A. MacDougall, "Group Therapy for Alcoholic Addicts," in *British Journal of Addiction*, vol. 54 (1958), pp. 127–132.

39. M. Brunner-Orne, F. T. Iddings, and J. Rodrigues, "A Court Clinic for Alcoholics: A Description and Evaluation of the Stoughton Clinic," in *Quarterly Journal of Studies on Alcohol*, vol. 12, no. 4 (1951), pp. 592–600.

40. M. Brunner-Orne, "Treatment and Rehabilitation of Alcohol Addicts in a General Hospital Setting," in *Journal of the American Medical Women's Association*, vol. 10 (1955), pp. 193–194.

41. M. Brunner-Orne and M. Orne, "Alcoholism," in S. R. Slavson, ed., *The Fields of Group Psychotherapy* (New York: Wiley, 1956).

42. M. Brunner-Orne and M. Orne, "Directive Group Therapy in the Treatment of Alcoholics: Technique and Rationale," Paper presented at Annual Conference of American Group Psychotherapy Association, 1953.

43. R. Fox, "Group Psychotherapy with Alcoholics," in *International Journal of Group Psychotherapy*, vol. 12, no. 1 (1962), pp. 56–63; R. Fox, *Behavioral Research: Therapeutic Approaches* (New York: Springer, 1967).

44. L. H. Gliedman, "Some Contributions of Group Therapy in the Treatment of Chronic Alcoholism," in P. H. Hoch and J. Zubin eds., *Problems of Addiction and Habituation* (New York: Grune and Stratton, 1958), pp. 214–227.

45. H. Greenbaum, "Group Psychotherapy with Alcoholics in Conjunction with Antabuse Treatment," in *International Journal of Group Psychotherapy*, vol. 4, no. 1 (1954), pp. 30–41.

46. R. A. Moore and T. K. Buchanan, "State Hospitals and Alcoholism; A Nationwide Survey of Treatment Techniques and Results," in *Quarterly Journal of Studies on Alcohol*, vol. 27, no. 3 (1966), pp. 459–468.

47. P. W. Haberman, "Factors Related to Increased Sobriety in Group Psychotherapy with Alcoholics," in *Journal of Clinical Psychology*, vol. 22 (1966), pp. 229–234.

48. C. McCance and P. F. McCance, "Alcoholism in North-East Scotland: Its Treatment and Outcome," in *British Journal of Psychiatry*, vol. 115 (1969), pp. 189–198.

49. E. M. Pattison, "A Critique of Alcoholism Treatment Concepts with Special Reference to Abstinence," in *Quarterly Journal of Studies on Alcohol*, vol. 27, no. 1 (1966), pp. 49–71.

50. P. Hartocollis and D. Shaefer, "Group Psychotherapy with Alcoholics; A Critical Review," in *Psychiatry Digest*, vol. 29 (1968), pp. 15–22.

51. M. M. Glatt, "Group Therapy and Alcoholism," in *British Journal of Addiction*, vol. 54 (1958), pp. 133–150.

52. *An Introduction to Alcoholics Anonymous Intergroup Association*, Alcoholics Anonymous Association (undated), pp. 6–7.

53. J. Alexander, "They 'Doctor' One Another," in *Saturday Evening Post*, December 1952, p. 31.

54. *An Introduction to Alcoholics Anonymous Intergroup Association*, p. 1.

55. *Ibid.*, p. 8.

56. H. Lindt, "The 'Rescue Fantasy' in Group Treatment of Alcoholics," in *International Journal of Group Psychotherapy*, vol. 9, no. 1 (1959), pp. 43–52.

57. A. Freud, *The Ego and the Mechanisms of Defense* (London: Woolf, 1937).

58. H. S. Ripley and J. K. Jackson, "Therapeutic Factors in Alcoholics Anonymous," in *American Journal of Psychiatry*, vol. 116, no. 1 (1959), pp. 44–50.

59. R. L. Custer, quoted in S. Cady, "The Gambler Who Must," in *New York Times Magazine*, January 27, 1974, p. 12.

60. A. Low, *Mental Health Through Will-Training* (Boston: Christopher, 1950);

S. R. Dean, "Self Conducted Group Psychotherapy: Mental Patients Rediscover Will Power," Speech before World Medical Health Assembly, Washington, D.C., November 8, 1969.

61. *Group Leaders' Guide, Recovery, Inc.,* rev. ed. (Recovery, Inc., June 1, 1971); T. Berland, *A Brief Explanation of the Recovery, Inc. System of Techniques* (Recovery, Inc., 1969).

62. H. J. Grosz, *Recovery, Inc. Survey: A Preliminary Report* (Recovery, Inc., 1970).

63. *Introducing Recovery, Inc.: The Association of Nervous and Former Mental Patients* (Chicago: Recovery, Inc., 1973).

64. J. Niditch, *The Story of Weight Watchers* (New York: New American Library, 1970).

65. A. Gold and S. W. Briller, *Diet Watchers Guide* (New York: Grosset and Dunlap, 1968).

66. M. Johnston, "An Experiment in Group Psychotherapy with the Narcotic Addict," in *American Journal of Psychotherapy,* vol. 5 (1951), pp. 24–31.

67. C. Batiste and L. Yablonsky, "Synanon: A Therapeutic Life Style," in *California Medicine,* vol. 114 (1971), pp. 90–94.

68. G. Endore, *Synanon: The Learning Environment* (Synanon Foundation, 1968).

69. D. S. Casriel, *So Fair a House: The Story of Synanon* (Englewood Cliffs, N.J.: Prentice-Hall, 1964).

70. L. Yablonsky, "The Anti-Criminal Society: Synanon," in *Federal Probation,* vol. 26, no. 3 (1962), pp. 50–57.

71. A. Bassin, "Daytop Village," in *Psychology Today,* vol. 2, no. 7 (1968), pp. 48–52, 68.

72. S. H. Foulkes, *Introduction to Group Analytic Psychotherapy* (London: Heinemann, 1948), p. 29.

73. I. D. Yalom, *The Theory and Practice of Group Psychotherapy* (New York: Basic Books, 1970), p. 5.

74. Special Report, Recovery, Inc., vol. 15, no. 3.

75. Sadoff, Roether, and Peters, "Clinical Measure of Enforced Group Psychotherapy."

76. T. Parsons, "View of the Changing American Family," in H. Rodman, ed., *Marriage, Family, and Society* (New York: Random House, 1965).

Chapter 5

1. Research included a comprehensive study of thirty nineteenth-century American communes, field visits to over forty contemporary groups of many varieties, a research project on urban communes, and long-term, in depth experience with two groups. (Some of Rosabeth Moss Kanter's research was

supported by the National Institute of Mental Health, grant number MH23030.) See especially my *Commitment and Community* (Cambridge: Harvard University Press, 1972) and *Communes: Creating and Managing the Corrective Life* (New York: Harper and Row, 1973), for further information.

2. B. Zablocki, "Some Models of Commune Integration and Disintegration," Paper delivered at 1972 Meetings of American Sociological Association, p. 10, mimeographed. See also L. Veysey, *The Communal Experience* (New York: Harper and Row, 1973).

3. D. H. van Zeller, *The Benedictine Idea* (London: Burns and Oates, 1959), p. 9.

4. N. Cohn, *The Pursuit of the Millenium,* 2d ed. (New York: Oxford University Press, 1970), p. 197.

5. T. Merton, *Mystics and Zen Masters* (New York: Delta, 1969).

6. Cohn, *Millenium,* p. 15.

7. *Ibid.,* p. 16.

8. *Ibid.,* p. 178.

9. *Ibid.,* p. 148–181.

10. J. Lofland, *Doomsday Cult* (Englewood Cliffs, N.J.: Prentice-Hall, 1966).

11. J. Bennett, *Hutterian Brethren* (Stanford, Calif.: Stanford University Press, 1967); J. Hostetler, *Hutterite Society* (Baltimore: Johns Hopkins University Press, 1975).

12. J. Eaton and R. Weil, *Culture and Mental Disorders* (Glencoe, Ill.: Free Press, 1955).

13. Bennett, *Hutterian Brethren.*

14. J. Seeley, *The Americanization of the Unconscious* (New York: Science House, 1967), p. 4.

15. L. Bradford, J. R. Gibb, and K. D. Benne, *T-Group Theory and Laboratory Method* (New York: Wiley, 1964), p. vii.

16. Seeley, *Unconscious,* pp. 55–56.

17. M. Halter, "What Must We Do to Be Saved?" Senior Honor Thesis, Brandeis University, 1970.

18. R. M. Kanter, *Commitment and Community: Communes and Utopias in Sociological Perspective* (Cambridge: Harvard University Press, 1972), p. 167.

19. V. Turner, *The Ritual Process* (Chicago: Aldine, 1969), pp. 106–107.

20. *Ibid.,* p. 123.

21. H. Schmalenbach, "The Sociological Category of Communion," in T. Parsons, E. Shils, K. Naegele, and J. Pitts, eds., *Theories of Society* (New York: Free Press, 1961), pp. 331–348.

22. G. Yaswen, "Sunrise Hill Community: Post Mortem" (mimeographed, 1971).

23. *Ibid.,* p. 25.

24. Kanter, *Commitment and Community.*

204   THE INTENSIVE GROUP EXPERIENCE

25. M. Buber, *Paths in Utopia* (Boston: Beacon Press, 1958), p. 134.
26. E. Bittner, "Radicalism and the Organization of Radical Movements," in *American Sociological Review*, vol. 28 (1963), p. 938.
27. Kanter, *Commitment and Community*, pp. 81–82.
28. Zablocki, "Commune Integration," pp. 9–10.
29. Bittner, "Radicalism," p. 938.
30. Kanter, *Commitment and Community*, p. 83.
31. *Ibid.*, pp. 83–86.
32. J. Howard, "The Making of a Black Muslim," in *Trans-action* (December 1966), p. 20.
33. G. Simmel, *Conflict*, trans. K. H. Wolff (New York: Free Press, 1964); L. A. Coser, *The Functions of Social Contract* (New York: Free Press, 1964).
34. P. Worsley, *The Trumpet Shall Sound* (New York: Schocken, 1968), pp. 249–250.
35. B. Zablocki, *The Joyful Community* (Baltimore: Penguin, 1971), p. 321.
36. Worsley, *Trumpet*, p. 252.
37. Quoted in Kanter, *Commitment and Community*, p. 106.
38. Buber, *Paths in Utopia*, p. 140.
39. K. H. Wolff, ed., *The Sociology of Georg Simmel* (New York: Free Press, 1950).
40. See L. Festinger, H. Riecken, and S. Schacter, *When Prophecy Fails* (Minneapolis: University of Minnesota Press, 1956). The authors found that, when faced with a disconfirmation of their prophecy of the end of the world, members of a group increased their proselytizing and refused to admit defeat. This was true, however, only of those members who heard the news together and not of those who faced it in isolation, indicating the role of social support in maintaining disconfirmed beliefs.
41. Zablocki, *Joyful Community*, pp. 308–309.
42. G. Hillery, "Freedom and Social Organization," in *American Sociological Review*, vol. 36 (February 1971), pp. 51–65.
43. Bennett, *Hutterian Brethren*, p. 263.
44. E. Z. Friedenberg, "The Synanon Solution," in *Nation*, vol. 200 (March 8, 1965).
45. Zablocki, *Joyful Community*, p. 157.
46. Bennett, *Hutterian Brethren*, p. 264. See also Hostetler, *Hutterite Society*.
47. A. Gladstone, "The War Between Us and Within Us" (Boston: 1972, mimeographed). Quoted by permission.
48. Y. Sugihara and D. W. Plath, *Sensi and His People: The Building of a Japanese Commune* (Berkeley and Los Angeles: University of California Press, 1969); Bennett, *Hutterian Brethren*.
49. Sources of information on Synanon include L. Yablonsky, *Synanon: The Tunnel Back* (New York: Macmillan, 1965); G. Endore, *Synanon* (New York: Doubleday, 1968), and Kanter, *Commitment and Community*, pp. 201–212.

50. For more information on urban communes and their use as temporary, transitional support communities, see R. M. Kanter, "Communes in Cities," *Working Papers for a New Society,* vol. 2 (Summer 1974), pp. 36–44; and R. M. Kanter, D. T. Jaffe, and D. K. Wersberg, "Coupling, Parenting, and the Presence of Others: Intimate Relationships in Communal Households," *The Family Coordinator,* vol. 43 (October 1975), pp. 433–52. On life style changes in general, see B. Zablocki and R. M. Kanter, "The Differentiation of Life Styles," *Annual Review of Sociology,* vol. 2 (1976).

51. M. Jones, *The Therapeutic Community: A New Treatment Method in Psychiatry* (New York: Basic Books, 1953).

Name Index

Ackerman, Nathan, 41
Adler, Alfred, 4, 5, 32, 45, 51
Al-Anon, 134
Al-A-Teen, 134
Alcoholics Anonymous, 10, 20, 123, 125,
    130–35, 138, 144
Alexander, F. M., 101–102
Allison, S. G., 124
Amana, 155, 172
American Group Psychotherapy Associa-
    tion, 43
Americanization of the Unconscious, The,
    157
Amish, 154
Anabaptist movement, 171
Antabuse, 124–26, 128–29
Anthony, E. J., 43, 51–52
Argyris, Chris, 70
Arthur Murray Clubs, 22
Ashton, Judith, 101
Assagioli, Roberto, 105–106
Association of Nervous and Former Mental
    Patients, 136
Avatar, 170, 175; *see also* Lyman, Mel

Bach, George, 39
Back, Kurt, 94, 96
Bakan, David, 56
Bell, Daniel, xiii
Bell, John, 42
Bell, W., 131
Benedictine monastery, 152
Bennett, John, 154, 179
Berne, Eric, 37–39, 46, 89; *see also* Transac-
    tional analysis
Bierer, Joshua, 25, 32
Bion., W. R., 25–28, 30, 32–33, 51
Bittner, Egon, 165
Black Muslims, 164–65, 167, 171
Breuer, Joseph, 6
Briller, Sarah Wells, 139
Brotherhood of the Free Spirit, 153–54
Brotherhood of the Spirit, 153, 170, 173–74,
    177
Bruderhof, 148, 168, 171, 180
Brunner-Orne, M., 126
Buber, Martin, 45, 89, 163, 172
Buchman, T. K., 129
Burrow, Trigant, 8–9, 31, 51

California Medical Facility at Vacaville, 121
Campbell, 83
Camphill Village, 148
Casriel, D. S., 143
Catalog of the Ways People Grow, A, 97
Chino, California State Prison, 115; *see also*
    Group psychotherapy, with criminals
Clark University, 4

Cohn, Norman, 152–153
Columbia University, Teachers College, 26
Committment and Community, 162–63, 166,
    170, 172, 175, 179
Congressional Review, 107
Coriat, Isadore, 3
Corsini, Raymond, 17
Coser, Lewis, 170
Culture and Mental Disorders, 155
Custer, Dr. Robert L., 136

Daytop Village, 143; *see also* Synanon
Dederich, Charles, 141, 175; *see also* Syna-
    non
Dejerine, Joseph Jules, 3, 19
Dewey, John, 57, 102
Diet Watchers, 139
Doomsday Cult, 154, 174
Draper Correctional Center, 115; *see also*
    Group psychotherapy, with criminals
Dunnette, M. D., 83
Durkheim, E., 169
Durkin, Helen, 43

Eaton, Joseph, 155, 179
Ego, Hunger, and Aggression: A Revision of
    Freud's Theory and Method, 92
Emerson, Ralph Waldo, 146
Emmanuel Church, 2
Ernst, F. H., 121
Esalen, 35, 56, 94, 150
Ezriel, Henry, 30, 32

Farrell, Michael, 43
Feldenkrais, Moshe, 102
Fenichel, Otto, 92
Fort Hill, 170, 174–75
Fortune and Men's Eyes, 122
Fortune News, 123
Fortune Society, 122–23; *see also* Group
    psychotherapy, with criminals
Foulkes, S. H., 27, 29–32, 43, 51–52, 143
Fourier, Charles, 156
Fox, R., 129
Frankfurt Psychoanalytic Institute, 29
French, Thomas, 34
Freud, Anna, 134
Freud, Sigmund, 4–6, 9, 11, 31, 37, 41, 45,
    48, 51–52, 102, 122, 157, 170
Friedenberg, Edgar Z., 180
Fromm, Erich, 29
Fromm, Marty, 92
Fromm-Reichmann, Freida, 29

Gam-Anon, 136
Gam-A-Teen, 136
Gamblers Anonymous, 134–36, 144
Gelb, W., 29

Gestalt Therapy: The Excitement and Growth in the Human Personality, 35
Gibb, Jack R., 83, 90, 94
Gindler, Elsa, 100
Gladstone, Arthur, 181
Glatt, M. M., 130
Gold, Ann, 139
Goldstein, Kurt, 29–30, 92
Good Templar's Temperance Lodge, the, 123; *see also* Group psychotherapy, with alcoholics
Goodman, Paul, 35, 92
Group Analytic Society of London, 29
The Guide for Diet Watchers, 139
Gunther, Bernard, 91
Gurdjieff, 102

Haberman, P. W., 129
Haigh, Gerald, 96
Harmony Society, 154–55, 164, 174–75
Hartman, 121
Haskell, M. R., 121
Hawes, John B., 3
Hays, David, 115–18, 120, 132–34, 137–40
Hefferline, Ralph, 35
Hein, 121
Heinrich, Jacoby, 100
Hillery, George, 179
Horkheimer, Max, 29
Horney, Karen, 28, 45, 92
Hostetter, John, 154
Howard, John, 167
Human Relations, 26
Human Side of Enterprise, The, 81
Hutter, Jacob, 154
Hutterites, 154–55, 179, 181–82
Huxley, Aldous, 102

International Journal of Psychoanalysis, 26

Jacoby, Heinrich, 100
Jacobson, E., 119
Janov, Arthur, 89
Jewish Board of Guardians, 12
Johnson, James, 48
Jones, Ernest, 4, 29, 92
Jones, Maxwell, 32–33, 51, 184
Jourard, Sidney, 90, 94

Kanter, S. S., 120
Kaplan, 179n.
Karpman, Benjamin, 117
Keleman, Stanley, 102–104
Kierkegaard, Soren, 99
Kingsley Hall, 184
Klein, Melanie, 26, 28

Laing, Ronald, 89, 184
Lakin, 80
Lama community, 175
Land, George, 89
Landauer, Karl, 29
Lazarus, Arnold, 47
Lazell, Edward, 4
Le Bon, 4
Lee, Anna, 155, 175

Lehner, George, 39
Lewin, Kurt, 30–31
Lewis, 106
Lieberman, Morton, 33–34, 43, 83–84
Lofland, John, 154–74
Lorenz, Konrad, 32
Low, Abraham A., 16, 136–37; *see also* Recovery, Inc.
Lowen, Alexander, 91, 103
Lyman, Mel, 170, 175

Mannheim, Karl, 29
Marsh, L. Cody, 9–10
Martensen–Larsen, 124
Maslow, Abraham, 90, 99
McCarthy, R. G., 123
McGregor, Douglas, 81
Mechanic, D., 124
Meng, Wilhelm, 29
Mental Health Through Will Training, 136
Merton, Thomas, 151
Mesmer, Anton, 1
Metelica, Michael, 175
Miles, Matthew, 43, 83
Minor, Charles L., 2
Mintz, Elizabeth, 99
Moore, R. A., 129
Moreno, Jacob L., 5–8, 51, 115, 123; *see also* Psychodrama
Moustakas, Clark, 90, 94
Mowrer, O. Hobart, 24
Mullan, H., 124
Murphy, Gardner, 8
Mystics and Zen Masters, 151

National Institute on Alcoholic Abuse and Alcoholism, 130
New Harmony, 156
New York State Division of Parole, 115; *see also* Group psychotherapy, with criminals
New York State Parole System, 120
Niditch, Jean, 139; *see also* Weight Watchers
Northfield Military Hospital, 25–26, 30, 32
Noyes, John Humphrey, 155, 175, 182

Oneida Community, 155, 164, 166, 168, 172, 175, 181–82
Orne, M., 126, 128
Owen, Robert, 156

Parsons, T., 144
Pattison, E. M., 130
Perls, Frederich S., 34–36, 39, 91–94
Peters, J. J., 120–21
Peterson, Severin, 97
Pfeffer, A. Z., 124
Plaut, 179n.
Polster, Erving, 92
Polster, Miriam, 92
Prather, Hugh, 89
Pratt, Joseph 2–3, 10
Psychotherapy Through the Group Process, 33
Pursuit of the Millenium, The, 153

Quakers, 155
Queen Elizabeth, 169

Rapp, George, 175
Reba Place Fellowship, 148
Recovery, Inc., 17, 136–39
Reich, Wilhelm, 38–39, 92, 103
Resoile, 120
Rickman, John, 25–30
Riker's Island Penetentiary, 121
Ritual Process, The, 160–61
Roether, H. A., 121
Rogers, Carl, 20–24, 45, 89, 96
Rolf, Ida, 100–101
Rosenbaum, Max, 49
Rosenfeld, 97, 104
Rossi, Ernest, 110

Sangiuliano, I., 124
Santa Monica, 143
Sartre, Jean-Paul, 45
Schilder, Paul, 11, 14, 29–30, 51
Schmalenbach, Herman, 161
Schmidenberg, 118
Schultz, William, 90, 94, 96, 98
Seashore, Charles, 90
Seeley, John, 157
Selver, Charlotte, 91, 99
Seven Steps, 122
Shakers, 151, 154–55, 166–67, 169, 171,
    174–75, 177
Shaw, G. B., 102
Sheldon, 88
Shields, Clarence, 8–9
Shinkyo, 182
Shostrom, Everett, 89
Simmel, Georg, 170, 174, 179
Sing Sing State Prison, 116; *see also* Group
    psychotherapy, with criminals; Hays,
    David
Slavson, Samuel, 12–14
Slawson, John, 12
Speck, 41
Spirit in the Flesh, 170
Spolin, V., 107
St. Benedict, 151

Stevens, 106
Stewart, 123
Stock-Whitaker, Dorothy, 33–34, 83
Stoller, Frederick, 39
Story of Weight Watchers, The, 139
Streitfeld, 106
Sullivan, 45
Sunrise Hill commune, 161
Synanon, 112, 141–43, 148–49, 170–72,
    176–77, 179–80, 183–84

Taylor, F., 115
Tavistock Clinic, 26, 30, 96
Thelen, Herbert, 26, 33
Turner, Victor, 160–61

University of California in Los Angeles, 39
University of Chicago, 26
University of Chicago Human Dynamics
    Laboratory, 33

Vienna Psychoanalytic Society, 4
Vienna, University of, 5

Waller, Gene, 39
Watts, Alan, 90, 105
Weide, T. N., 106
Weight Watchers, 139–40
Weil, Robert, 155, 179
Wender, Louis, 10, 14
Wisotsky, 118
Wolf, Alexander, 14–16, 26, 29, 34, 40
Wolpe, Joseph, 19
Worcester, Dr. Elwood, 2
Worsley, Peter, 170–71

Yale Divinity School, 155
Yale Plan Clinic, 123
Yale University, Department of Special
    Studies on Alcoholism, Laboratory
    of Applied Physiology, 123
Yalom, Irwin, 43, 83, 143
Yaswen, Gordon, 162

Zablocki, Benjamin, 148, 164, 170–71, 178,
    180
Zoar, 155

Subject Index

Activity group therapy:
    and group psychotherapy, 12–14
    and individual play therapy, 12–14
    modifications of, with preschool age chil-
        dren, 13
    and oral needs, 12–13
Adaptation:
    and group therapy, 48
Alexander technique, 1, 98, 100–102, 104

Alternate session (alternate meeting),
    with alcoholics, 128
    in group psychotherapy, 14
Anabaptist movement, 171
Antabuse, 124–26, 128–29
Aura, in human relations training group, 58
Authenticity, and personal growth, 88–89
Awareness:
    and bioenergetics, 91

and fantasy, 91
in personal growth, 91

Behavior therapy, 19
Bioenergetics, 1, 98, 100, 103–104, 108
Buddhism, 104

Catharsis, 6
Christian Science, 20
Client centered or nondirective group
    psychotherapy, 20–24
Communes:
    benefits of, 175–78
    definition of, 147
    millennialism, 152–55
    monasticism, 151–52
    psychotherapy and, 49, 156
    social practices of:
        communion, 167–70
        investment, 164–65
        mortification, 170–72
        renunciation, 165–67
        sacrifice, 163–64
        transcendence, 172–75
    urban communes, 147–48
    utopianism, 155–56
Counselling, 20–21; *see also* client centered
    or nondirective group psychotherapy

Depth therapy, 20–21, 48
Directive-didactic approach to group
    psychotherapy, 17–19

Encounter: *see also* Personal growth
Encounter group:
    foundations of, 97
    goals, 98
    and group psychotherapy, 43, 47
    and human relations training, 56
    and personal growth, 94, 96–97
England, group psychotherapy in, 25–33
Eros, 31
Experiential groups, types of, for therapy,
    human relations training, and per-
    sonal growth, 50

Family therapy:
    and group psychotherapy, 40–42
    nonverbal communication in, 41
    transference phenomena in, 41
Fantasy, and personal growth, 104
Feedback:
    in human relations training groups, 58, 60,
        67, 69, 73
    in personal growth groups, 95–96
Feldenkrais Method, 100, 102–104

Gestalt therapy:
    and group psychotherapy, 34–37, 46
    and personal growth movement, 91–94
Gnosticism, 151*n*.
Going around, 15, 40
Greek drama, 1, 6
Group process, and group psychotherapy,
    33–34

Group psychotherapy:
    and activity group therapy, 12–14
    and Adler, 4–5
    and behavior therapy, 19, 47–48
    Burrow's method, 8–9
    client centered, 20–24
    current, 43–44
    in Czechoslovakia, 43
    depth therapy, 20–21, 48
    directive-didactic approach, 17–19
    and encounter groups, 43, 47
    in England, 24–33
        Bion's system, 26–29
        Foulkes' system, 29–32
    existential-experiential approaches, 45
    family therapy and, 40–42
    and Freud, 4–5
    future of, 48–49
    gestalt therapy and, 34–37, 46
    and group process, 33–34
    history of, 2
    in hospitals, 9–12
    and humanism, 47
    and the marathon group, 39–40
    nondirective: *see* client centered
    psychoanalytic method of, 14–16, 21, 31,
        45
    and psychodrama, 5–8, 46
    regressive-inspirational approach, 19–20
    Shields and, 11, 12
    in the Soviet Union, 43
    supportive and adaptational approaches,
        48
    techniques of, 1
    transactional analysis and, 37–39, 46
    videotape approaches, 40
    Wender and, 10
    with alcoholics, 123–134
    with criminals, 115–123
    with gamblers, 134–138
    with narcotics addicts, 140–143
    with obese people, 139–140
Growth games, and personal growth, 106–
    107
The Guide for Diet Watchers, 139

Hare Krishna, 147, 150, 167
Hinduism, 104
Human potential movement: *see* Personal
    growth movement
Human relations training, laboratory con-
    cept in, 55–56
Human relations training laboratory:
    cohesiveness, 59–60
    cultural island, 66
    development of, 50–55
    disclosure in, 62–63
    dominance alignment, 61–62
    evaluation of, 82–85
    exercises used in, 73–77
    expression of emotion in, 61
    failures in, 78–79
    feedback in, 60–61
    leaders, 79–80
    nonresidential, 66–67

norms, 60
observations, 57–73
organizational development, 80–84
outlook for, 85–86
philosophical background, 56–57
residential schedule, 65t.
role differentiation, 62
and social context, 77, 78
therapeutic uses of group dynamics in,
    52–53
and therapy groups, 82
types of, 50

Intentional communities:
applications and assessment, 183–85
communal imagery, 148–50
communes:
    benefits of, 175–78
    contemporary, 156–59
    definition, 147
    social practices of, 163–75
    tensions and conflicts in, 178–83
historical background, 150–56
    millenialism, 152–55
    monasticism, 151–52
    utopianism, 155–56
Intentional groups with a specific problem
    orientation focus:
alcoholics:
    Alcoholics Anonymous, 130–34
    group therapy, 123–30
corrective emotional experience and, 111
the criminal, 115–122
    attitude toward authority, 120
    institutional obstacles in working with,
        118–19
    suitability for groups, 118
curative factors, 143–44
formally led, 113–14
the Fortune Society, 122–23
Gamblers Anonymous, 134–36
history of, 112
narcotic addiction, 140–43
obesity, 139–40
Recovery, Inc., 136–38
self-help groups, 112–14
setting, 114
and social norms, 144–45

Jesus movement, 173
Judo, 102

Marathon group, and group psychotherapy,
    39–40
Mediation, and personal growth, 104–105

Orgone theory, 39; see also Reich, Wilhelm

Personal growth:
awareness, 91
authenticity, 88–89
body work, 100–104

definition, 87, 89–90
future directions, 108–109
gestalt therapy, 91
group experience and, 94
growth approaches, 97–99
growth games, 106–107
growth models, 109–110
and meditations, 104–105
perspectives, 107–108
psychosynthesis, 105–106
sensory awareness, 99–100
Personal growth movement:
and existentialism, 88
origins, 87–88
and phenomenology, 88
Psychedelic drugs, 156–57
Psychoanalytic methods, 14–16, 21, 31, 45
Psychodrama, 5–8
and criminals, 15
instruments used in, 6–9
and Moreno, 5
and Perls, 36
and psychotherapy, 5–8, 46
purpose of, 6
see also Moreno, Jacob L.
Psychosynthesis, and personal growth,
    105–106

Repressive-inspirational approach to group
    psychotherapy, 16, 19–20

Safe emergency, 88
Schizophrenics, group treatment of, 4
Schizophrenics Anonymous, 133
Self-awareness, see Personal growth
Sensitivity training, 157
Sensory awareness, and personal growth,
    99–100

T-groups; see Sensitivity training
Taoism, 104
Thanatos, 31–32
Therapeutic communities:
of peers, 51
self governing, 51
Transactional analysis:
and group psychotherapy, 37–39, 46
and personal growth, 108–109
see also Berne, Eric
Transference in groups, 15

Videotape approaches to group
    psychotherapy, 40

Will training, 16

Yoga, 57, 102

Zen Buddhism, 57, 105, 107, 184